To Be Met as a Person at Work

This book provides an account of how the "Theory of Attachment-Based Exploratory Interest Sharing" (TABEIS) and the practise of Goal Corrected Empathic Attunement (GCEA) was used in a university setting to support staff. It works in three ways; firstly, it raises attachment theory, one of the pillars of self-understanding, into a central place in terms of reflecting on and learning from the dynamics of business and organisations. Neath explores how well this attachment theory sits with other theories of self and relationships such as transactional analysis and the person-centred approach. Secondly, it is an account of how Neath took an application of McCluskey's theory "The McCluskey Model for Exploring the Dynamics of Attachment in Adult Life" to the University of Leeds, with learning points made along the way, exploring the practise of a therapeutic-style of group facilitation, and reflection on good practice for professional adult learning and teaching techniques. Thirdly, it will act as handbook for anyone wishing to replicate Neath's work and it includes feedback from the participants both during and after the training process. It will appeal to those new to training, counselling, organisational developers and those wishing to enjoy and see the potential of the work of McCluskey.

Nicola Neath began practising as a psychotherapist in 2006. With over 20 years' experience in public and private organisations, she continues to develop a relational approach to work, and is passionate about synthesising her knowledge of organisations and theories of psychotherapy for the wellbeing of clients and organisations.

Una McCluskey is an Honorary Research Fellow at the University of York and a psychoanalytic psychotherapist. She is responsible for developing training for qualified psychologists, psychotherapists, social workers, GPs and others involved in the caring professions, interested in exploring the dynamics of attachment in adult life.

To Be Met as a Person at Work

The Effect of Early Attachment Experiences on Work Relationships

Nicola Neath and Una McCluskey

Routledge
Taylor & Francis Group

LONDON AND NEW YORK

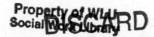

First published 2019
by Routledge
2 Park Square, Milton Park, Abingdon, Oxon OX14 4RN

and by Routledge
711 Third Avenue, New York, NY 10017

Routledge is an imprint of the Taylor & Francis Group, an informa business

British Library Cataloguing-in-Publication Data
A catalogue record for this book is available from the British Library

Library of Congress Cataloging-in-Publication Data
A catalog record has been requested for this book

ISBN: 978-1-78220-552-4 (pbk)
ISBN: 978-0-429-39797-4 (ebk)

Typeset in Times New Roman
by Apex CoVantage, LLC

MIX
Paper from
responsible sources
FSC FSC® C013056
www.fsc.org

Printed and bound in Great Britain by
TJ International Ltd, Padstow, Cornwall

Contents

Figures

About the authors

Nicola Neath graduated from York University in English and Philosophy in 1991. She gained her training wings volunteering with Greenpeace, where she ran non-violent direct action training, and coordinated groups and volunteers across the North of England over an eight-year period. She also spent over ten years in retail, developing business systems. Her training as a psychotherapist started in 2006 and she has been working with universities since then.

Neath started as a trainee psychotherapist with a student counselling service on a trainee placement, gaining her therapist hours and learning what therapy is in practice; what she was good at, and what specialisms she might wish to pursue. She remained with this service over five years while becoming accredited. She developed her own private practice, counselling, training and coaching with The Baobab Centre, working with various large public and smaller private organisations. This work deepened her skills and a separate opportunity arose to work with an internal staff counselling and psychological support service in 2011. This was a chance to synthesise all that she had learnt so far and to build upon her experiences. Neath was supported by the head of the service Sally Rose who suggested she might be interested in the work of McCluskey.

*****

Una McCluskey graduated from University College Dublin, did her professional social work training at the University of Edinburgh, and got her PhD from the University of York. She has written extensively on individuals, couple, family and group systems, and has developed her own model for exploring attachment dynamics in adult life. Her research on affect attunement in adult psychotherapy led her to develop a theory of interaction for caregiving. Using Heard and Lake's theory of a Restorative Process and her own theory of interaction for developmental change, she developed a form of individual and group exploration that she has called Exploratory Goal-Corrected Psychotherapy (EGCP). She has been offering training in this model since 2008 and has been carrying out research and publishing her findings. The model is being used as a guide in wide ranging situations such as psychological work with people with dementia, homelessness, people suffering from trauma, fostering and adoption, mental health issues, people described as having personality disorders, end of life and Hospice work and general individual and group practice.

***

The main voice of the book will be that of Nicola Neath in the first person singular.

Acknowledgements

Several peers and friends have helped us refine these chapters and we will acknowledge them as we proceed. Our special thanks here go to Sally Rose, Marcus Hill, Gayle-Anne Drury, Manar Matusiak, Timothy Knighton, Dr. Stella Butler, Gillian Felton, Abi Shearsmith, Mike Howroyd, Joanna Stevens, Eliane Meyer, Dr Elizabeth Sourbut and Sarah Wills for their suggestions and additions, as well as Helen Heard for the figures in Chapter 2. We should also like to thank all the other participants on the course, without whose willingness to explore and try the theory out, this book could not have been written. Thanks also to all of the training cohort who supported us in this venture. To our own mentors and to Nicola's clinical supervisor who continued to show support for the work this involved.

***

Nicola would also like to say thanks to her wife, Diane, and her daughter Charlotte, for their caregiving and interest sharing, and love they offered through many moments of fear and doubt. The model has been in action at home as well as at work.

***

Una would like to thank all who have contributed to her professional practice over the years, particularly the people that she has worked with from whom she has learnt so much and her mentors and colleagues J.D. Sutherland, Douglas Haldane, Dorothy Heard and Brian Lake.

Introduction

Exploring the dynamics of attachment and their effect on wellbeing and creativity at work

Using psychological theory to improve our understanding, and our experience, of what we need to give to and get from professional relationships at work

Attachment theory isn't much, if at all, used systemically or relationally within the field of professional organisational leadership in the UK (Harms, 2011). And yet, it is without doubt useful and applicable to organisations. Four years into my immersion into the innovative research and work of McCluskey I am now in a position to write with McCluskey about the theories developed with Heard and Lake and the McCluskey model. I will reflect upon how we brought her attachment model into the organisation I worked in. We will explore how it worked, how it altered along the way and how it still is having an impact on the individuals who came on the pilot and how it has impacted upon the organisation itself.

As part of my role in this organisation I design and innovate new proactive training for all staff, including: formal and informal leaders, professors and directors in academic and non-academic roles, all of whom have the possibility of impacting the organisation in a positive way. The modern workplace recognises that engaging with the creative potential of human beings and ensuring supportive collaborative work relationships is crucial for the survival and development of the organisation.

Following three years, two courses, two conferences and further training in exploratory goal-corrected psychotherapy (EGCP) I have now advanced the model McCluskey has developed, coined in 2016 as "The McCluskey model for exploring the dynamics of attachment in adult life", and incorporated an emulation of her skills with my own experience of working with people in my work environment.

Working in and with organisations for 25 years I have experienced, and understand, the deep attachments that can be made in teams. I am interested in the systems which people formally or informally create to make sense of their work practises and their needs. I have seen fear affect relationships, health and productivity and organisational culture. I understand how important rooms and office layouts can be for self-worth and creativity, and, how the strength of bonds, sexual or otherwise, can be formed. However, I had not previously found any single coherent system which described all of this, nor offered a framework with which we might support managers and leaders to help them navigate this landscape of humans at work. Therefore, I immediately recognised the value of finding a model which addresses, explores and explains all these aspects of human activity.

***

As an integrative therapist, I have relied on my integrative approach to find effective theories for different individual and work-based situations; the work of McCluskey, Heard and Lake (Heard and Lake, 1997; Heard, Lake and McCluskey, 2009/2012; McCluskey, 2005; McCluskey, Hooper, and Bingley Miller, 1999) really came as a gift in my work. Integrative practitioners like myself might have a base or core model, mine is humanistic person centred; the core element of this approach is to prize the experience (feelings, perspective, narrative) of the client in any intervention. My belief is no one theory fits for all at all times. Of course, this is a theory in its own right therefore we have a paradox in the explanation. However, in my work this involves integrating or otherwise employing and drawing upon models from a generally humanistic approach (emotional, behavioural, cognitive or physiological), and believing in the potential of human growth through relations and experience. Although there may be interpretative aspects to my work, my greatest learning and progress with my clients is made through our encounter, and what they understand of themselves and the theories which fit for them. Unless invited by the client (and even then, we might spend time exploring the invitation) I hold any inclination to make assumptions, pathologise, at bay, and spend time considering anything I might know from psychotherapeutic theory and practise which might help them make sense of and frame an understanding of their own experiences. I prefer to support them through the relationship – and any here and now experiences between us, to psycho-educate only if asked. Whilst I might remain knowledgeable in theories (whatever theories I know, so there is always a limit) they remain expert in themselves. All this I try to hold with Rogerian (Carl Rogers, 1902–1987 – see also Chapters 2, Three, 9, 12 and 14) core conditions of unconditional positive regard, congruence and empathy. Further key influences for me are the ancient dialectics of Socrates and Plato: philosophies of mind and phenomenology in particular. This integrative practice is one I bring into my training work, sharing my knowledge and insight and encouraging others to have experiences and deepen the knowledge they have about themselves and their interactions with others, if they are interested to explore ideas.

Utilising my experience as a trainer, coach, facilitator, and therapist, I worked on applying the McCluskey model in my workplace. For my audience to be interested it needed to have appeal across the Honey and Mumford (Honey and Mumford, 1982) range of learning styles; it needed scientific and managerial robustness and research, and from my point of view as a psycho-educator it needed the combination of didactic input, experiential encounter, reflection and case study.

A colleague in this organisation with influence at a senior managerial level training was fundamental in supporting my idea to pilot my work in this setting and he was key in disseminating my outline materials to targeted individuals. He was crucial in recruiting the first cohort, of which he was also a part. My intention was to parallel the specific experience of training I had encountered in learning the McCluskey model, to introduce the model to my training cohort, as developed by her. It is primarily experiential, therefore for this organisational structure, it ran as an experiential learning encounter. I had decided to use the structure initiated by McCluskey which she uses with experienced and qualified professionals in the caring professions.

***

The structure McCluskey uses invites participants to explore basic biological systems which are hardwired in every human being and to become curious as to whether an understanding of these systems would be useful in terms of their life and times, and work relationships.

In relation to my own context I was inviting members of the organisation to explore the following questions: Can you talk about careseeking and caregiving at work? Can you talk about fear? Can you talk about sex? Can you notice what helps keep us secure, creative? Can you talk about the interplay between our inner and our outer environments? It seems from what I discovered and plan to tell you about, that they could.

Essentially, I was transposing the model McCluskey had developed to the education system and I believe it can be transposed elsewhere.

***

I am going to talk about the construction of the session structure, my rationale, reasons and experimental ideas behind this structure and how these worked in reality. We are going to explain the process of goal corrected empathic attunement (GCEA) which is a key development made by McCluskey, and essential to the practise of the theory of attachment based exploratory interest sharing (TABEIS). The theory Heard and Lake developed, they described as a biological and instinctive restorative process which becomes activated once a person experiences a threat to their survival or wellbeing. We will give an overview of the seven systems which lie at the heart of the model. These systems are 'careseeking', 'caregiving', the system for 'self-defence' (this will include the fear system), the system for 'interests and interest sharing with peers', the 'sexual' system (this also considered sex and sexuality in the workplace), the systems for the personally created 'internal environment' and the personally created 'external environment' (home/lifestyle). Full accounts of these models are published in McCluskey's books *To Be Met as a Person: The Dynamics of Attachment in*

Professional Encounters (McCluskey, 2005) and *Attachment Therapy with Adolescents and Adults: Theory and Practice Post Bowlby: Revised Edition* (Heard, Lake & McCluskey, 2012). I will give a detailed account of how I applied this work and provide for the reader an account of the instant and enduring impact of the pilot. The last sections of the book will consider some theories of leadership and change, our considerations of the direction of travel for this model and its continued potential and applications, as we can see them and how this contributes to notions of wellbeing in the workplace. Participants from the pilot have kindly agreed to offer their experiences of the pilot and their voices will appear throughout. The final part of the book will offer lesson outlines and handouts for anyone wishing to take the application further.

***

We both wish to say very clearly that none of this is intended to be a quick fix for workplace stress, professional inequalities or conflict. It is not something anyone can apply anywhere—it needs to be used as part of an embedded approach to supporting people at work. Anyone wishing to get to know and understand the model in full should aim to read more and will benefit by attending the experiential and trainings which McCluskey and others immersed in her model run. It is becoming apparent these models cannot just be learnt at a cognitive level, they need to be felt, embodied in some way and it is through this permeation that the real magic starts to happen. So, this book might give you some good ideas and practices to consider, and really we hope it starts you on, or helps you along a path of, exploration and self-discovery.

This book will make use of the term "self" at many points; you will find our understanding for self for this purpose in Chapter Three. We also reference the developments of ideas of self further in Chapter One. For now, it is a reference to that aspect of you that is currently processing and connecting, in whatever way, with these aspects of us, now as writers, communicating with you.

Chapter 1

The application, theory and why try it

Exploring the dynamics of attachment and their effect on wellbeing and creativity at work

McCluskey's hypothesis is:

> If careseeking is effectively regulated through an interaction with an exploratory caregiver this can then promote the exploratory system in that person.

My aim was to explore whether leaders, managers and employees could become interested in the underlying dynamics of the way in which they behave towards other people when they are under stress or frightened. Also, I was curious if they would become interested, and curious about themselves, in how they respond when others approach them in fear-driven or stressed states.

Outline of the Theory of Attachment Based Exploratory Interest Sharing (TABEIS) in the workplace

This theory offers a framework to explore the notion "that as a matter of course we all work in jobs that require us to respond to the needs of others, have our own needs, and often don't create the conditions to support our own personal and psychological development" (McCluskey and Gunn, 2015).

According to attachment theory (there will be more description of the development of attachment theory later in this chapter), experiences of careseeking and caregiving have their roots in infancy and shape our expectations and responses to careseeking and caregiving in adult life. My project was to explore how these manifest themselves in our working patterns and relationships. Heard and Lake developed a theory based on our biology about what enables wellbeing, and they constructed the idea of a restorative process which becomes active when faced with a threat to our survival or perceived survival. My plan was to use the theory that they had developed of attachment based exploratory interest sharing (TABEIS), subsequently applied and operationalised by McCluskey. At the heart of McCluskey's work was the process of goal corrected empathic attunement (GCEA) (McCluskey, Roger, and Nash, 1997; McCluskey, 2005; McCluskey, 2005a). If we regulate our affect, the systems of careseeking and caregiving can be appeased and leave us biologically and emotionally more equipped and free to work and communicate well with our peers. McCluskey's research provided some support for Heard and Lake's understandings of biologically based goal corrected interpersonal systems. The work that McCluskey asked those who came on her courses to do was to consider these ideas in an exploratory way. To explore is to wonder (and to wander), not to judge or criticise, not to diagnose but rather to find what is there to find. Clearly the terms "careseeking" and "caregiving" were going to arouse some reactions in a work setting but I decided to deal with those as they arose.

The theory suggests these systems work together as a single process to contribute to and maintain maximum wellbeing (McCluskey and Gunn, 2015). By taking this into the workplace I was asking participants how they saw this theory and this approach applying to them at work, and indeed if they could.

**

We know working with others can be a scary business; our competence, and our skills in role and with each other are constantly put to the test. We bring with us our unique histories, myths and family structures. Sometimes this causes great disturbance in our "selves", our bodies and our minds. We may not recognise our own needs, and we may not tune into the way we impact upon the needs of others. Left uncared for too long, unassuaged needs push us to the brink of fear. We fear for our survival (this might mean losing our job), we may over or under compensate for the situations in which we find ourselves. We may get caught up in dominant/submissive dynamics in relation to colleagues, team members and those for whom we are responsible. We may work too hard, or not enough. We may find ourselves going around in circles spending hours not achieving very much. We may become ill and forced off work, or become ill and remain in work. Both absenteeism and presenteeism are challenging features of the modern workplace. Our ancient systems trigger ancient responses, our past haunts us in the present, and our natural fear hinders us because we don't know how to heed it anymore. If we can consider these biological systems and catch the unassuaged needs before they trigger fear we may help each other stay healthier in work, or go appropriately off work for recuperative periods of time to heal and recover in order to get back into the fray.

This pilot was pitched at certain potential participants selected by my training colleague, to avoid unconscious bias on my part. It was pitched to help participants consider various factors which affect performance and their own wellbeing; to consider the way they worked with others through a new lens, offering a different way to review their impact on their immediate teams and stakeholders, and on the organisation, and vice versa.

It was delivered as a collaborative learning opportunity; collaborative in that each person's contribution was recognised as valid and important, each person's exploration offering the potential of learning for others. For instance, asking the questions: am I the same as or different from someone else, and in what ways?

What might this mean for me? A chance to bring real case studies under a new scrutiny and develop reflective practise skills, providing a fresh way to think about their own needs and expectations. For McCluskey and I, a chance to get a fresh look at the hypothesis and our thinking.

We were clear this pilot was a further development of the approach taken by the staff counselling and psychological support service using different psychological perspectives to enhance professional work and leadership skills. So, it had a broader frame within which it could comfortably sit.

Recruitment involved me meeting with each of the participants to give a brief outline of the McCluskey approach. I explained the organisation had an internal staff counselling and psychology support service, which could be accessed to support participants should the process cause any unhelpful emotional or psychological disturbance. I explained while the systems were to be presented in a group setting it was not group therapy. This is also the way McCluskey describes her work, as "courses" not therapy. It is however evident to McCluskey and myself that these courses nevertheless often seem to have developmental impact which may include therapeutic effect; either way having a positive effect on how they manage their relationships. After recruitment was completed the course was delivered to nine participants over nine sessions of two-hour group meetings over the period of time between April and October 2015.

Group structure

Recruitment of participants was conducted by working closely with a colleague from our Organisational Development and Professional Learning unit (OD&PL). This colleague circulated the outline of the course to various members of staff, but actual participation in the group was by my invitation. I asked all interested participants to commit to all the group sessions, and I asked them to be willing to provide review and feedback of the course after its completion.

I organised meetings or phone calls with each participant individually first before we started. This introductory contact was an opportunity for me to outline the intentions of the course and gauge their fit for it. They got to meet me and ask preliminary questions. The final nine were selected through these conversations. Attachment work is relational, therefore, it seemed only fitting to start on a relational footing. The group met for nine sessions with as many participants as were able to attend on each date. Sessions were mainly at no more than two week intervals; however, I made a mistake by not having all the dates set at the outset. When we tried to set the outstanding dates, congested diaries meant some sessions had greater gaps between them than I was really happy about, but these pragmatics impacted upon the planning. This become the first learning point, it is a simple one and I would have fared better to have remembered it (LP1) – it is much easier to have all dates set prior to the course commencement. Different intervals between sessions have different impacts – at two weeks it feels very much like a structured taught course, more than two weeks moves the experience toward a more reflective practice/action learning set nature. The longer gaps also required greater work from the participants to hold the new model in their minds, not conducive to application at this early stage. In hindsight, having established a strong connection with the participants compensated for my mistake in some ways as they were willing to be as flexible as they could to attend. To rerun this without such a connection could easily reduce attendance. I initially set up a system to bring anyone who missed a session up to date by inviting them to a one-to-one session with me. Whilst this offered them a good chance to gain the didactic input it became evident from the pilot that actually the group and shared learning was more important to the participants than just having didactic input from me. This became LP2 – participant application and exploration in group and cross learning gave the course greater impact than just my teaching and coaching. Additionally, it offers us here a parallel bit of application; if the number of people requiring one-to-one became overwhelming, I would have struggled, which would not have been good modelling of caregiving to myself.

***

Session one was designed as an opportunity to meet each other as equals interested in the course, to consider what they would like to get from it and what the plan of the next sessions would be. In principle, it was deliberately not for people to ferret out how important they were in the organisation by dropping in job titles, thus avoiding activating a fear-driven dominant/submissive culture from the outset. I explained this directly to them. I asked they respect the approach and not head off after the session to find out who they all were. I couldn't guarantee they weren't guessing or already familiar, of course, but they certainly appeared to be respecting this principle. This is a principle used in the McCluskey approach which I happily replicated. However, it aroused their curiosity as most of my participants were used to presenting themselves as their roles not as themselves. The session also functioned to outline the rules and boundaries of the course, the history and genesis of the theory and an outline of the remaining sessions and the session structure. This included explaining the reflective activities I was asking them to complete in between sessions.

Sessions two to eight: each session focused on one of the biological systems involved in the instinctive restorative process (as defined by Heard and Lake), the subjects of: careseeking, caregiving, sexuality, exploratory interest sharing with peers, the personal system for self-defence, the internal supportive or unsupportive environments and the personally-created external supportive environment (home/lifestyle). In each of these sessions participants had an opportunity to review their progress, a short didactic input from me on the biological system to be explored, with time put aside for discussion of their observations and their integration of these ideas at work. Specific time to identify what people were learning, discovering and applying to their own ways of being, operating, thinking and feeling, was allocated in every session; this is a key aspect of the McCluskey approach.

Session nine was a summary session, reflecting on the course impact, on themselves, their teams, their ways of working and was very important for managing their wellbeing. It became a summary stop in what turned out to be an ongoing process, and the review was also an opportunity to establish if there was an interest in any rolling ongoing activity for the group.

I will explain each session in detail later in the book.

***

The theory

In an evolutionary, heritage or genealogist type of style, McCluskey and other attachment practitioners seem to take considerable pride in making explicit the legacy of the development of the theory where other psychological theories may only reference and nod to the key figures. One of the advantages of paying detailed homage to the minds that have gone before is that you make explicit the splits in theoretical development and you can bring the theory right up to date in the room with the people who are your collaborative pioneers. This is a wonderful way to help people take ownership of their place and inventiveness in the development of thinking (LP3). Whether this is done deliberately or not it has powerful impact, as it locates the work we do together in the thinking and the ongoing genesis of attachment theory. I was also operating in a knowledge economy, where legacy and clarity are currency.

However, whilst it might be possible to reference every great mind that has contributed to the evolving form of attachment theory, we are not going to do so here in this book: it has been laid out explicitly elsewhere in other texts for that purpose. I realise this may upset some readers who might feel especially bereft without more reference to say, Freud. Certainly, no offence is intended here but we really do wish to give the time and space to this application and therefore to references that most apply to this application.

As an integrative practitioner and philosopher, I do not see the thinkers below as the only great contributors who have had impact on attachment theory. However, I hoped that understanding the particular impact of some of the figures, ones that made particular landmarks, could give my participants structure and landscape to this theoretical history.

Based upon what I have learnt from my own study and my work with McCluskey, I introduced this theory by headlining a few key figures. **Sigmund Freud** (1856–1939) developed ideas about self (Freud, 1923). **Charles Darwin** (1809–1882) developed ideas about the evolution of systems to deal with the world and hierarchical pecking orders (Darwin, 1859). In the 1930s Human Ethology is developed by **Irenäus Eibl-Eibesfeldt,** who considered the study of human adaption, survival, character and its formation (Keller, Scholmerich and Eibl-Eibesfeldt, 1988). I didn't talk about, but should have also mentioned these next three influential scientists, my thanks here to Butler who kindly reminded me they should be included. **Walter Bradford Cannon** (1871–1945) published his book "The Wisdom of the Body" describing the fight or flight response in 1932. The fight or flight response is our autonomic instinctive biological response to real or perceived threat (explained in more detail in Chapter 6). It is typified by a burst of adrenaline, causes psycho-physiological change and the experiences of anxiety through to terror in mobilised or immobilised manifestations. Cannon built upon the notion of an "inner world" coined by **Claude Bernard** (1813–1878). Bernard theorised that body systems function as they do to maintain a constant internal biological environment – which he called the "milieu intérieur". Both scientists expounding the then revolutionary idea that our bodies self regulate. It was Cannon who consequently encapsulated this idea in the term "homeostasis" in a paper he produced in 1929 called "Organization for Physiological Homeostasis". Homeostasis is recognised as the ability of our bodies to organise themselves to maintain an equilibrium. And we should also wish to include **Aristotle** (384 BC–322 BC) and his earliest ideas on perception and a concept that the whole may be greater than the sum of its parts.

William Ronald Dodds Fairbairn (1889–1964), a Scottish psychiatrist and psychoanalyst brought explorations of our intent to form supportive relationships born with components of personality hotwired in (Fairbairn, 1952). He expanded notions on splitting, defence and repression from early hurts, ego and self-to-self as well as self-to-other (objects theory). He theorised that our primary motive was to form supportive relationships; this was a key difference to Freudian theory at that time. **John Macmurray** (1891–1976) contributed ideas about the essentially relational nature of human beings. **Thomas Kuhn** (1922–1996) influenced by, amongst others, the philosopher Ludwig Wittengenstein, made some excellent elucidations on the nature and cause of paradigm shifts. Relevant here are aspects of his work that included exploration and statements about how paradigms become a dominant frame through which we make sense of the world. These paradigms often then become self-referencing theories; theoretical revelation and shift occurs when perception, experience, and cognition of anomalies drive forward the motivation to form a new paradigm (Kuhn, 1962).

John Bowlby (1907–1990), a psychiatrist asked by the World Health Organisation in the 1950s to look at how to support children affected by homelessness because of World War II – stated that adult mental health was adversely affected by separation and loss in childhood, through his work he deduced that we have two instinctive complimentary goal corrected systems. These systems, amongst other functions, enable affect regulation.

Mary Ainsworth (1913–1999) worked with Bowlby, and expanded the knowledge of place and sense of security as essential for survival, exploration, and play. It was Ainsworth who brought the notion of security as a secure base to Bowlby; this is often attributed to Bowlby who of course used the idea. It was Ainsworth who brought the idea from a hypothesis presented to her by her lecturer Blatz (1940). Both Ainsworth and Bowlby could instantly see the biological and emotional sense in the hypothesis of a secure base being needed before an infant moved into exploration.

We will come back to some of these philosophers, practitioners and theorists later on in the book.

***

The birth of goal corrected empathic attunement (GCEA)

Brian Lake (1922–2007) qualified in medicine, and later in life worked as a psychiatrist and psychoanalytical psychotherapist. During the 1950s he was employed as ship's doctor on the RMS Queen Mary sailing from Southampton to New York City. On board, he developed an acute interest in the internal organisation of the ship in terms of crew and passengers and seriously began to study, at first hand, organisational dynamics. When the volume of passenger travel changed from sea to air in the 1960s Brian left the Cunard Company and joined his brother Frank, also a psychiatrist, who had established the Clinical Psychology Association (CPA). This was a massive movement within the Church of England aimed at introducing clergy to insights from psychology. Brian parted from his brother when Frank began to move into more controversial practises which Brian felt there was less evidence for at that time, such as birth trauma. This was very new territory. Instead, Brian sought analytic experience and training for himself from the psychologist Harry Guntrip. Guntrip was himself analysed by Fairbairn and later Donald Winnicott, paediatrician psychoanalyst. Brian was given the first post of consultant psychotherapist at St James's University Hospital in Leeds, where he established a very successful day care service for people with mental health problems using a dynamic form of group therapy. One of his key observations was to notice many of the people using the service had few if any interests in their lives, and had no peers with whom to share any interests they may develop. In Brian's view, having, developing and sharing interest was a source of vitality, creativity and wellbeing and which contributed to social and interpersonal competence. This was a theme he was to bring to the theory which he and Dorothy Heard later established.

Dorothy Heard (1916–2015) – her first degree was in medicine, after the war she worked as a scientist at Addenbrooke's Hospital, Cambridge, producing with her colleagues many articles subsequently published in the journal *Nature*.

In the early 1950s she was widowed with three small children from her marriage and whilst bringing these children up she retrained as a child psychiatrist with John Bowlby. She worked with him in the department of children and parents at the Tavistock Clinic in London for 20 years. Heard was part of a research team with Bowlby, Ainsworth, Robert Hind, James and Joyce Robertson, amongst others on their early work on separation and loss. She was an integrative thinker, who could see how observations of behaviour could be understood within different theoretical models. Heard and Lake formed a productive and creative relationship when they got together in the late 1970s and developed their understanding of attachment dynamics which changed our understanding of the paradigm developed by Bowlby and Ainsworth.

Heard's primary focus was in the biological nature of individual and interpersonal systems and what happens biologically if we are overstimulated. Heard also challenged Bowlby's idea that the caregiver had to be older and or wiser; her research indicated a peer could give goal corrected care, and this could lead to interest sharing separately or evenly together. This is a fundamental factor for the workplace pilot application of the theory. An effective, creative and productive workforce is one with effective interest sharing across its staff resource.

Una McCluskey graduated in social science in Dublin but did her professional training in social work at Edinburgh University. There she was influenced by Megan Brown, a psychologist, who had a phenomenal understanding of research into human growth and development and the work of child and adult psychoanalysts, particularly the work of Anna Freud. Esmee Roberts, also on the social work staff was concurrently staff with the A. K. Rice Leadership[1] courses and introduced McCluskey to such theorists as Bion (1961), Emery and Trist (1973) and Tom Main. JD Sutherland had returned to Edinburgh having retired as medical director of the Tavistock Clinic.

Having originally trained as a psychologist in Edinburgh, Sutherland came under the influence of Fairbairn (who was lecturing at Edinburgh University) and decided to study medicine in order to train as a psychoanalyst, which he did in London. His return to Edinburgh was facilitated and supported by many colleagues, including Dr Douglas Haldane. On his return, Sutherland set about establishing the Scottish Institute of Human Relations, with a view to training individual and group analysts who could take the insights from psychoanalytic work into the broader fields of health, education, community work and social services. McCluskey subsequently trained with Sutherland in Analytic Group work. After qualifying as a social worker McCluskey went to work with Douglas Haldane. Haldane, was an innovative child psychiatrist working in Fife, who developed a unique organisation for working with family systems (highly influenced by staff at the Tavistock Institute of Human Relations, such as A.K. Rice (1965), E. Trist and Emery (1973) and Harold Bridger. In collaboration with Fife Health Board, he established a residential facility for working with whole families within the child and family services (see Haldane, McCluskey and Peacey, 1980). Bowlby visited that department every year on his way to Skye for his summer vacation. In the early 70s McCluskey sought consultation with Bowlby on the impact on child development of an emotionally unavailable parental figure. This started an interest in the use of attachment theory as a guide for clinical practice that McCluskey was to pursue many years later.

Around this time (mid-1970s) McCluskey was assigned by Haldane as family therapist to the first family admitted to the family unit. The challenge to think systemically, produced what was later described by Sue Walrond Skinner at an

Association for Family Therapy (AFT) conference, held at the University of York, as the middle school of family therapy in England. McCluskey had developed a model of family therapy addressing individual and group dynamics which she called theme-focused family therapy (McCluskey, 1987; McCluskey and Bingley Miller 1995). The original work on theme focused family therapy (1987) was strongly influenced by the work of Bion (1961) and his focus on the "primary task" of the workgroup. Another paper published at the time had within it the prototype for the theory subsequently developed by Heard and Lake. Published under a somewhat obtuse title ("Teddy Bears: facilitators of therapy", 1983) it carried within it observations of the fact that different interpersonal systems within the person seem to interact with each other, i.e. working with a person on their interests could affect their sexual relationship with their partner, the nature of their caregiving to their child, and their capacity to seek care for themselves. McCluskey noticed how observations of these interrelating factors could be used to good effect to enable change in the direction required by the person seeking help (McCluskey, 1983). Also in this paper is evidence of McCluskey's inclination towards empathy; that is, really valuing another person's experience, from their own frame of reference.

McCluskey met Heard at an AFT week-long conference in Cambridge in 1976, and later when Heard and Lake came to work in Yorkshire, McCluskey, Celia Downes, Liza Bingley Miller, Dorothy Whitaker, Ian Sinclair and others formed a regular research seminar on attachment and object relations theory, with Heard and Lake, at the University of York.

In the 1980s McCluskey and Haldane worked as part of a staff team from the Tavistock Institute of Human Relations in London running week-long workshops for staff from industry and the health service on "understanding and working with organisational dynamics". These workshops were based on the work of Harold Bridger, a psychoanalyst, social scientist and a founder member of the Tavistock Institute of Human Relations. He is well known for his concept of the "double-task". This involves helping members to examine the process by which they go about achieving the "primary task" of the organisation and at the same time insisting that they observe the process by which they achieve or fail to achieve this aim. He is known for his innovative work with companies such as Philips, Unilever and Shell.[2]

In 1986 Heard and Lake published a seminal paper on the attachment dynamic and later produced their book *The Challenge of Attachment for Caregiving* in 1997, outlining five instinctive biological systems including Bowlby's established two of "careseeking and caregiving", they added a system for affectionate sexuality; a system for interest-sharing with peers; a system for self-defence. Around this time McCluskey was engaged in her PhD research and put together a theory of interaction for caregiving (2001), based on her understanding of the literature emanating from the field of developmental psychology and her own research. Through micro-analysis of the process of interaction in psychotherapy and psychoanalytic sessions she suggested that the offer to "treat" seemed to arouse the dynamics of attachment in both parties. This she set out to examine, and with her two external raters published her findings on the phenomenon of goal-corrected empathic attunement (GCEA) with her colleagues (McCluskey, Hooper and Bingley Miller 1999). Heard and Lake could see how this work provided evidence for the theories they were developing and led to the subsequent close collaboration of the three.

Heard and Lake went on to develop their theory to include two other systems which are operant along with the other five; these systems they describe as having the function "to support the self when no other caregiver is available" (Heard, Lake and McCluskey, 2012). These are: the "internal environment", which could either be supportive or unsupportive, and the personally created "external environment". At this point Heard and Lake deduced the seven systems operated as a single process which becomes active when a person experienced a threat to their survival or wellbeing; the function of which is restore as much wellbeing as possible. These ideas are published in the book, co-authored with McCluskey, first published 2009, and reprinted in 2012.

Independently considering affect attunement in adult psychotherapy, McCluskey (2005) worked using an understanding of Sterns' work on the external micro-analytic findings and ratings (Stern 1985; 2002) mother/infant observations. McCluskey recognised that the offer to treat in the interaction between therapist and clients aroused the dynamics of attachment. While working on the process of getting an external rating analysis of the process of interaction between the careseeker and caregiver, she could see some of these interactions were effective, and some were frustrating and challenging to both parties. On closer examination, she found effective interaction was linked with the effectiveness of the caregiver to be empathetically attuned and responsive to the verbal and non-verbal signals of the careseeker. She observed this was a highly fluent and fluid process involving rupture and repair, and when effective, both parties experienced relief, and in addition there was also a noticeable shift in vitality affects of both parties which could be captured on camera. This process was reliably rated and referenced in the article earlier mentioned and was coined as GCEA.

Together Heard, Lake and McCluskey then explored the idea of a restorative process to achieve wellbeing (some might call this actualisation) and created an approximation of the dynamic of the careseeking/caregiving relationship in diagrammatic form. They concluded that central to the restorative process working to an optimum level was the presence of an effective (suitably attuned) responsive and exploratory caregiver. Within this process, their work begins to identify how these seven individual biological goal-corrected systems interrelate. This gives an opportunity to identify biological goals (needs) and to work out the best way to obtain satisfaction of those goals (needs). They observe how the internal environment and external environment are all in constant construction. On the back of her research McCluskey set up courses for training practitioners in GCEA. Later she set up nine-week courses to explore the systems identified by Heard and Lake in the restorative process. Originally she facilitated the group exploration of these different systems through using a form of group therapy that she had trained in Philadelphia called systems centred group therapy (SCT) and it took a few years for her to use her own work on the development of a theory of interaction for caregiving (TIFC) as the primary medium for facilitating these groups. By then she had realised the importance of the facilitator as an exploratory caregiver. This shift in emphasis had a profound effect upon her training cohorts. Eventually McCluskey went to print on the difference and similarities between SCT and TIFC. In 2010, she delivered a lecture at the University of Porto on the relevance of TICF to organisational life. The lecture was called "Fear-Free Exploratory Caregiving: An Essential Component of Leadership in Organisations".[3]

Using this as a model and her ideas on goal correction through the systems, she helps attendees to understand how they might interpret and experience the arousal of instinctive systems, and the impact on the self when these systems remain unresolved (not "goal corrected"). She facilitates and supports members in exploring their histories, assumptions, and finding new openings to know and assuage their needs – to explore their potential and track changes in vitality.

I believed these ideas could be usefully brought into business and organisations. The focus of my work was to ask: "What does it feel like to be a member of this team, this group, this organisation?"[4] This clearly sets the person as centre and recognises the notion that if we don't address people's feelings and their experience of the job and their relations with others we create a culture where people feel like cogs in a machine and fodder for the organisation rather than a creative (and essential) part of it. Taking us to the proposition if we haven't been met as a person – if we don't meet others as people, we are likely to move into dominant/submissive activities in order to control our environment. Dominant/submissive relationships are not the best for individual nor organisational wellbeing. The job of the pilot (and McCluskey's model in general) is expressed by her as working on how we ease off the fear and work in non-competitive ways delighting in our own and others skills and competence, sharing in competition not being threatened by it.

***

What I set out to test . . .

There hadn't as yet been an organisational application of TABEIS, although it is being used by others working in organisational settings, such as but not limited to: education, therapy, social work, palliative care. Being a psycho-educator I really wished to see it applied in an organisational context. McCluskey was also really interested to see if I could operationalise it.

The questions I set out to answer with my pilot group were:

- Is there any impact from the course on your interpersonal encounters with your colleagues? If so can you describe what it is?
- Has the course impacted the way you think you might be working? If so can you describe what it is?

- Has the course impacted how you regard yourself, and take care of your "self"? If so can you describe what it is?
- Can you imagine this course for other groups or members of staff?
- Any unexpected outcomes, surprises, learning, satisfactions, dissatisfactions?

***

Group ground rules

Creating an environment for people to learn, based on the McCluskey approach

A safe and well-constructed learning environment maximises our potential to learn. When we are frightened our chimp brain (basal ganglia) gets in the way and we can't access our cognitions. We generally need some cognitive competence for learning, and whilst we may look present, when driven by our chimp brain we won't be present for learning. A safe and well-constructed learning environment maximises our potential to grow, thrive, explore and tackle the business of being frightened, being a human being at work. In the model McCluskey frequently notes that, if we are to ask people to put themselves out on the edge of knowledge, we have to support them looking over the edge, help them feel there isn't a precipitous fall ahead, that they aren't going to be (metaphorically) beaten up by the facilitator or their colleagues. Therefore, it is crucial to have good boundaries and rules. Through McCluskey's considerable experience of working with groups, through her studies and reflections on the group work she has done, she has honed some principles which really do support effective group orientation, containment and nurture. I combined these principles with ideas from my own therapeutic practise and training background.

How good group structure works: key messages

- Spot and try to move away from anything dominant or submissive – move to joint exploratory relating.
- Try to create a fear-free exploratory process – we aren't here to be better than anyone else.
- Bring big questions to the facilitator, not each other. This reduces dominant/ submissive activities by accident or intention.
- Work alongside each other: don't be a voyeur on someone else's discovery – whatever they are looking at, consider what it might mean for you. This is a lovely technique – whilst one person might be thinking about how they give care, everyone else can also think about how they do it too – rather than just ride on the back of one person's hard self-reflection.
- You aren't here to problem-solve someone else's problems.
- Pay attention to what happens in your body – it is your biggest database.
- Tolerate difference in the room.

- Be open about your responses – don't just say what you think you ought to say to each other or to the facilitator.
- If you have a mind-read about me or another person in the room say so – we can look at these, there may be important information in your mind read, accurate or not.
- As you start to become conversant with the systems, as you learn to tune into yourself, notice which of the systems is being aroused, and by what.
- Come as people not as roles.

In order to facilitate this last one, as I mentioned before, I emulated McCluskey's model (which she learned from Yvonne Agazarian (1997)) by not letting any of the participants know who their colleagues were going to be prior to the course. On the first meeting I only used their first names and asked them to talk about themselves, but not about their jobs or their seniority or status. This had instant impact; we weren't bantering about remit or exerting or challenging authority – they were from that moment in it together. Each equal to the other.

The other thing I did was to use a combination of settings for holding the sessions. The first location was new to all of us, the subsequent five in one room and the rest we booked as we went along. The new room for the first session was important for all of us, including me; it signalled in an external way that we were all doing something different here. The settling in one room for a subsequent set offered some stability again for us all; they knew where to come and I knew the room and its equipment. Some large organisations are like small villages, with a myriad of buildings, routes, passage ways. This organisation was no exception to this rule. It involved clinical activity for medicine and dentistry, it was located next to a hospital, some of its areas are distinctly clinical. The first room was quite tricky to find and this had a most marvelous and unintentional effect. They were all really proud of themselves when they had found it. I had inadvertently brought them into a state of self-competence. After the use of the same room for a while, the movement and experience of finding new rooms for most, became so preoccupying the participants detached from their previous activity of work. The group arrived chuffed and ready and open to whatever came next. The evidence speaks for itself, the external environment matters. Consequently, after checking it caused no-one unhelpful anxiety, I resolved to find new and interesting spaces for some of the other sessions – and as a group we explored the impact of this as we went along. After the pilot had finished the ongoing meeting of the group continued to take place in different locations

What became very evident, as all skilled group therapists and trainers will know, is group safety is crucial for productivity and contribution. The rules and boundaries need to be fair and the facilitator has to be consistent, available and vigilant. It is not always possible but every moment of deviation from this is worth exploring reflecting upon for the facilitator, and sometimes for the group. I worked on this throughout the pilot with differing levels of success. A colleague, who offered her reflections on the book, Gayle-Anne Drury kindly helps me notice how in this attentiveness the care seeking/caregiving dynamic is at play, and perhaps this small piece here reflects and demonstrates the power of the theory.

Not only did this first meeting, and subsequent ones, tell me more about the systems and how they permeate once we start to explore them, but also each and every encounter taught me more about myself as a person, as a facilitator, and about working with groups.

So, we have a theory, we have a means of constructing a group, forming it to explore, we have all the systems ready to go and we have a group of people really willing to see if this work matters at work.

Notes

1 The A.K. Rice Institute is a community of teachers, students and practitioners of a discipline known as group relations. Group relations offers a powerful and unique methodology for understanding how our unconscious thoughts and feelings significantly impact our lives when we are in groups; from family to workplace to nation.
2 See Guardian Obituaries, 2005. Available at: https://www.theguardian.com/science/2005/jul/12/highereducation.guardianobituaries
3 Una McCluskey, 2010, lecture, University of York, UK. See: https://vimeo.com/14417615
4 Reflecting McCluskey's primary question in her work with families (1987) when she asked, "What does it feel like to be a member of this family?", immediately capturing the individual and group components.

Chapter 2

Introducing GCEA and TABEIS for the workplace

A key skill for any manager, leader, trainer, therapist, or in fact anyone in a leading or caring role, is to ascertain exactly what the problem is when a colleague or client approaches or signals for help. The greater the skill the more we are available to offer appropriate responses and effective care to the person presenting the problem. Essentially this is goal correction. The concept of a goal is used in a very specific form here. Goal setting is a very well-known feature of cognitive behavioural therapy (CBT) and brief therapy. In these contexts its purpose is target or aim-setting, something definable, measurable. A goal which a coaching or therapeutic client is aiming to achieve, feel, think. Unlike the CBT or brief therapy (although there might be the same experience), goal correction in the model being introduced here is intrapersonal, interpersonal and is biologically based. Goal correction in this form is extremely productive. It means that when the goal is reached the system that had become aroused is assuaged and the primary, natural exploratory system is engaged. Without effective strategies, tools, or talent in asking astute questions, a manager, for instance, might find herself on wild goose chases. An apparently satisfactory answer is given but the person returns, with the same question or query, or a slightly altered version of the same question or query. This can be frustrating for both: the manager might find herself repeating the same answer over and over again, the colleague consequently hearing that same answer over and over again. But neither finds satisfaction. The manager might find herself attending to, or working furiously on, mythical problems, coming up with care for the wrong issue; genius solutions, ideas or strategies to problems or concerns which may exist but aren't actually the real problem. Therefore, whilst a task or an issue might be satisfied the underlying problem remains. The colleague returns, needing more help, having new but similar issues, finding themselves repeatedly enveloped in similar predicaments. Does this sound familiar?

This is a huge cost to energy, time, relational quality, productivity and creativity. We have to learn how to tell the difference between the words, the behaviour and the need or needs being expressed. Learn to detect when we are being thrown off the scent (consciously or unconsciously). Wade through the morass of the other person, keep our heads above the morass of our own histories or even mind out for transference (see section on transference below and also in Chapter 4).

Mind out for, say, specifically transferential shame, where the experience of having been shamed when asking for help earlier in life has become internalised, or at a deeper level, prompted a behaviour of indirect manipulation, manifesting as pressure to seek from others or impose help on others. I believe that if I can support myself (and others) to discover more about this I might be able to improve the ways I (and they) give help and get the help really needed. This really matters at work, with competing agendas and priorities. It is my view these goal correcting, focusing skills are under-rated, under-valued and in general under-nourished in training for workplaces. Doing this well (identifying and resonating with needs) can look like alchemy, instinct and skill weaved together. It is however, eminently and phenomenologically recognisable. You know it when you do it (resonate with another person's need), and you know it when you are on the receiving end of it (having your need resonate with them).

These nuggets of content, these tiny colossal, refined forms (not unlike the Platonic (Plato 1987, c.427–347 BC) idea of 'Form', Penguin published 1987) of human meaning are everything inside and outside of work communication. Without refining skill, we miss each other's meaning, confuse, confound, annoy and hurt each other at work and elsewhere. In transactional analysis, these moments of resonance could be called "strokes", "a unit of human recognition" (Steiner, C. 1971). Spenceley describes it as "A transaction which provides a person with either recognition or stimulation" (2016, p. 4). It is a phenomenological moment of connection; where contact and response chime meaningfully. Antonio Damasio (2006) might call it an element of a somatic marker a biological entity as part of a neurological pathway that registers mind/body data of the past in the present. Irvin Yalom (2004, p. 50) might call it "the patients' idiosyncratic response" something the therapist picks up with their "rabbit ears". Carl Rogers might call them "molecules of personality change" (1980, p. 62). We might know them as conscious synapsis awareness. These phenomenological encounters occur in excellent therapeutic moments, when the therapeutic alliance is effective. If we can bring this skill into workplace encounters, without inferring an inappropriate therapeutic relationship, we can perhaps help colleagues access each other usefully, productively, creatively. Having learnt about phenomenological ideas through the work of Maurice Merleau Ponty (1964, 1973), and having thought long about what these vessels of meaning might be, there seemed to me enormous value in exploring the McCluskey Model because of the various ways the model endorses and considers mechanisms for this effective interpersonal chiming.

Whatever word or phrase we use, these small but Tardis[1]-like entities are crucial for connection and effective relating at work. They underpin how well we meet each other, they underpin successful work relationships and productivity. Success in giving and receiving these entities may be indicated by a moment of psychological and physiological relief. Goal correction, in this description, allows us to include the idea we are a set of biological systems and these interpersonal goals are biologically based. There is a physical sensation, a moment when you know the other person has got you – it is the equivalent moment when you know you have got the other person. In some ethereal resonance, there is implicit or explicit understanding. It is easy to see how they could fall into the notion of alchemy. McCluskey has recorded and mapped hours of one to one and group encounters, working hard to capture the moment of face to face, body to body, synchronicity which often symbolise this resonance (McCluskey, 2005). My humanist therapeutic training took me into the territory of advanced empathy. I know that, like many experienced or intuitive practitioners, I have reasonably good skills in detecting these tiny but hugely important units of individual nuggets of meaning. So, it was with great enthusiasm that I recognised the significance of her development of GCEA.

*****

McCluskey's training involves considerable practise of advanced listening skills and slow pacing over small encounters of enquiry to find and experience these moments of mutual congruence and meeting.

Goal correction is about eliminating all the things which stand in the way of getting at real meaning, the real problem. In Egan (2001) it is in stage two of the skilled helper model to ascertain what the client is seeking, but in GCEA it is far more subtle; empathetic attunement is the difference.

However, before we move to attunement perhaps we need to say more about why this matters in the workplace. I think it is fair to say that most people interested in workplace behaviour and wellbeing are all, more or less, in agreement that some emotional nous is useful at work. We don't leave our personal lives and histories at home and enter the workplace free of our own current relational and life preoccupations and operate in automaton ways. We may struggle to differentiate between one patterning of relational history to another, but we are, in the main, emotional creatures in the workplace. We have needs, we get frightened, we get angry, we like or dislike routines, we attach to others, objects, or our office spaces. We can ignore all of this of course, but might find ourselves bemused at why our colleagues become dispirited, de-motivated, antagonistic. We might find ourselves dealing with more disciplinary processes, recording more time off sick. Mental health issues alone have a huge impact on the UK economy and the UK workplace:

> Mental ill health is the single largest cause of disability in the UK, contributing up to 22.8% of the total burden, compared to 15.9% for cancer and 16.2% for cardiovascular disease. The wider economic costs of mental illness in England have been estimated at £105.2 billion each year. This includes direct costs of services, lost productivity at work and reduced quality of life.
>
> (Department of Health, 2011)

As well as lost health and lost productivity, there is lost creativity, lost edges of competitiveness, and lost time. Time is perhaps the most precious commodity. Good skills in the here and now equate to really good use of time! Now, just to be really clear we are not propounding the idea where everything needs to be done quickly, some relationships need to grow slowly over time, some conversations should take a long while. But if we can blend in these relational focusing skills, we can use time well and have better quality in our exchanges and communications where possible, and less wear and tear on the self.

***

Attunement

The idea of psychological attunement (rather than Reikian or chiropractic attunement) could be said to originate from Heidegger's ideas of internal/external settling in the self by finding the right place to be (Heidegger, 1929). For our purpose here though we are thinking more of the work and descriptions of attunement between mother and infant by Daniel Stern (1985). Attunement is a really interesting idea. There is an excellent article which explores the role of mirror neurons in attunement by Gallese, Eagle and Migone (2007).

It is this Stern attunement and resonating which I believe is crucial in the workplace. We know from the work of Ainsworth in particular, and later Gibson and Walk (1960), that there can be an iterative connection between mother and infant, both conscious and unconscious. This echoing and resonating is learning attuning skills as a baby. It is the echoes of smiles, turning toward, turning away, which occur every second when the infant is in contact with its caregivers. We can attune – look towards and engage, we can deliberately fail to attune – withhold our attention, we can mis-attune – pretend not to get the message – over-attune or offer an over simple attunement. So, there is an intentionality (conscious or unconscious) on both sides. Attunement in parenting is connected to affect regulation. Teaching the infant how to manage the impingement of needs effectively, teaching them to put needs on hold or even ignore them altogether sometimes. Through numerous repetitions, we teach soothing skills (down-regulation) animation skills (up-regulation) and stabilising skills. These ideas for work, are explored further in the innovation of Workable Ranges by Rose (2016). Rose furthers the theories of Porges (2001) and Siegel (2007), and explores the notions of up-and-down-regulation across the biological, psychosocial, cognitive and emotional systems. She posits the idea that we all have a range wherein we are at our best and most functional; most competent to work.

Through our explorations of the systems, as you will see later, the pilot group began to consider, that is really tune into, how and how often their colleagues might come to them in a state of agitation or enquiry, but what they needed was not a solution but a moment of human connection to manage the agitation. Of course this is time consuming in its own right, but mastered in the right way, with phrases, attitudes, appropriate attention in the moment, the encounters my pilot group have with others start to take on a different quality altogether.

In the pilot, I spent less time talking to my group about honing these goal corrected attunement skills, and more about using the systems to help eliminate the obstructions to finding out what was going on for them and for the people they were dealing with. I offered them ideas and processes to identify aspects of their past histories which may be shaping or distorting their encounters with themselves or with others.

***

Transference, counter-transference and projection

Chapter 4 further explores the contribution of Freud (1949), but let's here have a quick reflection of transference, counter-transference and projection: three of his very enduring descriptions of inter-personal tangling. Transference is where I move an emotional response I hold about one person onto another, often to their bemusement. Counter-transference is where they respond back to the transferred emotion.

Something like this, perhaps:

> I have a history of issues with Bill, a person from my past, who I found to be manipulative and annoying. Sarah, someone in my present life approaches me with a problem, but she inadvertently expresses her issue just like Bill does. I consciously or unconsciously respond to her as though she was Bill, off-hand and quick to get away. Sarah is disappointed with me, as this is out of character for our interactions and tells me off for being off-hand. She is confused, caught in my transference.

The potential for transference and counter-transference is all around us at work. The transference can be positive feelings too: watch for favouritism here. Colleagues accidentally behaving in ways which have meaning for us. If we are not able to catch these echoes, we find ourselves in fraught exchanges, punishing innocents, praising without merit, overvaluing someone, failing to discern reality, withholding care unconsciously. If we can tune into these dissonances and recognise them we will be able to get back into relationship and competence much faster, back to good work, good interest sharing.

Projection is similar and different. Projection is where I feel angry, but perhaps don't feel justified in my anger. Sarah comes to me and says something, and blinded by my own anger I say, "Why are you speaking so angrily to me?" Sarah heads off confused again. Poor Sarah is having a rough day with me. These "snags" as McCluskey might call them, these bruises from our past are a part of us. Using the skills of TABEIS and GCEA can help us to manage these in our here and now.

***

Empathy

Empathy is a similarly complex simple phenomenon. It too might belong in the world of alchemy and mystery or become a skill to hone. Like attunement, we can use empathy well, or respond in a mis-empathic way, or with apathy. Empathy skills in the workplace can enable us to relate to and identify the state of our colleagues, see what may be hindering or affecting them so we can then start to decide if we need, or even can, do anything about it – and chime with their experience. Language plays a huge part in empathy – think of the way you might describe a pain to another person. We tend to use metaphors and similes in abundance. There is something very important about describing our experience to others, and then finding out and believing they, in some way, get it (Merleau-Ponty, 1973). Good or advanced empathy requires something like Yalom's rabbit ears – ears, or rather a body, that hears all the messages being sent by the other. It requires the skill to set aside enough of oneself and let the world and priorities of the other drive the definition and rules of whatever is being described by them. It is the Mr Benn[2] of work. You need to don enough of the clothes and outfit of the other person, and to walk around in their skin enough, to get a sense of what their experience is to them (their experience of a chill along their spine) and not how you imagine you would feel with that experience (your experience of a chill along your spine). Although your equivalences could be informative, you need to check them out. Empathy can be very hard to grasp and not everyone can experience it either. If grasped though it is through this window of empathy that the nugget of meaning from the other might be viewed, received or understood. I believe you have to have empathic skills to attune well. One can only be truly empathic (and therefore effective in terms of attunement) when one is in exploratory mode. We can only be in exploratory mode when we are not being blinded or inhibited by the arousal of our biological systems. There are many layers of attunement.

***

Bringing them together – Goal Corrected Empathic Attunement (GCEA)

If managers and helping professionals can develop enough of these attunement, goal correcting and empathy skills they can have, in my opinion, enormous purposeful impact at work. If we can help people refine their conversations so the real issues (not just work issues, but worries, concerns and agitations) can be safely aired expediently, we might have shorter but more effective conversations. This is a large portion of McCluskey's concern, if we can get to the "nub of it efficiently", we might still have to manage fear and anxiety and perhaps recognise we cannot provide the environment where all problems can be resolved.

The caveat on this has to be psychological and emotional safety. We cannot expect everyone to receive all that others communicate, if every aspect of the other person were to be received, we would become overwhelmed and confused very quickly. We want here also to be clear, we do not see people as containers, which become over-full. This conceptualisation of people might lead to an inference that some people are better containers than others, suggesting a rank of skill of containership, this ignores the fact we are talking about living organic human beings with systems which change and develop on contact.

However, nuanced and intelligent exchanges minimise the overall drain and stress of these encounters. It takes practise. With practise though these individuals go on to have good conversations or even know when to avoid getting into conversations because the conversations are smoke-screens for something else that needs little or a different response. A well timed and genuine acknowledgement of the content of the other may well see your colleague back on track, accessing the resources they need, using their skills, resting or changing direction, or in McCluskey's terms, back in competence, back to exploratory interest-sharing and creative working.

GCEA in the workplace has the potential to help colleagues differentiate between someone needing to sound off, let off steam, to when they actually need something from you. Gifted questioning might help your colleague refine something for themselves too. Done well it is the dissipation of blocks and hindrances to whatever other (work) activity we are supposed to be getting on with.

***

The Theory of Attachment Based Exploratory Interest Sharing (TABEIS)

As explained in the introduction, TABEIS was developed by Heard and Lake. I called the pilot TABEIS because it was both what I was teaching and doing with the group. We were exploring and sharing interest in attachment. It also meant we started using the words straight away.

Attachment theory, is, in my opinion, absolutely one of the key pillars of self and self-understanding. It is based on the quality and nature of the interaction between infant and parent/guardian. Through the seminal works of Bowlby and Ainsworth we began to understand that the resonance between infant and parent is key in the structural development of the child's mind, personality and emotional processing. Attachment research introduced the idea of four attachment styles: secure, avoidant, ambivalent, and disorganised (Ainsworth and Wittig, 1969).

Having insight into your own or the presenting styles of attachment of your colleagues can be helpful in effective communication. It could tell you about how you might need to be to talk to them in order to meet them as the people they are.

***

Why do I think this matters at work?

Let's just overview it a little.

Every day at home and work each of us will have others careseeking (needing care, time, solutions) from us, or wanting say, for us to share their passion about a subject or work issue – whether you like this or not, your attachment systems will be consequently firing up and down at the same time. This dynamic takes its toll on us as persons, it is physiological, and if we can observe the dynamic and work with it, we can do things which improve our own overall wellbeing and to help manage, and work with, any anxiety the careseekers or interest sharers (people we share interests with), may be experiencing in regard to us.

Work is essentially interpersonal. The biological systems described by TABEIS are both intra and interpersonal. The McCluskey model includes a diagram developed by Dorothy Heard (see below) – showing how if our care-seeking is active but unmet we very quickly become anxious, as our system for self-defence takes over as the dominant emotional and behavioural presentation. In other words, left unchecked the anxiety fuels our primitive fear system. By this point the person is at the mercy of their fear system. Our fear system interferes with being creative. Our fear system prevents the "self" acting in any way that is not useful for the survival of the "self", as the "self" determines at the time. For instance, over time it might manifest as focusing only on a job promotion rather than the team effort, when the team effort might in fact be the activity which keeps me in a job in the first place. The "defensive self" becomes the sole object of determination, the bigger picture gets lost. If, however our care seeking is met, the fear system is either not activated or alleviated, we get on with or return to happily interest sharing, data entry for instance. For instance, I am busily working on the annual report, but have a thought about something I think my service should do, it's in my mind, I go to my boss, but she can't give me the attention I need, I leave, brewing a little. This brewing becomes preoccupying, I start to invent or catalogue instances of not being listened to. I am not interested in the data anymore, in fact I make mistakes. However, if I can replay it, go to my boss, park the idea that I need to talk to her about something, get sufficient acknowledgement, I have no angst, and get right back on with my work. It's a simple example, but they happen probably on a daily basis. Please note here, there is no idea of criticism in the behaviour, rather understanding of it and explorations of ways to work with it to support wellbeing and interest sharing. Interest sharing is working well with our colleagues, sharing our skills or knowledge for the organisational objective in which we have a personal and real investment. If we can use our talents and skills we can discharge our individual responsibility and make a real tangible contribution to the organisation. The relationship between us and the organisation is symbiotic.

Both have a biological effect – one good one not good. In Figures 2.1 and 2.2 (developed by Heard) we can see how when the careseeking goal is not met it

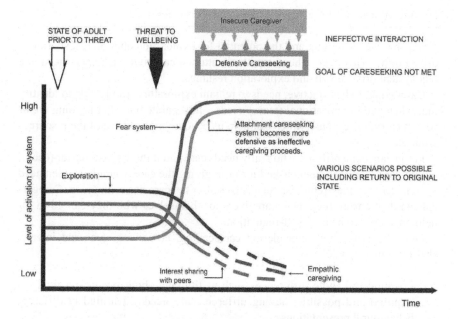

Figure 2.1 Insecurely attached adult responding to a threat to wellbeing

Note: Original by Helen Heard, from *Attachment Therapy with Adolescents and Adults: Theory and Practice Post Bowlby* (Karnac, 2012)

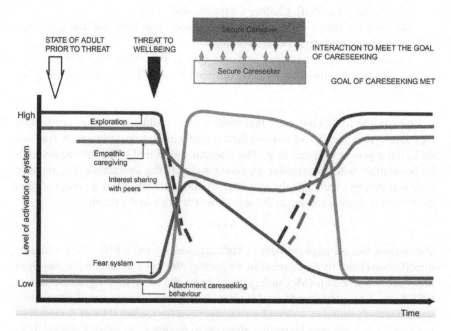

Figure 2.2 Securely attached adult responding to a threat to wellbeing

Note: Original by Helen Heard, from *Attachment Therapy with Adolescents and Adults: Theory and Practice Post Bowlby* (Karnac, 2012)

drives the fear system up and the potential for exploration and interest sharing is driven down. However, when empathetic attuned caregiving is experienced, the fear system drops down and exploration resumes.

Caregiving, to be effective, needs to remain exploratory. Being able to identify individual and organisational (team) needs – to separate out what is going on, or who is carrying responsibilities can help us become more aware of the resources around us.

For instance, identifying who really needs care and if there is an ulterior (useful but hidden) motive in being asked for or in giving the care. Caregivers then need to consider how they replenish themselves after the care has been given. Caregivers can then ensure they have caregivers for themselves who they can go to for help, this leads to healthy self-regulation.

Other benefits about considering careseeking, caregiving, fear and interest sharing could include

- Learning to handle difference. Such as thinking about what care giving is required and possible, having different care needs identified in different behavioural presentations.
- Negotiating the fear system. Learning to communicate with the understanding that fear paralyses, stifles and obstructs creativity (i.e., if I have evoked fear in another I should not expect them to be effective and functional until this fear has subsided). Chapter 6 explores this in full.
- Minding for dominant submissive behaviour watching out for defensive caregiving – or defensive care seeking.
- Interest-sharing: Chapter 7 explores this in full. Matching and noticing vitality levels: noticing shifts in our energy and vitality and encouraging others to notice theirs.

You can see from Figure 2.2 that when a secure adult feels threatened while their fear system is quick to respond their careseeking systems trumps the fear and seeks out a person who can help. The diagram shows that when the secure adult makes contact with an effective caregiver and gets the interaction they require; their fear systems immediately goes back to normal levels. Over a period of time their interest sharing returns to the level it was at prior to the threat.

***

We suggest that an improvement in staff careseeking more effectively could be directly correlated to an increase in wellbeing. We have evidence for this from McCluskey's research (McCluskey and Gunn, 2015). A training in the use of GCEA can help participants on the pilot identify work instances of attunement and mis-attunement, i.e., by emphasising my need for feedback I was demonstrating how GCEA operates by paying attention to feedback. In short, I needed them to let me know when I had got it right.

TABEIS, like other good models of self and its attributes (such as TA), considers the ideas of development, preference and predetermined hotwired genealogy.

We may easily develop an understanding of any one of these systems more than the others. Those of us who are therapists, may be in our professions because of over-developed systems of caregiving, developed so perhaps because of whatever family situation we found ourselves in. Might the architects and builders of the world have also an over-developed sense of the system concerned with the external environment?

The system for creating a personally fashioned external environment, as we see fully in Chapter 10, is a powerful source of wellbeing. At work, it is filled with pitfalls and bear traps. I might not get to even choose what my external environment looks like; at work, it might be someone else's idea of what is aesthetic. This might perturb me. I lose my creativity, my sense of place and self, think back to Heidegger's ideas of internal/external settling in the self by finding the right place to be. Now my external environment might not be something I can entirely influence but a little influence and tailoring might go a long way to feeling a creative resonance around me enough to feel creative in the workplace. One of my pilot participants has a great example of this in the chapter on the external environment.

And what about the internal environment? If my inner sense of myself is disturbed how can I be expected to engage with my staff review processes? How can I cite my attainments, think about goal setting? My boss gets left with the idea I don't like my job, when maybe the reality is I don't like me.

The fact is you may be able to tune into some systems better than others. All of them firing up and down at work from the minute you arrive. Caregiving as you respond to the colleagues who need you, careseeking from the colleagues who you see as caregivers. Interest sharing with those who have the same passions as us, being sexually attracted to or repulsed by others (whether you like it or not). Getting angry or fearful when a threat is perceived (or a need not met), analysing ourselves or our performance (internal environment) and creating a story about what is most likely going to be based on your life narrative. Reflecting all of this in the world around you, on your desktop, on our desk in our office – wherever you may have the freedom to express.

***

Exploratory

The McCluskey model embodies a practise of remaining exploratory. We look at the theory from an exploratory perspective, we look at ourselves from the same viewpoint. Not to cast judgement, or assign blame, but to find out what is there and decide what we might like to do about it, if anything. This curiosity-based approach helps us be open to possibility. This exploratory approach is not dissimilar to one of the core conditions of therapy as laid out by Carl Rogers, the father of person centred theory. This is to approach a client in the spirit of "unconditional positive regard", one which is free as far as possible from judgement. To relate to the client from the point of view of openness and enquiry: traits which are currently very alive and evident in the growing development of mindfulness (Chapman-Clarke, 2016) for the workplace. So, these ideas, this theory of attachment based exploratory interest sharing sits in excellent company, it is a gift for work, a gift for living, a real addition to thinking about being human at work.

The next chapter looks at the structure of the sessions and thoughts about how adults learn.

Notes

1 A "TARDIS" is a Space Machine of vast size disguised as a 1930s British Police Box that a character called the Doctor travels around in. It was created for a BBC TV series called *Doctor Who* by Sydney Newman, Donald Wilson, C. E. Webber, Anthony Coburn, David Whitaker and initial producer Verity Lambert.
2 Mr Benn, a character created, written and produced by David McKee for the BBC in 1971 and 1972.

Chapter 3

The session structure

This chapter will look at: the structure of the sessions in the pilot; the rationale for the structure; its purpose from my point of view; its impact on the experience of my group; and a review of session one, which was the introductory session.

The theory

I hope this chapter will draw out the nuances of good adult workplace learning, nuances which I believe are sometimes taken for granted. I shall explain the ideas I used and why. For those readers who teach, you might find the parts of this chapter which talk about group facilitation and group work, only tell you what you already know. You should feel free to skip to the second half of the chapter.

This chapter has had the benefit of considerable review and contribution from Marcus Hill, who helped me to put the pilot together. Amongst others, my secure attachment with Hill has been key for the success of this work. We have a collaborative and supportive professional relationship, where we interest-share and cross-coach. We actively support each other's competence and whilst not always fear-free, we work together to talk about the fears we experience. Hill helps me bring out of my unawareness aspects of training and facilitation I would otherwise take for granted and not state explicitly for your benefit. Therefore, this chapter is better for his kind and generous contribution.

***

Structure

Each session of the pilot had broadly the same structure to it; this is called "constructive alignment", where your learning design and pedagogy reflects your learning outcomes (Biggs, 2007). The format evolved a little through the course with adaptations based upon my ongoing assessments of what the group needed. Essentially, my pilot group needed less didactic input from me (LP3) and more time to explore their own understandings and application of the systems and the model. We will explain more of this in the chapters covering the different systems too. For working with a small group, my style is very much to move in and out of different modes – from teaching (didactic) to facilitating to holding a space noticing a moment of learning, to coaching, questioning, and exploring, to training and giving tips, to mentoring, and asking second order and meta questions (see Griffiths in Fry, Ketteridge, Marshall, 2003). Sometimes I don't notice doing this anymore, Hill's observations help me bring this knowledge out of my unconscious competence into observations which I hope will be of interest to you, the reader.

***

The rationale, purpose and impact of the structure

The session structure functioned to keep me steady (my fear system in check) and the participants safe. If they remained safe I optimised the possibility for them to learn. As a rule, I preferred to have a detailed session plan, rather than rely upon improvisation. Hill refers to this as Parker Palmer's "paradoxical tensions" in the classroom, for example, "The space should be bounded and open" (Palmer, 1998), it's a challenging task! However, when achieved well it left me with mental capacity to focus on the subjects and my participants. I would let the structure go a little, if the group work moved into creative and learning flow. By flow I mean those moments of learning when participants embrace and play with ideas, moments of energy. Assessing the ebb and flow of the learning experience meant vigilantly watching the group, being guided by their responses as well as asking them directly for feedback on the structure. A pre-ordered structure supports fear-free work, modeling exploratory interest-sharing behaviours in my facilitation style as best I could. It also left me with something to fall back on should any flow stop. As a facilitator I needed to not have to entirely rely on my pre-frontal cortex or cognitive mind, which I knew would be periodically taken off-line with anxiety.

Even the most confident presenter or facilitator is liable to anxiety, a natural fear response when standing in front of a group of people. I heard from a colleague it may be ancient instinct which makes us fear being watched; that from a primitive point of view it is possible the only time we would have several sets of eyes upon us was prior to being attacked or eaten by a pack of predators! Plus, I knew that when I want to do a good job I can become anxious. Therefore, the TABEIS fear system was very alive for me. As the work of Damasio (2006), Rock (2009), and Rose (2016), show very clearly, a burst of adrenaline can have the effect of de-activating my prefrontal cortex (thinking in the here and now), hindering access to my hippocampus (memory/competences), and if very anxious the basal ganglia puts me into survival mode (often referred to as chimp brain these days but I prefer the notion of primitive brain). These are not the states to be in for exploratory interest sharing. It takes me into survival mode, alarmed, nervous, defensive. All this could also be true for my participants. Therefore, working towards minimising fear in me, as well as in them, is a constructive way to work, unless we wish to experience the fear response in the present tense.

My session structure was:

1   Arrive, welcome and centre.
2   Introduce the session.
3   Cover any questions or feedback.
4   Discuss the system in hand and any relationship to any other systems.
5   Learning and reflection.
6   Surprises, learnings, satisfactions and dissatisfactions.
7   Headline the next session subject and any reflection to do.

***

The sessions and pilot structure also paid attention to people's different learning styles. I have great faith in utilising the concepts of learning styles as expounded by Honey and Mumford (1982). My faith comes from ten years of training experience using it, and hours upon hours of participation and observation in meetings. I was first introduced to these learning styles through my colleagues at The Baobab Centre in York. I will be eternally grateful for what they taught me. Honey and Mumford described four learning styles: theorist, activist, reflector and pragmatist (TARP). Those of you reading this who are activist will be wanting to do something with what you are reading, if you like it, straightaway. You might have already penned a note suggesting an action of some kind, you may have made notes. You'll know yourselves as being keen to get going with things – you might find meetings super hard work.

Broadly speaking, those of you who are theorists will be paying particular attention to our theoretical references. You will probably be making assessments of how credible or not these theories and theorists are. You might be thinking of alternative theorists, you might be making references to other names in the margins of this book. You think and know a lot about theory, about the philosophy of learning and knowledge. You dislike a poorly structured argument.

Reflectors are cogitators, you take time to absorb an idea, turn it over, feel it and think it through to know it. You are most likely to have not yet made your mind up about whether you like these ideas or not. I should come back and ask you later what you think. If I ask you now, you are likely to either go blank or tell me you don't get it.

And those pragmatists amongst you will be thinking about how it can be applied, requiring hands-on details. I hope this chapter will be of particular interest to you.

You will want to know about the practicalities. And you will judge us on the effectiveness of the impact. You will consider many things so long as they have the desired influence. You are great negotiators. You help others see the benefit of any activity which you decide has value.

Our learning styles are not fixed, we can easily have a combination of some or all of the styles, and our style is affected by work and life circumstances. I used to be a reflector; cogitation was a key process in gaining confidence in a subject or a skill. Having a neurological familiarity with a concept used to be very important. To this end I would rehearse, and talk through anything I planned over and over again. I sometimes still do; I still like to check that whatever I have intuited in my mind is close enough to what I expected to learn. I am now, however, far more activist. This is noticeable in the fact that once I had recognised the potential of McCluskey's work, I wanted to bring it in to my workplace quickly. An effect of my work as a trainer/facilitator means I have developed responses in the moment skills; learnt how to react faster to the multifarious requirements of my organisation. My payoff is I find they are very receptive to new ideas posed as suggestions for problems which might have occurred, and therefore I have reinforced this behaviour in my ways of working. However, the pitfalls of working this way are that I might panic a little if I don't take advantage of an opportune moment, and yet a quick, knee jerk response sometimes is not the right response, and limits how much knowledge I am able to gain about a situation. Upside though, a quick response does certainly reinforce and deepen good listening and focusing skills. I can be in that moment the mother tuning into the needs of the organisation.

There are positives and negatives with each style: activists can be too impetuous, move too fast for others, as above, and leave people in a state of confusion. I have to mind this in my workplace, and remember that ideas I have adopted and absorbed as part of my practise and understanding for supporting people at work, might be completely new, or new variations of ideas, they may have heard of before and they might need other things from me in order to learn. I needed therefore to know how I operate in order to keep an eye on it negatively affecting the pilot course. Hence also the importance of the contribution here from Hill who could observe me doing this or not.

Success, as I learnt from the Baobab Centre, in working with others is to ensure that any learning activity has a range of elements which appeal to the differing learning styles. Therefore, my sessions include something to do in the moment (activist), discussions of application and benefit (pragmatist), theoretical references (theorist) and over time reflection (reflectors) with a handout to use if needed. I find following these ideas helps build any workshop plan.

In addition to the insights from Honey and Mumford, I also paid attention to VAK/VARK[1] Fleming and Mills (1992) came up with additional ideas about learning described now as VAK/VARK, they suggested from their observations people have certain inclinations in their ways of absorbing information: visually, auditory, through reading/writing, or kinesthetically. I can see it and copy it, I hear it and follow instructions, I write it down myself and learn it, or I learn by doing it physically. Like the Honey and Mumford's TARP there is no suggestion you only have one modal learning style, but you might have a preference – a good teacher/ facilitator will provide a mixed medium of modes to maximize the opportunities participants and learners have to acquire the learning. If you like, TARP is about mental embodiment of learning, VAK/VARK is about the medium – the tools.

I addressed VARK by having visual aids, sometimes drawing up on a white-board. Auditory is my didactic delivery and group discussion. Reading material, and periodically encouraging them to write to me, offering them constant opportunities to feel the experience of the systems and by the nature of having a group talk to each other – having the additional opportunity of other people's experience to learn from as well. Hill is kind enough to suggest that I addressed this in many more ways: "'for example visually – painting pictures with my words, using visual metaphors, providing a colourful systems chart, kinesthetically – my gathering exercises, asking them where in their bodies they were experiencing the systems, auditory – using expressive language to describe the systems etc.". A learning point here then is about maximising the ways we communicate if we want to communicate.

***

Offering training as a therapist

Being a psychotherapist offers me the opportunity to bring therapeutic skills to the training and the group work that I do. One of the most useful of these skills from my practice is being able to work in a present way with thoughts and feelings being expressed in the here and now. These are all forms of information and content which may be useful to the experience and learning of the group. I recognise also there is constant learning and development for me in noticing and reflecting this content back to either individuals or the group. I abide by a code in my therapeutic practise this code is called "the ethical framework for the counselling professions" (BACP, 2016). Through this framework I try to embed some principles of being in my practise amongst these are non-maleficence and beneficence. These guide me to reflect upon and check my interventions come from the principle of not causing harm (as well as I can reasonably be expected to know this) and check I have some rationale that an intervention will in some way benefit the other person. For instance, this means I interrogate my natural curiosity to see if a question I wish to ask might have value beyond satisfying my own curiousity. I might tune into my gut instinct as indicative information rather than compulsion. Another principle of the code is "prizing client autonomy", this means as much as I might be interested in something someone says or does, and however I might believe some insight is just in your sight, I need to allow the other person to go at the speed they wish to, in the direction they might wish to. So I might offer an observation, or offer them a chance to pause on something, but if they choose not to, then I prize this choice above my own belief. I might come back to it if the appropriate need or opportunity arises again. This selection and filtering is going on all the time. It was the grist of my therapeutic training. And even having an intuitive take on an instance, I have to be prepared to professionally account for anything I might suggest. I bring these skills to my training, I notice lots, I feel lots, I use as much as I truly believe has value and recognise (as in noticing less didactic input from me was better for them even if I had a strong urge to explain what I knew) the learning and insight which each individual makes for themselves has infinitely more value than my describing or formulating it for them. This is not to say however, that a well-placed formulation can't be of great use, at its very best when it is a fair and compassionate reflection of the person I am meeting. These practises underpin what I hope is my respectful and open approach to my colleagues. These principles underpin my essentially relational way of being at work. It's not easy sometimes, but I find it is deeply satisfying in the main.

In tandem with the ethical framework, my training had a predominately humanistic element to it and the work of Carl Rogers and his formulation of the core conditions also underpin the stance I take to supporting and working with others. We look at Rogers later on.

***

The room

As I have mentioned in Chapter 1, the sessions were held in different locations. The consequence of this was unexpected and delightful.

The first room was in a building unfamiliar to all but one of us. The room itself was new to us all. The effect of this was neutralising. The room was a blank canvas. There were none or few associations. Sometimes associations can be unconscious. Unconscious or not, though, they can impact upon how our bodies and our minds might be available to be present for new information or learning. If a room is like some room we have experienced before, our minds and bodies are designed to recall these positive or negative associations. It is such a clever way of being – but if we don't notice it, it can be distracting. A funny or unexplained feeling can become diverting, and left unchecked I might start casting around for external reasons to explain these sensations. I might become hyper-vigilant, looking for something in the other people to prove I should be feeling jumpy. Whilst all this is going on I won't be as available for learning, that is for sure. And again, we see here the fear system and its connection to both the internal and external environment. More on these later. I changed the room periodically as we progressed through the systems. The consequent work group which formed after the pilot always meets in different rooms. We have traversed across the campus, sometimes closer to some participants' places of working, sometimes away from everyone's. By moving into different spaces with the group, I was shifting the pitch and the sources of association all the time. This lent itself to a kind of resetting for us all. It tuned into the impact of the external environment very well, which we will cover in detail in Chapter 10. All participants experienced a sense of mastery in finding the room, which in a complex of hundreds of rooms in 24 buildings, is no mean feat. This could have been a disorganising and anxiety-raising process, so it was important I checked how it was for them to know whether to do it again. My inclination, as Hill observed, was to enable them to be in a place of "competence" to start the sessions well, an example perhaps of the value of finding ways to help others be in a state of unconscious competence before you ask them to engage in a task. In other words, to feel competent and not be in a state of anxiety or fear from the outset. Furthermore, I can only wonder that perhaps we miss small opportunities to change our perspectives at work – like exploring our work environment, and miss too, opportunities to celebrate different skills – like finding different buildings, different rooms. Mastery is crucial in the workplace. With a sense of mastery, we can feel emboldened to take on new ideas, we open ourselves to possibilities rather than defend against the unknown. This also created a bonhomie amongst the group. Forming as a learning cohort helps participants support each other and learn with and from each other too. The impact of this technique in moving room also played out through the continuance of group meetings – whereupon asked if they would like me to settle on one room they all declared they preferred the changing spaces. Hill experienced this as my inclination to allow the cohort to be in a place of "competence" to start the sessions well. Again, a technique learnt from McCluskey about how if we can reduce any activation of the fear system, we support our colleagues in being exploratory to do the work and learning.

Another learning point (LP5) then – do we really consider the spaces we use for training and learning? Might there be different spaces we can use? Does a lesson (especially management or leadership training) always need to take place in a classroom? When we need to balance resources against practicalities do we pay enough attention to the learners' needs over the facilities we favour for certain activities?

***

I: Arrive and centre

In response to a new stimulus, it is usual for humans to experience a burst of adrenaline. A warm and genuine welcome when we arrive in a new setting can help us manage the effect of adrenaline (excited or nervous) that might not be helpful. Adrenaline is useful of course, it can help us become sharp, but it can also intensify or distort those first few moments of encountering a new situation. A poor start can ruin a whole experience (as the fear system activates), if someone feels missed out, criticised, frightened in any way. As mature adults, we underestimate the impact this has upon us; it is our nature at work though, pay attention to it and we open up the possibility of improving our encounters no end. My insight from TABEIS and the learning of group facilitation of the McCluskey model made these notions very evident to me.

Remember, all the time we have the notions of attachment theory behind us; attachment places great relevance upon up and down regulation. Regulation is biological and emotional. My mother regulates my need for food by feeding me. I regulate the hunger of the learner by giving them food for thought. My mother regulates my anxiety by soothing me. I give my cohort time to consider a new idea which might rattle them and reassure that it is ok to like or dislike it. As a facilitator working with attachment dynamics my charge was to anticipate some of the dis-regulation or spot it and soothe or animate my cohort. It was my job to anticipate the potential regulatory impacts of this whole experience upon them, address it and in the meantime, model a behaviour for them to consider using in their own work activities. If I could offer them a felt sense of this way of working with others, they were more likely to consider employing it themselves.

After all, it is the belief of McCluskey and I that regulated colleagues are col-laborative, healthy and creative ones. This warm and genuine welcome is very present in McCluskey's teachings and group work. Whilst as a trainer I might have known this was good etiquette, I didn't really grasp why such a welcome matters. As creatures we like to feel we are in the right place, we belong. Using the principles of attachment theory we could suggest this taps into our early baby/child experiences of belonging to an entity of which we are a part. We were all once intact with our mother, and this primitive attachment is etched through our being. And whilst we may have learnt separation skills this doesn't mean that we aren't affected by these primitive anxieties. Perhaps you can notice the physiology of this the next time you go to or attend a new meeting? Upon arriving, what welcome do you receive? If there is none, do you feel open and inclined towards the other people there, or do you wish to keep to yourself a little bit? Can you notice anything going on in your body? What might your heart rate be like, are you hot or cold? What thoughts might be going round in your body? How able are you to attend to what is going on? Notice humour – adults use humour as a chief way to release tension.

Stepping into a new experience is risky; if we are unknown to others do we exist, are we secure enough on the inside to engage with and become known (or rejected) by others? It is remarkable how quickly we can become terrorised by the existential fear of being abandoned or non-existent. But, of course, this isn't a global truth, as I hear all the introverts amongst you say that you might wish to remain anonymous, quite right, but I still believe that you prefer a quiet welcome and acknowledgement of place before you are left to you own devices. Essentially it is about recognising that we will be in a range of states (securely or insecurely attached) and preferences and be meeting others at work in a range of states with different preferences. These meetings and differences need to be navigated in some way.

The techniques and approaches in the model are to reduce people's fear, manage and support them so that they can bring as much as possible of themselves, their wisdom and their curiosity to the business of thinking about these TABEIS systems. It's all parallel process too. If I can model being curious, non-critical self-reflective behaviour congruently and genuinely I hope that I can support my participants in thinking about adopting these techniques for themselves and with their colleagues. As a workplace therapist, I know the workplace is full of bear pits, poisonous fruits, dead ends, unexpected mountains and difficult terrain. As we progress through these terrains, we need as much of ourselves as we can bring to the endeavour, and if we can reduce the times we frighten each other we can really work well. You see this fear system gets in the way of all sorts of things. But as a system it is crucial for our physical, emotional and psychological survival as we will see in Chapter 6.

***

Centering

One of McCluskey's approaches is to use the technique of "centering". You might find centering in yoga, pilates, meditation. Centering is all about settling ourselves in the moment, using gentle breaths to notice any physical tensions in the body, unhelpful or nagging thoughts, back or foreground information that could hinder how we might receive information in the moment. Breathing and focusing on these bodily and mental sensations helps us set them aside, to allow our meta-awareness to choose its focus rather than be tugged away by a physical niggle or repeating neurological or mental factor. Centering is not about becoming sleepy, zoning out. It is taking the time to clear enough physical and mental space to attend to whatever it is you are up to.

The key aspects to centering are to stop, notice, breathe, keep your eyes open and then spend some good time getting into a really healthy, comfortable sitting position. McCluskey promotes the concept of finding your sitting bones, by shuffling on your bottom until you feel your posture change and correct. Good posture enables us to be present and alert, our bodies feeling supported in the chair we are in and not collapsed forward or back. Training colleagues who studied with McCluskey have taken the element of centering on to focus on it alone – such is the power of this particular activity.

Each session started with centering, a period of shuffling and settling in the chairs. A chance for them to arrive, set aside thoughts of where they have come from. I encouraged them to notice and release any tensions they tuned into. We have the tendency, especially at work, to crash from activity to activity, without pause. We erroneously believe we can move from writing an email to talking to a colleague, to running a meeting. The false notion claiming that multi-tasking is a good thing! Yet, in reality multi-tasking is doing more tasks with less attention. Good work is focussed work. It is no wonder we might relax on holiday when we permit ourselves to focus on less for longer. Bring this back into the workplace and notice the shift in work effectiveness but also the reduction of anxiety. If it is true that our prefrontal cortex only accounts for 4% of our brain mass (Rock, 2009) and we are limited in how much we can do with it in any one time, why try to make our minds carry more?

***

2: The introductory part of the session

The introduction to the first session was of course different to the rest in that I needed to convey the history of the model and outline my plan for the pilot; to explain their participation and to hold on to the principle of allowing them to come as themselves, not as roles, not as ranks in hierarchy but to encourage and allow them to participate as equals. This also clearly set me out as the facilitator. I was indeed in role and needed to remain in role in order for them to know that I would hold the group and the boundaries for them. This is perhaps another key learning point (LP6) which is that group dynamics (in workplaces as well as in therapeutic settings) are greatly benefited by clear and fair leadership of the group facilitator. I had to have a rationale to be working from, I needed to be able to share this with the group and without being a dictator I needed to set the pace and rhythm for the work – these are notions key to good group work and foundational elements of the McCluskey model.

The introductory portion was our map for the following two hours – it gave them a sense of where they might be going and also supported their learning. Sometimes I skirted the outline of the session plan and received feedback that this left some of them feeling distracted as they wondered about what might come next. Again, it is a basic idea, but so fundamental. We might use agendas in formal meetings but do we offer structure enough in learning encounters too? I had an agenda and a plan for each session and when I shared this with the group, they could see the map too.

The introduction also served each time to remind the group about the pilot model. It is worth reiterating here, the model considers the idea of a restorative process to achieve wellbeing (like Maslow's notion of actualisation). To remind you, the restorative process consists of the interaction between seven instinctive systems, each with a discrete goal working independently. Using awareness of these systems can help us establish when one of them has been activated and think about what we might do differently. This puts us back in the driving seat, i.e. if our system for self-defence is aroused and we are not aware of it. Using the idea of the restorative process enables us to choose to focus attention on which system is active. The activation might become noticeable physically or emotionally. The trick is to develop the skills to notice. Consequent to noticing the activations come the opportunity to consider if there are unmet biological goals (for instance if self defence has activated but there is no need for it), and then the option to work to the best of our ability to meet those goals or at least learn enough about them to set them aside to manage later (see Chapter 2 for more on goal correction and attunement). We were learning and reflecting upon these seven systems of care-seeking, caregiving, self-defence (including fear), interests and interest-sharing, sex and sexuality, the internal environment, and the personally created external environment. These systems are either intra (self-to-self) or interpersonal (self-to-other) or both.

Our systems for self-defence and careseeking are imprinted from birth in most cases. Interest-sharing with peers, then sexuality, develop at later stages. Care-giving develops in toddler stages and is very dependent upon the parent/child dynamic. The system of the internal environment and our skills for expressing our personally created external environment are developing from birth and become noticeable in teenage puberty stages onwards, but all the systems essentially remain forever in constant construction.

Therefore, these systems are present at work, in work. On the pilot, while we worked in the here and now, we also aimed to find "lookalikes" from the past which might be "snagging" our movement forward or influencing how we are working with others as colleagues. Finding these "snags" is an underpinning McCluskey technique and a key part of her innovation.

***

3: Collaboration, questions and feedback

Participants were consistently offered opportunities to ask questions as we went along. My experience is that if I can allow for questions to be asked in process, I am most likely to be able to discover places where I may have been too quick in explaining an idea, made an assumption or indeed forgotten to say something at all. Allowing questions also adds to the collaborative nature of the learning activity. I needed to manage my fear most around this and trust that a question is a question and not an assault on my knowledge. This consideration is very relevant not just in an education setting but anywhere information and knowledge is prized; a learning environment where knowledge is currency. I was actively supporting the idea of collaborative learning and working on my own fear all the time.

But also from a cognitive competence point of view by allowing for questions along the way (or at least making sure they record them) I affirm their competence to have questions and allow them to free their minds from holding on to these as the time progresses.

Good questions really assist others to access their competence and their knowl-edge. Great leaders and managers know how to ask great questions. Great ques-tions do not have to be long ones, possibly the best question anyone can ask is "What do you think?". To add to the learning points we have included an appen-dix of the questions we used at the end of this book – we hope you might like some of them.

***

4:   Discuss the system in hand and any relation to any other systems

The approach McCluskey takes when introducing people to her model is to over-view the history of the development of attachment theory, to explain how her professional development brought her to develop the model with Heard and Lake and then to take course participants through the systems in stages. I emulated this stepped approach in the pilot. It allows for a kind of immersion and permeation. Each system is introduced succinctly and historically and then participants are invited to consider and explore how a particular system might be evident in their ways of being. This exploration often takes us back to childhood or significant life moments. By using a system as a lens, it focuses our minds on a way of thinking about ourselves. It is less intense (although certainly not without intense moments) than trying to assimilate the model all at once. By starting with the most well known of the systems (Bowlby's three careseeking, caregiving and self-defence) it taps into any pre-existing knowledge anyone might have about the terms and ideas. By starting with careseeking it also perhaps means participants might start bringing any new self care learning into the present, perhaps even prac-tise them with others. As the experience increments up, the terms become more familiar, a competence grows. Another crucial aspect to McCluskey's approach is to encourage participants to work alongside each other (i.e., apply this idea or questions to yourself) and not sit in study of others; again this approach means everyone works for themselves, with the similarities and the differences anyone might share, becoming points of interest, not of competition.

***

5:   Learning and reflection

Learning to handle difference

This brings me nicely to the notion of difference. In the multi-faith, multi-cultural society which exists within the UK, I think we are still woefully poor at managing our differences. McCluskey propounds the richness of difference. As a therapist, I experience and welcome difference. When we are learning or teaching, embrac-ing difference is crucial. Potentially our worlds open up when we are offered another person's perspective or experience. We lose this when we try to make everyone swallow ideas in the same way. But knowledge has a seductive quality and sometimes we can feel frightened if our version of knowing the world is challenged. It takes us into uncharted territory, where we might need to rely on someone else, and this creates a vulnerability.

Some of our past inheritances embody themselves as psycho-physiological habits – neurological pathways embedded through repetition and not necessar-ily thoughts, feelings or behaviours which have to have a hold upon me now. Our understanding of neuroplasticity (Jerzy Konorski (1948) developing the work of Ivan Pavlov) means we now know, assuming no other limiting factors, each and every one of us has the potential to change (structurally) how we think, how we respond. We know from our increased understandings of conditions such as autism for instance, some of us have different neurological typologies which impact upon how flexible this wiring and rewiring can be. And sometimes, well a certain idea or approach is just not for me, either ever, or at this point in time. Either way, I am better for knowing my associations, lookalikes, or at least recognising when I might be getting snagged, than not knowing it and leaving the snag to hold me back in the darkness of my unconscious. This can lead into behaviours coined by Freud as "transference" and "projection". I pile my own content into the exchanges with others as I desperately try to manage my own disturbing internal content. Transference and projection are explained in a little more detail in the next part of this chapter.

***

6: Surprises, learning, delights, satisfactions and dissatisfactions

McCluskey adopts the notion of surprises, learning, satisfactions and dissatisfactions from Fran Carter and Yvonne Agazarian (1997) and adds "delights" to it. This technique helps me and my participants tune into their personal learnings their blocks, resistances. Everything is information, everything counts (LP7). This approach also allows the cognitive mind and instinctive body to mark in memory, significant learning and awarenesses, which might have otherwise been subject to falling into overly unconscious or fear-ridden reactivities. Fear-ridden because thinking and learning about ourselves can be terrifying.

***

7: Headline the next session subject and any homework to do

At the end of each session I set the cohort some homework. Their first homework was to think about how they sought care (careseek) at work – they were asked to reflect upon any ideas they might have had about how they learnt to do this. Remember we said earlier how this work is aided by a permeation of the ideas and terms. The homework here serves not only to get them thinking about themselves but also kept the participants thinking about the systems between sessions, and progressively increasing their self-awareness and familiarity with the ideas – Hill noticed this for me and rightly deserves the credit for this observation.

So before we get going again, is there anything you (the reader) can notice for yourself as you have read thus far? Is anything resonating with you, challenging you, what are your disagreements, those rich differences? Can you notice any surprises, learning, satisfactions, delights, dissatisfactions for yourself? Is there anything here making you consider how your past might be influencing your present at work? Perhaps you can also work alongside us as this book progresses?

How it worked in practice

Session One: The introduction to the pilot

1　Arrive, welcome and centre.
2　Introduce the session and context.
3　Cover any questions or feedback.
4　Discuss the model and its history.
5　Learning and reflection.
6　Surprises, learnings, delights, satisfactions and dissatisfactions.
7　Headline the next session subject and any reflection to do.

1: Arrive, welcome and settle

So all participants arrived, having found the room as explained previously. I invited them to settle and centre on their seats as explained above. In wishing to avoid the hierarchical banter, I prevented them from introducing themselves to each other, and was so anxious myself (my fear system charged up – would this work, how would this affect my professional reputation, would they engage?), I forgot to even let them share their first names. Whilst I wished to preserve their non-professional personhood they still needed the means to communicate with each other!

Hill was the only other person who knew everyone else, and his contribution explains beautifully the impact this had upon him (see Chapter 13). It did therefore mean his experience was also different from the others and meant he had to work differently at times, he trod an invisible course of both being my collaborator and a participant.

Introducing myself

As I had already met with or spoken to everyone, this didn't take long. I did recap on my training with McCluskey and her interest in this specific pilot, what we were embarking upon and McCluskey's encouragement and support for our endeavour. Connecting, I hoped my participants to the historical steps we were taking.

***

2:   Introduce the session and context

Context of the pilot

It was very important to explain where I was coming from organisationally. Not all staff counsellors or many staff counselling services work with such a mind for organisational application. Our psycho-education principles mean we elect to share our knowledge to help this staff group develop their competence at being themselves. We do not doubt this benefits the organisation; a more self-aware leader has the potential to manage interpersonal relationships and conflicts with greater skill. A more self-aware leader may be inclined to take good care of themselves, leaving them more available to contribute to the organisation. This is not to say work harder, but to contribute with greater skill. This staff enrichment helps these leaders influence the organisation, we hope for the ultimate betterment of all. This organisation won a prestigious award in 2017, a principally student-led vote; the student experience was largely determined by the ability of the staff to support the student journey with well regulated, competent, self-caring members of the organisational group. Therefore, whilst they might be thinking about themselves, their childhoods, their ways of being inside and outside of the organisation, the organisational benefit is writ large in our work. By saying it out loud, we legitimise, we hope, and really give people permission to look at themselves in this way at work. We also model some self affirmation practise being out and proud about the work we do.

How you were selected – no bias from me

This was a recap on the selection process and Hill's support in finding them. This recap also meant I was able to explain how I wished to invite them to participate as individuals not as jobs, as people not as roles. Fortunately, this was where one of the cohort kindly and respectfully asked me to let them know each other's first names so they could use their names to address each other. As I mentioned in my anxiety and, indeed in my relief, they had all arrived and I had forgotten to do this. Sometimes I find, if I am passionate about an idea, I become immersed in my own passion and can forget or even dare to hope what it means to have others share an excitement and interest. Having them all arrive, was one of the many experiences of joy as the pilot progressed. It was in my distraction of nerves and excitement I made this error, and I was very grateful for the question. Whilst I was aware this oversight of mine was absolutely down to my own fear system kicking in, I felt it was too early to say so. To have said could have aroused their caregiving – wanting to look after me, or even their self-defence – wondering if I was equipped to run this group work? And I did not wish to arouse any systems any further than they might already be. Whilst, I considered I might confess it later, I did not then have sufficient confidence I had established enough of a learning alliance, to risk showing my own vulnerability.

This was something I reflected upon throughout the course, and remains an area for my own personal development.

Confidentiality

The first session also covered confidentiality. Group therapists will be very familiar with the notion of setting confidential boundaries for group work – this might not occur so much in learning activities. Confidentiality rules are there to support each participant to express their experience without fear of it being a source of discussion for others outside the learning setting. Honest and deep reflection really helps us learn. It leaves less going on in the mind too – which leaves more room for the precious "presencing" (being in the moment) to happen. Whilst this was not a therapeutic training, I wished to set up group rules which helped them keep safe in the knowledge they could share their inner most thoughts with impunity, free from judgement, in so far as was possible. We also agreed we would all respect the privacy of our colleagues outside of the training, in mentioning challenging interpersonal situations; others would not be named or described so well that anyone might guess at who they were. The pilot group embraced these ideas with great respect and consistency.

***

3:   Cover any questions

Given the executive functioning and role of the prefrontal cortex, and its limited size and capacity (Siddiqui et al., 2008), it is a good idea when embarking on a training session to check if there are any questions before you set off. Whilst we might know it is good practice, we perhaps don't know why it works. Forcing people to hold content in their minds occupies the mind – leaving it less free for the learning. But also, the question held may be fear inducing, so a quick scope around means there is the opportunity to express rather than fester.

I then invited subsequent centering and settling, using a phrase which McCluskey uses all the time in her three to five day experientials, which is an invitation to "centre – get in your seats – on your sitting bones – eyes open – attentive". I knew I was about to launch into considerable detail and wished to prepare them as well as I could for it. McCluskey also uses centering through the course of her training and group experientials, she does this especially when a tense moment may have occurred. I was less confident at doing this through the sessions – if I had, however, I know I would have also been working on my own fear a little better. This would have stopped me talking too much sometimes! I believe my technique got better the more sessions I did. Again, this points to the powerful incremental effect of working in this way for both myself and the group.

***

4:   In the introductory session this meant covering some theoretical history

History of attachment theory and the evolution of the systems

The session gave a whistle-stop-tour of the figures below – with the luxury of the book we offer here a little more detail than the time limits of the session afforded, but it's still only a brief résumé here.

Historical context

Sigmund Freud (1856–1939). Freud changed the course of our understanding of the inner world of human self. For our purposes, here we are making an assumption of self as an interior meta and non-meta-awareness of sensations, feelings, thoughts, which shift and change according to neurological, psycho-social, biological stimuli Heard, Lake and McCluskey explore "self" in their 2012 book if you wish to read more and there are many works which explore the notion further. To proceed what we need is to agree that everyone has some way of formulating their experience, the notion of having an inner world which holds, processes, evaluates and sometimes determines our behaviours and encounters.

What Freud explicated particular to this theory, was the idea of psychoanalysis. The Institute of Psychoanalysis describes it in this way:

> While studying, Freud developed a particular fascination with neurology, and later trained in neuropathology at the Vienna General Hospital. In 1885, Freud travelled to Paris to study at the Salpêtrière Hospital with Jean-Martin Charcot, a famous neurologist studying hypnosis and hysteria. Freud was deeply affected by Charcot's work, and upon returning to Vienna he started using hypnosis in his own clinical work with patients.
>
> Out of these experiments in hypnosis, and in collaboration with his colleague Josef Breuer, Freud developed a new kind of psychological treatment based on the patient talking about whatever came to mind – memories, dreams, thoughts, emotions – and then analysing that information in order to relieve the patient's symptoms. He would later call this process 'free association'. Early forays into this new 'talking cure' by Breuer and Freud yielded promising results (notably in the famous case of 'Anna O'). A year before marrying his fiancée Martha Bernays, Freud published *Studies on Hysteria* (1895) with Breuer, the first ever 'psychoanalytic' work. In this book, Freud and Breuer described their theory that the symptoms of hysteria were symbolic representations of traumatic, and often sexual, memories. By 1896, Freud had abandoned hypnosis and started using the term 'psychoanalysis' to refer to this new clinical method and its underlying theories. The following year, Freud embarked upon a self-analysis, which he deemed necessary both as a means of expanding and testing his theory of the mind, and as

an exercise in honesty and self-knowledge. This self-investigation led him to build upon his and Breuer's original theory that neurosis was caused by early trauma, and to develop substantially his ideas about infantile sexuality and repression. In the coming years and decades, Freud's clinical work with his patients – among them the famous 'Dora', 'Rat Man', and 'Little Hans' – would remain the basis and core of his work, and would provide the vital material for his continual advancement and refinement of his theory of the mind.

(Institute of Psychoanalysis, 2017)

We see here the formation of a theory of mind, which suggests that through dialogue and narrative one person can make an interpretation of the state of the other, which may enable the other to gain insight into themselves. Freud influenced and taught many, one of whom – another key figure – was Carl Jung (1875–1961). Jung also contributed to these new theories of mind and exploration of human experience. Whilst he and Freud regularly disagreed on approach, what they did was bring into society the ideas of exploring the inner world of being human; of seeing how our past experiences and history contribute to how we are in the here and now. Freud coined the terms "ego", "super ego" and "id". Jung became very interested in dreams, the self, the collective unconscious, and synchronicity amongst many other ideas.

Alongside the vast and readily acknowledged works of these men come the long line of female and male clients with whom they worked, who should also be acknowledged as fundamental in the development of their theories. Without the participation of these clients these theories could not have advanced in the ways they did.

We should also like to acknowledge the work of Melanie Klein (1882–1960). Relevant to this model is her work on the development of the child's inner world and the importance of the child's relationship with their primary caregiver. She provided us with the concepts of the life and death instinct, part object relating, splitting experiences and our experiences of other people into good or bad, the concepts of projection, introjection and projective identification. She gave the psychoanalytic world a rich vocabulary for understanding previously less well understood phenomena. Her work is still influential though many do not agree with her thinking and have reformulated her ideas in the light of an understanding of whole person relationships.

The thinkers above espouse, in my view, a notion of the existence of an inner world, or furthered the long-established Socratic approach of dialogue and encounter (with object or other) leading to learning, into new paradigms. Two or more minds in conversation. Meeting each other and discovering something new of their inner selves, whether this be rediscovery or new discovery. They also contributed transference, counter-transference, dominance and submission, projection; all ideas very much alive in attachment theory, with its focus on interaction and relationship.

Transference and counter-transference

For detailed explanations of transference and counter-transference you may wish to explore Ackerman (1959) or Racker (2012). McCluskey is embarking upon the task of defining from the point of view of attachment theory in another book due to be released sometime in the future. For our purposes and the purpose of the pilot, transference was explained briefly as the way in which early experiences of a relationship can be triggered by look-alikes in the active present. At work the trigger might be a manager or colleague. My emotional, relational learnt responses (positive or negative) to person A are overlaid onto person B because something in person B reminds me of A, and it may happen consciously or unconsciously. It may well be a part of our systems of somatic markers, which collate and record positive and negative experiences to help us keep safe and pursue positive survival patterns. For work, for example, say Fred my team leader, uses the same aftershave that my Grandad did. At some level, consciously or unconsciously my responses are to the familiarity of this smell. My Grandad used to repeat himself a lot and I learnt to tune out of his repetitions and sometimes him altogether, as a consequence. As a child, the repetitions made me quite angry with my Grandad, but I could never say I found him boring because that would have transgressed family rules of respect and get on with it. When I sit with Fred I find it very hard to be attentive, my previous feelings towards my Grandad are overlaid or re-directed towards Fred. In unconscious moments, I even stockpile in my mind times when Fred repeats himself, to validate perhaps, my feelings of annoyance. I unconsciously (in this instance) behave to Fred as I learnt to behave with my Grandad. I may even deride Fred in some ways either directly or behind his back.

Understanding counter-transference is the skill of identifying unconscious communication from the other person. Fred detects my annoyance, and without understanding my redirection of feeling he could feel attacked, deskilled. Whilst he may know there is no reason for this, he responds defensively (his counter to my behaviour) because he feels attacked by me. If we can pick up the transference or counter-transference it gives us information about the state of the other person and what is being communicated. So, Fred notices I appear bored or tuned out every time we work together, and instead of extrapolating from this I don't like him, and feeling insecure and angry with me, he instead first decides to explore with me if there is any other reason why I might be responding to him in the way I am.

We believe such insights into interpersonal tangles should not just be confined to the therapeutic relationship but have great value at work. Transference and counter-transference can be very helpful in the therapeutic setting, left unchecked at work they are the source of much confusion and conflict.

Projection

Projection is the term used to describe imposing a feeling that belongs to me on to another person. For example, I was very scared by the proposal to write this book, anxious and talking to my collaborators, I fail to assess what they actually present as their feelings but decide that whatever they are doing is a representation of their anxiety. I might easily conclude they have no faith in my ability to do this, whereas the reality is my own faith in my own ability is wobbly, to say the least, and I do not know if my collaborators will help. This projection is often because there is some trouble I have with owning the feeling myself. Or if I am angry, instead of saying to my partner, I am angry with you, I might say why are you behaving so angrily to me?

Again, at work this can lead to very messy and confusing encounters with each other. My group did not need extensive knowledge of these terms, however a cursory idea of them was offered to give them some tools to pick up these crossed and confusing encounters through the exploration of the systems.

Dominant/submissive behaviours

One of the things I asked the group to consider throughout their reflections was to identify behaviours which might fall into the category of either dominance or submissiveness. These behaviours are natural normal human tendencies, and can occur when our fear system is activated, and can become habitual ways of working. They have their place. However, they can cause problems in interpersonal relationships if left unchecked or are unconscious behaviours. Put simply, I either muscle up or pull back. A member of staff who grew up in a large family may have learnt to fight to be heard, be a bit louder, overt, even proclaim their needs louder than the rest, and this can easily transfer into the way we work. Equally so the same upbringing may have led to a preference to retreat, especially in the face of dominant others. A member of staff unable to express their needs may become overwhelmed or resentful at work, leading to illness and or conflict. We will look at these tendencies more when we discuss the fear system.

***

The evolution of the theory

Charles Darwin (1809–1882) is lauded for his ideas about evolution. He wrote of systems which exist throughout the animal world to deal with the world, its threats and its stimuli to progress, and he talked about hierarchical pecking orders. This idea of hierarchy also exists within the systems themselves (Darwin, 1859).

Ethology is a science emerging from the notions of evolution and is the study of what might be evolved behaviour, development, control and function; a now broad field encompassing many others. It is relevant to this model in the exploration of how and why we exhibit the behaviours we do, what might be instinctive, what a consequence of habituation and environment. Key figures in ethology are

Niko Tinbergen (1907–1988), Konrad Lorenz (1903–1989) and Irenäus Eibl-Eibesfeldt, who continues to this day to further the study. Bowlby was very taken with the ethnological approach; parenting, he said:

> can usefully be approached from the same ethological inspired viewpoint. This entails observing and describing the set of behaviour patterns characteristic of parenting, the conditions that activate and terminate each, how the patterns change as a child grows older, the varying ways that parenting behaviour becomes organised in different individuals and the myriad of experiences that influence how it develops in any one person.
>
> (Bowlby, 1988, p. 4)

For our purpose here, the interest is also that if these patterns can be observable in the person, they can therefore be observable in the way the person relates at work. Bowlby also noted the emotional component of these observable behaviours and makes connections to preprogrammed biology and neurophysiology. These ideas permeate his descriptions of attachment theory.

William Ronald Dodds Fairbairn (1889–1964) was a Scottish psychiatrist and psychoanalyst. Fairbairn was interested in our mainly innate intent to form relationships. He also suggested that we are born with components of personality hot-wired in. Fairbairn explored ideas on splitting, defence and repression from early hurts, ego and self-to-self as well as self to other (objects theory) but his main understanding was that the infant was born with a unitary psyche that was not split, and that our primary motivation was to seek another person who would support our development as a person. This is an important consideration if we are thinking about how we are with others in the formation of professional relationships.

John Macmurray (1891–1976) wrote about the essentially relational nature of human beings in his 1961 book *Persons in Relation*. This is important in this context as we were about to embark upon exploring the notion of being relational at work.

John Bowlby (1907–1990), a post-Second-World-War 1950s psychiatrist was asked by the World Health Organisation (WHO) to look at how to support children affected by homelessness because of the war. Through his research he deduced that we have two instinctive biological complimentary goal-corrected systems. These are the systems for careseeking and caregiving. Bowlby and Ainsworth (below) began to formulate ideas around what counts as healthy or unhealthy attachment experiences based on these biological systems working well or failing in the early experiences of life. He concluded that a key factor in adult mental health was to have had the experience of a continuing warm experience of interaction with a caregiver within which both parties experienced satisfaction.

Mary Ainsworth (1913–1999) – A psychologist, who collated phenomenal quantities of data from studying interactions between infants and their mothers in

Uganda, and then in Baltimore, USA She joined Bowlby in 1950 at the Tavistock clinic. Her data exploring the verbal and non-verbal connection and interactions between mother and child enabled her to devise "the strange situation test" which produced clear differences in the pattern of interaction between mothers and their one-year-old's on reunion after a brief separation. In a nutshell, she showed us how resonance, affirmation and acknowledgement between the mother figure and baby provide a sense of security which is essential for survival, exploration and play of the developing infant. Dorothy Heard noticed while visiting Ainsworth in Baltimore that it was the quality of the interaction between mother and toddler on reunion that determined the level of exploratory play to which the child returned. This was a significant observation and one which McCluskey confirmed through her own research on adult to adult interaction in the context of psychotherapy and absorbed into her practise with adults. Through these studies we see the emergence of different attachment styles and the further development of the concept of the "secure base", a concept introduced to Ainsworth by her former PhD supervisor. Later on, through the work of Daniel Stern (1985) we can see that most infants are born with a capacity to attune to those around them. Again, McCluskey incorporates this insight into her practise with adults, helping them to explore whether they may be carrying emotional experiences from very early times which may in fact belong to significant people to whom they were attached.

Donald Winnicott (1896–1971) also wrote about play and how play is a process to find meaning. Play figures significantly in interest sharing. Winnicott coined the phrase "transitional object" expressing how we invest objects (often teddy bears or other soft toys) with qualities of individual significance. Objects will matter when we come to think of the external environment. Think of your office, your desk, it is likely to have a few transitional objects on or around it.

Daniel Stern, as we have already seen, contributes to the ideas of attunement and the existence of micro-events and nuanced communication between mother and infant. He is also one of the authors to write about the forms of our sense of ourselves (Stern, 1985, 2002).

Thomas Kuhn, as mentioned in Chapter 1, interested in the structure of the scientific revolution and paradigm shifts. Kuhn brought us the notion of scientific revolution and conceptual thinking changes. His work is particularly relevant as he explained "paradigm stands for the entire constellation of beliefs, values, and techniques 'and so on' shared by members of a given community" (cited in Heard, Lake and McCuskey, 2012, p. 15). His definitions of paradigm and revolution help us recognise Ainsworth's work in particular (for instance utilising the moment an infant cries as a base for measuring the speed of response by the caregiver and the effectiveness of soothing) but Bowlby's work as well, as paradigm changes; challenging the given theories of the time, challenging the sometimes austere analytic diagnostic practises of the time.

I suggest we are in another new era, drawing upon these great ideas, there is perhaps a chance now for less silo mentality. There is the possibility of a paradigm change in how we imagine and theorise about ourselves as employers and employees. In our current zeitgeist, we have greater knowledge about neurological differences, greater sharing and cross discipline working (could the joint honours degree even make a comeback?). The power of our minds seems to be back on the agenda for discussion and study, and meta-awareness and meta-skills development is occurring more widely in the take up of work based practises such as applications of mindfulness. Indeed, there is a strong program of mindfulness based stress reduction running in my own organisation through the innovative work of Sally Rose. Mental health has become a reality – we know there are psychological emotional tools out there which can help us function better as people and as workers and we have become explorers again.

I explained to the group recruited for the pilot how I see attachment theory in this light, and how I believe that it underpins a huge area in psychology, psychiatry and psychotherapy. As a means to understand how we are as people, I explained how I thought it could be relevant in helping us to explore how we are as people at work. I then gave them the detail we have set out for you, in the introduction to this book about Heard, Lake and McCluskey.

I referred my group to an excellent paper on the origins of attachment theory (Bretherton, 1992), pulling out highlights. The other key text is "A Secure Base" (Bowlby, first published 1988). As the book moves in and out of theory I won't go into any more detail here about Bowlby and Ainsworth but really encourage anyone interested to explore the writings of these most excellent scientists.

***

I am also interested in some of the other ideas developing in parallel to thinkers listed above Carl Rogers (1902–1987), the grandfather of person centred theory, moved the dialectical notion of therapy along again. Rogers signalled that attention to the position and relevance of the clients' world and their own interpretation, was more significant and therapeutic, than analysis. Empathy figures significantly in his writings. Rogers also described what he called "necessary and sufficient conditions" of therapy (1957). This is the idea that six particular conditions need to be in place in order for a therapeutic encounter to happen. Three of these became known as "core conditions". Rogers named these as unconditional positive regard, congruence and empathy.

For constructive personality change to occur, it is necessary that these conditions exist and continue over a period of time:

1   Two persons are in psychological contact.
2   The first, whom we shall term the client, is in a state of incongruence, being vulnerable or anxious.
3   The second person, whom we shall term the therapist, is congruent or integrated in the relationship.
4   The therapist experiences unconditional positive regard for the client.

5   The therapist experiences an empathic understanding of the client's inter-
    nal frame of reference and endeavors to communicate this experience to the
    client.
6   The communication to the client of the therapist's empathic understanding and
    unconditional positive regard is to a minimal degree achieved (Rogers, 1957).

These conditions outline the need for some form of transaction, engagement, agreement or relationship to exist between the two parties. Client incongruence means that there needs to be something which the client is either directly aware of or sensing as not matching in their experience and awareness. The therapist (helper or caregiver) needs to be able to tune into themselves, be aware and be genuine to the intent and purpose of the therapeutic relationship. They cannot be acting, manipulating or faking this intent and they should be able to bear their own experience and information in mind to help their understanding and communication in the process appropriately (and only if there is sound assessment of therapeutic benefit). The helper or therapist needs to be able to offer warm acceptance (this does not mean subscribing to someone else's value systems or ways of being) of the client without judgment, without conditional disapproval or approval. This act of acceptance Rogers observed, facilitated the potential for increased self-regard in the client. This condition helps the careseeker consider how they experience and view themselves and offers the environment where the therapist provides a space for the client to have a non-judgmental look at themselves, to see perhaps any distortions of others, but perhaps more importantly, see any of their own insights or distortions of themselves. The last condition being the summation in that all of the previous ones need to be experienced to some degree by the client (careseeker) in some way.

I like to bring Rogers into the mix because of his prizing, using and knowing your inner content when working in psychological contact with others. He clearly appreciated the relationship between the therapist and client and valued the client's understanding of themselves. It is perhaps a different take on attunement. It was core conditions that I practised developing for hours and hours in my training, learning to listen to my inner content, to value what the client was saying. These skills and ideas remain key features of not only my therapeutic work but also of my support for leaders, managers and staff in organisations.

I also nod to Abraham Maslow (1908–1970), who contributed the idea of a hierarchy of needs. He developed the notion that, if given a good enough space and environment to grow and thrive we will aspire to actualisation, to reach our biological potential, but only given the right circumstances. And clearly, we have not mastered making this a universal truth on the planet.

These are the lines of insight merging into the formation of thought that brings me to Heard, Lake and McCluskey in this extraordinary and delightful joining of specialisms, sciences, and approaches.

This is an indicative though not exhaustive map of the ideas and innovations which took me into this work. Trying to show the integration and weaving of these founding ideas is complex. It is possible to head off on all sorts of diversions. I encourage you to explore these diversions and follow them a little, that is exploratory interest sharing, after all.

This finally brings me to a main point with TABEIS. The point is, if I can know my feelings, know the causes and experience of my arousal, I can begin to make choices. If I can learn to see the systems alive in me and others, if I can detect when a system is aroused and consider what I might do, I might do something different and not reactive. If I can learn to understand how these systems work together, I can access them as a restorative process to achieve my wellbeing. And I can share this with others. I can model it. Through this attachment based exploration I can value my interests, and interest share with others, understand the triggers that take me out of competence. Using this as a restorative process, we have the opportunity to identify biological goals and then work to the best of our ability to have these goals met or satiated. My belief really is this can be usefully brought into business. So, the focus of this activity is to ask as explained in Chapter 1 – what does it feel like to be a member of this team, this group, this organisation? Can we consider McCluskey's proposition that if we haven't been met as a person – if we don't meet others as people, we are likely to move into dominant/submissive activities which do not support good creativity, good work, healthy businesses? It is worth repeating a key learning in the McCluskey model, which is, the job here is to work on how we ease off the fear and work in non-competitive ways – delighting in our own skills and experience, sharing in competition together not threatening each other with competition.

I then explain goal corrected empathic attunement (GCEA, see previous chapter), and draw out a diagram for them to consider using along the way why I think it matters at work. Each of us will have others careseeking (needing care, time, solutions) from us – whether we like this or not, we will have our attachment systems firing up and down all the while too! This takes its toll, it is physiological, and if we can observe it and work with it we can do things that improve our own overall wellbeing and to help manage and work with any anxiety the careseekers may be experiencing in regard to us.

Working with the systems the picture can look like figures 3.1 and 3.2. Both have biological effects – one good one not good.

The McCluskey models exemplifies the idea that to be effective, caregiving needs to remain exploratory.

Being able to identify individual and organisational (team) needs – separate out what is the organisational need, might indicate there are others with organisational responsibilities that can help in a situation. As we mentioned earlier, it allows us the opportunity to really utilise the resources around us.

Thinking in this way also allows us to identify who really needs care and consider if there is an ulterior (useful but hidden) motive in being asked for care. It means we might reflect upon how we replenish ourselves after the care has been given too. Looking for our enablers and our empowerment and discovering

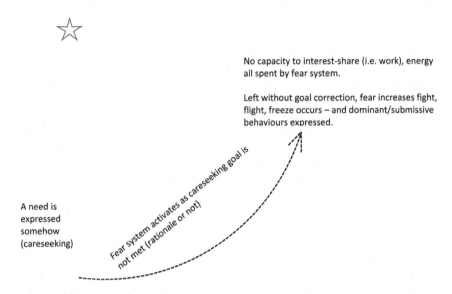

Figure 3.1 No capacity to interest-share

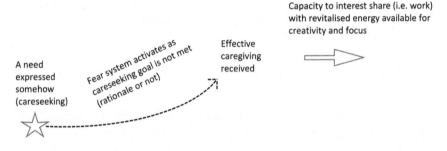

Figure 3.2 Capacity to interest-share

how to do that for others. Another benefit I saw as potential in the pilot was to enable participants to trust their differences, and appreciate that it is ok (and not organisationally damaging) if someone views or experiences something differently to them. So, all the way through the sessions I heralded their differences and encouraged them to enjoy their own take on the systems, and embrace their own views and enjoy, and find interest in the differences with each other's views. This is interest-sharing. Not grandstanding knowledge or declaring right and wrong. It is about embracing the rich and varied nature of human beings. This is another staple in the McCluskey model, exemplified in her practise and her group work. If I have learnt nothing other than how important this is, and how readily it can be acknowledged, I have learnt a lot. This alone is a crucial aspect of her work.

The chief LPs so far are that we are together going to be negotiating with our fear systems. We will be minding out for dominant submissive behaviours in the group but also out there in our interactions with others. I shall be matching and noticing vitality levels as part of my attunement activity with them. As I notice shifts in their vitality, I encourage them gently to notice these shifts themselves and perhaps notice it in others too. We will also be interest sharing, trying to figure out how this matters to any of us and to any of us at work. Watching out for defensive caregiving – or defensive careseeking (we'll see more of this in the next two chapters). Learning to communicate with the idea that fear paralyses, stifles and obstructs creativity and that improvement in effective staff careseeking is directly correlated to an increase in individual wellbeing, and that an increase in individual wellbeing is directly linked to an increase in creativity and organisational wellbeing.

***

5:   Learning and reflection

I offer them a handout with the key historical landmarks on it and these ideas of group structure to take away and absorb. These are key messages which McCluskey conveys:

- Trying to move away from anything dominant submissive to joint exploratory careseeking and interest sharing.
- Trying to create a fear-free exploratory process – we aren't here to be better than anyone else.
- Bring big questions to me not each other.
- Work alongside, don't be a voyeur on someone else's discovery.
- You aren't here to problem solve someone else's problems.
- Pay attention to what happens in your body – it is your biggest database.
- Tolerate difference in the room.
- Be open about your responses – try not to say or do what you think you ought to say or do, but rather what you want to say or do and feel to each other and to me.
- If you have a mind read about me or another person in the room say so – we can look at that.
- As you start to become conversant with the systems, learn to tune into yourself and notice which of the systems is being aroused and by what exactly?
- Session structure – I will introduce the subject (system) very briefly and then we will explore how that system operates at work. We work in the here and now but will aim to find lookalikes from our past that might be snagging our own movement forward.

As this was a really new way of working with them, I wished to give them as many tools as possible to engage with the process as much as with the theory. The following diagram shows the systems and was offered to them as a constant reference source.

The order of the systems (and the chapters from now on in this book) was:

1 Careseeking
2 Caregiving
3 Self-defence/fear
4 Interest and sharing with peers
5 Sexuality
6 Internal environment
7 External Environment

The final session was set to be for reviews – overall surprises learning satisfactions dissatisfactions – leading to another meeting and an opportunity to meet McCluskey in person.

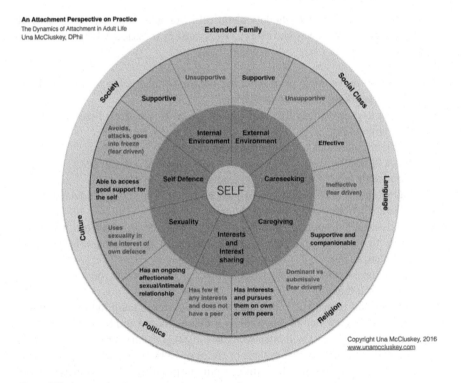

Figure 3.3 An attachment perspective on practice

I took this opportunity to get them to work together in pairs, looking at the wheel (Figure 3.3) and thinking about the descriptions of the systems on the handout. I invited them to wonder which of these systems they might feel interested in, and which might they be more unsure of. It was very important to get out of the lecture style approach, and my motive was twofold. I wished to put them back in relation with each other (and help them stop feeling sleepy, if they were), and I had to manage my own fear system too. I needed a break at this point; I went for a walk to the toilet, tuned in myself, the impact of my fear and self-defence systems in flow, the adrenaline and buzz of my caregiving system and interest sharing systems all active. I noticed that my careseeking was expressed through a request for them to do this exercise and be compliant on this occasion and be responsive to each other and to me.

It was with some delight that I returned to find the room buzzing with energy and conversation. The group really had absorbed much of the information I had offered and were delighting in it; it seemed to me in applying it to themselves. They were thinking about what worked so far, what jarred and jangled. There was no doubt that they were indeed interest sharing using the attachment paradigm as one to think through, the vitality in the room was tangible, delightful and represented engagement in every way that I might have hoped for. My fear system was allayed, my own capacity for interest sharing in full force! Vitality was in evidence for themselves.

*** *

6: Surprises, learnings, delights, satisfactions, dissatisfactions

As already mentioned, McCluskey also uses the technique of encouraging participants in her experiential and training work, to reflect upon the emotional, psychological, theoretical work they have done. She frames this as "surprises, learnings, delights, satisfactions, dissatisfactions". I asked the group these questions in every session and used that knowledge to go over un-grasped systems and fine-tune future sessions. It is a lovely way to consider the ideas that have been introduced, to notice how they might have impacted, to explore whether a dissatisfaction lies in the self or in the delivery of the session. This approach is also a great way to develop reflective practise tools. The trick is to get at our learning, imbed what is useful, find parts that may not have resonated so well and double check them out; a kind of Jungian looking for the gold in the shadows. Sometimes I might reject an idea because there may be a painful conscious or unconscious association, or a "look-alike" as McCluskey would name it, to something difficult for me. But if I can nail that association, find that lookalike, uncover a Rogerian (of Carl Rogers) "condition of worth" (Rogers, 1959), script or schema, I might just be able to unshackle the hold it has upon me.

The focus of this pilot was to reflect actively upon what it felt like to be in their teams, this group, this organisation? Did they know what their needs were, did they notice unmet goals? Could they notice the activation of the systems, careseeking etc. and then if the system is goal-corrected could they tune into the sensation of assuagement? For example, if they were excited what would it be like to be met with something flat? Is it disheartening, might they give up asking or expecting help or support? Or if they give care and get it rejected which system is affected, what might they do? These moments are the opportunities to explore, and see if they haven't been met as a person – if they don't meet their colleagues as people, with these systems in play, are they likely to move into dominant and submissive activities? Fear based interactions that distract us, prevent us being creative. So, if we ease off the fear and work in non-competitive ways – delighting in our own skills and experience, sharing competence not fighting in threatening competition what is the difference?

The question and the message takes time to permeate through. It needs to be repeated. It is my belief that the message is hugely important for wellbeing at work.

The subsequent sessions followed the order in which I learnt them. There is a coherence to the order, the original Bowlby systems of careseeking and caregiving, and the subsequent systems named by Heard, Lake and McCluskey. Following careseeking by caregiving is logical, self-defence next, because failures in careseeking and caregiving arouse defence. When care needs aren't met, careseeking and defence arouse. Defences interfere with interest sharing. Our capacity to develop our interests fully, and share them with others, depends upon our careseeking system being assuaged and our sense of self being affirmed and our self-defence (fear system) regulated. With these regulated, our affectionate sexual relationships can flourish, and tend to follow the same trajectory as our interest sharing. All are influenced by the scenarios and templates of interaction laid down in our internal environment and full functioning is expressed in whether our home and work environment is a suitably resourced and supportive place for us to live and thrive.

***

7:   Headline the next session subject and any reflection to do

Session 1 homework: think about how you careseek at work.

1   Where/how might you have learnt to do this?
2   When is it effective?

3　　When is it ineffective and might that be described as dominant/submissive?
4　　Is there a particular careseeking culture in your team that you can describe? (Instead of 3, as it reads, a clearer question would have been to ask when might your behaviour be described as dominant or submissive?)

I also provided a table for them to complete which includes the questions listed in the appendix. I wanted the group to begin embracing these notions from the outset, so that they might begin to track the heritage of such behaviours and consider them in the present and to help them develop the skills to notice when these behaviours might be helpful or not, or might be indicative of past struggles. If they could begin to tune into these behaviours, they could consequently choose whether to carry on in the same vein or try something different. Either way, feeling compelled to behave dominantly or submissively can be a real drain on personal resources. Given that we were running the pilot in the organisational setting we make explicit the notion that being drained reduces what we have to offer at and in work. It can feel wearing, and left unchecked give others an idea about us that might not be entirely true. I did not wish to overburden the group with lengthy descriptions of these behaviours, but rather invite them after a brief explanation, to consider what these meant for them. This was another way to model the exploratory interest sharing and try to avoid overdominance.

In structuring the homework however, I was asserting one point; this was that I wished them to think about themselves first. As straightforward as that sounds, it can be really hard to get professionals to consider a positive or negative impact on themselves. They can be driven to want to apply good practises models, techniques, to others, if they believe their team might benefit. I have worked with employees with this conscientious work style for many years, and I have seen the cost of it too on numerous occasions. I wanted them to have a really good sense of what this all meant for them as individuals. To consider the wear and tear upon their lives. Work can be very hard. Good leaders and managers, or carers, dedicate so much time to the plight of others or an organisation's mission, that their own wellbeing might fall by the way. The framework for the homework therefore was quite rigid at the beginning. In this instance, my dominance was well intentioned.

This was my target: to get them thinking about a restorative process through the systems for their individual wellbeing first – and then to encourage them to consider it for others much later. I wished to encourage them to have a phenomenological experience change through the model, knowing (and hoping) it would be good for them and then later it would help them pass the skills on. My hope and plan was to reconnect them with their innate skills (competencies) of parent child symbiosis as they manifest in the riches of their professional relationships.

So reader, as with McCluskey's writings, experientials, and our pilot, the next chapters will work through the systems in detail. Are you ready, do you need to centre – get in your seats – on your sitting bones – eyes open – attentive? Find the tension and let it go.

Note

1 VARK Copyright (1998) held by Neil D. Fleming, Christchurch.

Chapter 4

Careseeking

In this chapter I will cover the session that introduced the system and concept of careseeking from the McCluskey model. We will look at the session structure, offer more detail on the genesis of the theory relevant to careseeking, and how we introduced this in the pilot at work.

From Session 1 the participants had been set the questions:

Think about how you careseek at work:

1　Where/how might you have learnt to do this?
2　When is it effective?
3　When is it ineffective and might be described as dominant/submissive?
4　Is there a particular careseeking culture in your team that you can describe?

As outlined already our intention was to introduce these ideas and these terms. I had asked my participants to send back their feedback to the questions in this first instance as I wanted to encourage them to use the questions to think about themselves (not their colleagues) and to begin a process of allowing this model to start permeating into their awareness. This also enabled the participants to raise some questions with me about the model and about the terms I was using. This iterative approach meant the participants had a say in their learning and helped keep my facilitation on track. This was with McCluskey's encouragement and was to help them to be reflective, to support the notions and that one liner responses were good enough in the feedback, it all counted as data. This certainly seemed to encourage them to respond.

I met with McCluskey prior to as many of the sessions as I could, so that I might share my intentions for the session and gain invaluable guidance on whether my ideas seemed sound. McCluskey offered clarifications or corrections where I may have misinterpreted or become confused. In terms of leadership and training development, this mentoring behind the scenes was an example of the model at work. I was careseeking and we were interest sharing, McCluskey met my needs, and this directly filtered through to allay the fear I experienced which, in turn, was of benefit to the group. Less fear in me, more competence for them, a perfect example of how mentoring can be really effective at work. My participants were all aware that I was in supervision with McCluskey, and it meant they had a conduit to her as well.

McCluskey and I set the scene, we agreed that an organisation is essentially an interpersonal environment. As laid out before, we followed the structure of:

- Welcome
- Centre – get in your seats – on your sitting bones – eyes open – attentive.
- Find the tension and let it go.

1   Outline of the session:

Overtime reflections, clarifications, subject introduction, discussion, surprises learning satisfactions etc.– next subject.

2   Feedback and reflections (not homework) from session 1.
3   Various clarifications and feedback from me.
4   Would you like a recap of first names?
5   I'll recap on the history as I explain and introduce the careseeking subject – but I will draw it out visually as well when we come to it.
6   Explain more about dominant/submissive careseeking concept.
7   How you can contribute (what I want from you) – statements in the sessions but also from feedback – I'll invite a midpoint evaluation – plus the new reflection forms (can be emailed to me).
8   What I mean by bring big questions to me.

Any questions?

These questions arose from feedback that I received very helpfully from Hill about clarifications on my approach but also from correspondences from various participants after the previous scene setting session. Therefore, I modelled the approach by respecting their needs (actually for the wellbeing of the whole group) and by attending to them. This left us free to interest share in the model, because these needs are both acknowledged and met rather than remaining unsaid and unmet, and left to fester.

This session involved reminding them of the genesis of attachment theory and the evolution of the systems. Why do this? It was important to keep locating them in the history of the thinking behind the theory; also, to acknowledge their place as pioneers, and as pioneers we were exploring new territory together. Therefore, there weren't any wrong or right questions, all content was valid, all queries of interest, a hesitation or reservation as important as acceptance and agreement. Furthermore, every subsequent group will be pioneers in their own right, so these rules will continue to apply. As we explained in the introduction, acknowledging the legacy of the model is part of its impact. Being able to locate oneself in a chain of thinking can be quite empowering. For me it meant that as well as pioneers, we become explorers of knowledge, working in a knowledge economy. It is only reasonable to offer credence to an approach. Some leaders (theorists for instance) need to have a sense of where the theory comes from, it can be the thing that makes the difference as to whether they might give it a go or not – permission to engage, if you like (see Chapter 3).

Back to the notion of careseeking then, in the main we can deduce that we all have an:

1   Urge to attach – that is a pre-programmed unlearnt behaviour in most human babies/children, we call this careseeking – the goal is to seek and get care.
2   To give care – caregiving from often an older/wiser other with whom an affectionate bond has been established (Heard, Lake, and McCluskey, 2012).

Daniel Stern (1985) and his team noted that most of the mothers they were observing tended to accurately attune to the vitality state of their infant. However, they also noted that when this did not seem to happen, there were significant consequences for the infant's wellbeing and vitality. For example, a mother could be "out of tune" with her baby's emotional state and engage in excessive jiggling and other forms of intrusive behaviour when her baby had a much less aroused internal state. It was obvious that the baby experienced distress at this level of mis-attunement. Accurate attunement and purposeful effective mis-attunement (McCluskey, 2005, p. 49) contributes to one of the building blocks in promoting an effective careseeking caregiving partnership. When these two instinctive biological systems of careseeking and caregiving are met both parties carry on about their business whatever that might be. The meeting of the goals of these respective biologically based systems is what we describe in the tradition laid down by Bowlby, as goal correction.

This is the human version of the open beak of a chick. An instinctive, hotwired biological need in most humans from birth, for assistance. Initially biologically driven for the sake of seeking help around all our physical entrances and exits. Ainsworth described it as a biological dependency on a key caregiver, or health and nourishment giver (Ainsworth, 1969). It is something that you can see clearly in the behaviours of the infant and mother after periods of separation. Is there a reconciliation between the two, a reuniting, or is there a block or failure to reconnect? A failure becomes an unfulfilled need. In this way therefore the unfulfilled need (isolation, abandonment) fills us with fear; it's a threat to our survival. Without food we starve, without attention to defecation and urination we get infections or disease. The unmet need for care risks death. Therefore, careseeking and fear and needs are inextricably linked together.

There is a chemical response – fear fills us with adrenalin, it energises us, but left unchecked it changes how our brains and our bodies function, it is also motivational when we get what we set out to get, then we also get a rush of dopamine. When we share these kind of experiences with the good company of others we generate and benefit from other positive hormones (such as oxytocin and vasopressin), hormones that support relationality and social bonding. This works because we experience a chemical lift, the body becomes charged and if it feels good we are likely to repeat it, therefore the behaviour is likely to be repeated too.

This system swings into action whenever an infant, child, or adult senses an occurrence that acts as a threat to his or her sense of wellbeing. At that point, the biological system for careseeking and the system for personal defence are activated; then after an empathic caregiver has interacted with a careseeker in the appropriate manner, the experience of well-being (contentment) is restored for that moment (as far as is possible, depending on how empathic the caregiver has been). Our strategies for seeking care develop as we experience different forms of caregiving responses and become part of our natural survival strategy in adult life. For some of us they work very well, for others, based on frustrating, ambivalent or destructive/persecutory responses from early caregivers, our strategies may remain ineffective and frustrating. We may overly rely on trying to dominate or bully others into taking care of us, or become submissive to whatever form of help is offered, regardless of whether it is useful or not.

The effectiveness of careseeking is having some skills, tools, language to discern our needs, being able to express them in a way which makes sense for the other, and then seek satisfaction. It is complex. Successful careseeking depends upon some awareness of the care sought (an un-met need) and the identification of a caregiving person or activity – some completion of the cycle to affect a restorative process – effective or temporary.

These skills are learnt as a baby, and as a child. If the parent used purposeful mis-attunement maybe as a learning cycle, to up or down regulate the child, or if there were problems with the caregiver – repetitions (and not many) of mis-attunements key in (register, neurologically) different responses into the care seeking behaviour of the child. Imprinted if you like. If I never get what I want, I might give up, get angry sad or try to get it by manipulation.

***

At work this might manifest as something like this. Let's say I find it very hard not to say yes to requests to take on work or offer support, especially if others are excited by the work or in some way needy or vulnerable. I learnt this pattern as a child. The intense emotion of adults was often expressed or at the very least discernible, I was expected to manage their emotional content but without great help in learning to manage my own, and even inferring from their behaviour to me, that my emotional content should not be expressed. When vulnerable myself I tended towards physical ill health, either from actual physiological depletion, or as a maladaptive, defensive, fear-ridden coping strategy to get out of the emotional arena or seek care. Maladaptive in that, it kind of gets me out of trouble, but only perhaps to get me into more trouble and difficulty. If I need to be ill to escape trouble I can't manage myself or find a caregiver, then I am left ill, even if I have got away from trouble. I learnt therefore to manage other people's emotional content and diminish or hide my own, sometimes hoping this brave and noble behaviour would be rewarded. Sometimes it was rewarded. In transactional analysis terms, this could be described as "pleasing adaptive". At work this plays out as adapting myself and my behaviour to please (meet the needs) of others, more often than I tend to myself. I might even fool myself that tending to others first is meeting a need in me. However, my workload becomes untenable. Without sufficient means, I have no way of asking for help, and I begin to get ill. I might project my needs onto others. I am transferring my experience of childhood into work. I might express this very submissively, like saying "Wouldn't it be nice if I could get more reports done?", knowing full well I have no way of doing so. Imagining others might decode this for me and offer to help. Or overwrought, I become vulnerable to illnesses or get burnt out and might eventually just go off work sick. This risks a cost to my health, and a cost to the organisation I work for. The Chartered Institute of Personnel and Development (CIPD) 2015 *Absence Management* survey arrives at an overall annual median cost of absence per employee of £554. As they say, however:

> this figure is unlikely to capture the full impact of employee absence if all the potential indirect costs (such as lost productivity, impaired customer service and lower employee morale) as well as the direct costs are not taken into account, as these less tangible effects are very difficult to quantify.
>
> (CIPD, 2016, p. 16)

If my organisation is losing productivity, then I am losing productivity with them. Effective careseeking therefore really matters at work!

The careseeking system weaves in and out of all the other systems – a bit like a stealth weapon or unexploded bomb depending upon a person's history.

In her studies of interactions McCluskey identified five careseeking presentations (McCluskey 2005):

Careseeking presentations

1   The careseeker wants to discuss feelings, conflicts and concerns.
2   The careseeker is reluctant to discuss feelings, conflicts and concerns.

3   The careseeker brings in issues which tangle and confuse the caregiver as they try to help.
4   The careseeker brings in issues they are concerned about but dismisses the caregiver when they try to help.
5   The careseeker is overwhelmed, incoherent, and disorganised in presentation of feelings, conflicts and concerns.

The group members were were offered a handout with these careseeking presentations on them for future reference.

In considering these presentations I also introduced ideas for the group to think about what fear does. After reading LeDoux (1998), Heard and Lake observed how:

> the self defended itself, against the pain and distress that follows failure to reach the goal of careseeking and the goal of interest sharing with peers, especially failure to experience exploratory interest sharing with like-minded peers . . . Heard and Lake realised that human beings have two quite separate systems for looking after themselves, the fear system as described by Le Doux and the attachment/careseeking system. The goal of the fear system (survival) can be reached in many circumstances by a person, without help from anyone else; in order to reach the goal of the attachment and careseeking system (survival of wellbeing), it is obligatory to be in contact with effective trustworthy and protective caregivers, whose behaviour towards a careseeker ought to be such that it enables the goal of careseeking to be reached.
>
> (Heard, Lake and McCluskey, 2012, pp. 57–58)

Neuroscientists such as David Rock (Rock 2009), show how it actually affects brain function, toward reward and away from pain. So careseeking can be very risky indeed, in fact it is a little bit like putting a portion of the self on the line each time. If I express my needs and they are ignored or belittled a portion of me gets hurt, gets frightened, angry – all potentially leading to me acting out in dominant or submissive ways.

This means then that careseeking is intra and inter personal. In the work of training, teaching, facilitating or therapy, we might find ourselves managing (or being) the threat. The development or assuagement for the careseeker depends on the availability of the caregiver. Is the caregiver able to attune, are they attentive, do they have any capacity to offer care? Can the caregiver endeavour to understand and handle any defensive behaviour of the fear ridden seeker? Caregivers need to be able to do all these things to some degree if they are to attend to the wellbeing of the careseeker. Please refer back to Figures 3.1 and 3.2 on page 56 to consider interest sharing again.

Heard, Lake and McCluskey (2012, p. 123) explain how any seeker of care needs to find a caregiver who can be expected to give effective care. So perhaps we might extrapolate further and suggest that, amongst other things, one of the functions of leadership is to help careseekers rehearse seeking care and getting it met – colleagues take away a new pattern of behaviour (cognitive and neurological) and perhaps some refinement of what might count as a reasonable expectation of managers in the workplace.

Goal correction in the system of "careseeking" represents the biological meeting of these needs so as to settle the biological system of fear before it fires up out of control, or even only sufficiently to interfere with adult to adult relating. It is with the exploration of these patterns that we can really start to think about the application to work and organisations.

Thinking of themselves, I encouraged my participants to consider some of their careseeking behaviours in the light of these presentations. It was hard sometimes to stop them heading off in the direction of thinking about those who sought care from them and then getting involved in discussions of how they responded (caregave). And of course, there was validity in considering this aspect too, but I wanted them to focus on themselves first.

To help them focus upon themselves, in the course of this session I stopped and checked with the participants to see if they were tracking with the content. One of questions I used to illuminate this was to ask – what is goal correction in careseeking – and have there been any examples in the room so far?

***

Why I think it matters at work

I addressed their interest in thinking about it from the caregiving point of view by reminding them, that each of them will have others careseeking (needing care, time, solutions) from them – whether they liked this or not. Consequently, their attachment systems will be constantly activating (biological systems of fear, careseeking etc.) firing up and down all the while. This takes its toll, it is physiological, and if we can observe it and work with it we can do things that improve our own overall wellbeing. Understanding this dynamic may enable us to tune in to the anxiety the careseekers may experience when seeking help from us.

From a work point of view, it was quite easy to persuade them to the idea that interest sharing equaled work, therefore they were taken with the notion that in fact poor careseeking could lead to an interruption in work. A concept framed this way was entirely new, entirely new to probably all of them. Important to catch I think, because I believe it is this connection between careseeking and interest sharing that especially matters in the workplace. I would suggest it is precisely this connection that legitimises us to consider our needs and careseek in the workplace rather than boldly pretending there aren't any needs, or worse that these needs aren't important. Whether they are appropriate for work is entirely different, and whether they should or could be met at work is again an entirely separate matter. Having ways to know what we need, however, is essential.

Bringing it back to them, I explained that, according to the model, if careseeking is to be effective it needs to remain exploratory. The exploratory approach allows us to consider what might be going on, to try to stay away from pathologising ourselves or finding fault, but rather think about possible causes and consequences. It is the power of the exploratory approach as was explained in Chapter 2. It means that we can use our inquisitive natures, not be self-critical or judgemental. We can allow ourselves to observe patterns or habits. We can wonder about any inter or intra personal dynamics and consider why we might be feeling and behaving in these ways. It can support a way of reflecting to understand if we might be caught in an old maladaptive routine (developed in our childhood) and might in fact have the opportunity in the present tense to do it and feel it differently. Furthermore, it offers us the opportunity to separate between being able to identify our own individual and organisational (team) needs. This means separating out what is going on and who is carrying responsibilities. This in turn leads to considering the uses and availability of the resources around them.

I asked them to reflect upon and really identify who really can offer care to them or those in their teams. I asked them to wonder if they have a way in which they might tune in to see if there are ulterior (useful but hidden) motives in asking for care. I asked them to consider how we might replenish ourselves after the care has been given. This approach is to look for our enablers and our sources of empowerment and then we can consider how we might do that for others. Care and observation of self first before attending to others. Careseeking is designed to influence others to get what we want – I want to have an effect on the other person, in order to regulate an affect in me, an uncomfortable feeling that I am experiencing, so the more I know about that the better I can resource myself and know if I have what is needed to attend to my colleagues.

To back up this particular system I showed the group a YouTube video which McCluskey had introduced to my training cohort. The video was located online[1] at the time, however, these media files do move. If you search for "elephants" you may find it just as easily.

In this video clip, we see an elephant calf covered in mud, struggling, struggling to get out of a river bed. The video lasts a few moments and we see one of the elephants, possibly the calf's mother, work hard to get the calf up the bank. Other members of the herd gather and retreat as the episode goes on. The noise of both the calf's distress and the adults' frustration is palpable and clearly demonstrates careseeking and caregiving active in nature.

I used the video to consider the nature of how my participants and their teams might respond to the distress of one of their number. Who comes to help quickly but recedes quickly, who sticks with the problem situation, and what might it be like for them to be stuck in the mud sometimes with nowhere to go, without reliance on someone else.

The video was a lovely change of pace and medium, a way to regain some vitality, if there had been some collapse because of information overload. The video presented a fine metaphor for what goes on at work. It also offers a way to draw attention to the difference between exploratory caregiving and defensive caregiving. I left them with the questions "what can help you get back out of the water" vs. "how did you get yourself in that mess?"

If the caregiver is responding in a defensive way the careseeker is likely to remain in some state of distress. This is very apparent in the video. Some of my group explained to me how the video had enabled them to drop their fear a little. It gave us all a different focus and a starting point (LP). In discussion it became apparent that one of my participants was already starting to take these terms and ideas back into his work. He was exploring the notions of helping colleagues acknowledge their careseeking needs at the end of each week, encouraging them not to fester over the weekend but inviting them to address their needs in work time. This participant observed how an attempt to get his team to articulate needs before the weekend was received warmly, but he also recognised he needed to be consistent with the message that this wasn't about blame or intended to increase workload expectations, it was instead, a real effort to help them clear their mental work decks before the weekend so that they might better enjoy their weekends. So first he has to manage their fear, earn their trust, repeat his expressions of genuine care and remain exploratory with them. For instance, saying: "Shall we see if trying it this way works?" to change things with them.

***

Learnings

Several of the group had begun to recognise through reflection on the subject matter, how they prepared for careseeking with a presumption of fear of not getting what they needed, or fear of admitting they needed help. Their fears were that their requests or appeals would lead to attack or undermine the perception of their professional competence. This is such a significant matter. Careseeking at work is essential. However, if we are paralysed by the terror of attack or the inference of incompetence how can we persuade ourselves to get answers to problems, develop our competence and skill or seek professional relationality? When discussing this issue with my colleague Drury, her response was to ask me "But how do we help others or ourselves to deconstruct how we ask for care and whether or not this impacts on the results – on whether we get the care or not? How do we reflect on times when care is not forthcoming when we ask?" These are good questions to ask.

This slowly began to reveal a real hesitation in the group about using the word "care". It seemed that work and care do not sit comfortably with each other. And yet there was also clear recognition from the group that when any of them let their careseeking needs go unmet for too long they became physically ill, exhausted. I can only guess if this would be the same in another workplace, I suspect it would be. Sometimes it seemed this utter debilitation was then the only legitimiser for getting help. This was a fabulous discussion as a real recognition of the dilemma of getting help for oneself at work, and a discussion that was repeated many times. The message of the theory clearly being that if we leave our needs unmet for too long, ill health and burn-out are the risks that we run. So how is it then that we legitimise the process of noticing our needs and seek their appropriate restoration at work?

Participant 5 also noticed that not only was not seeking care bad for her, it was potentially a very dangerous model for her team. If she didn't resource herself, perhaps they would not either. Everyone working as hard as they could, getting no restoration, the potential was that this behaviour could lead to the collapse of the whole team. This seemed to be a very powerful observation to make, highlighting how significant a leader's modeling of self-care is for wellbeing and establishing a resilient culture.

All of them were very interested in thinking about who their caregivers were, in thinking about the concept of collapse in the face of unmet careseeking goals and interested to take these ideas back to their teams in various ways. It was an exciting session, as it seemed to me, that though sometimes rattling in part – the model was arousing their curiosity. They were applying it to themselves and thinking about what that meant for work. The following is an example of application.

> Careseeking was an interesting idea, as this was something I historically did not do well but improved upon after my breakdown. That being said, I rarely did it at work, and didn't do so effectively, and by seeing how integral this is to the self I have dramatically improved and felt comfortable with care seeking from colleagues and managers in an effective way.
>
> Course participant 3

This participant had really gotten hold of just how careseeking had become omitted from his conscious awareness in the workplace. By allowing himself to know this he has been able to change how he operates and utilise different mechanisms to support his wellbeing at work. More of his story is offered in Chapter 12.

I had drawn up a self-reflective grid for the homework to use for this session onwards. The grid was supplied in hard and soft copies for the purposes of this pilot.

Heads up for the next session

Session 2 homework: think about how you caregive at work

1   Where/how might you have learnt to do this?
2   When is it effective?
3   When is it ineffective, and might that be described as dominant/submissive?
4   Is there a particular caregiving culture in your team that you can describe?

We agreed both forms, so that they might choose the method best for them, and those who wished could email their feedback to me. This further supported adult learning across different mediums by trusting them to take their own reflections seriously, but in the style that suited them.

Note

1 Available at: https://youtu.be/KTHsyIQI2L0 (accessed 12 February 2018).

Chapter 5

Caregiving

In this chapter I will cover the third session that introduced the system for caregiving. So, lets remind ourselves briefly, caregiving is the second of Bowlby's biological systems looked at in the model. This is a system designed to notice that care is required by another, and some ability to supply some satisfaction to that need. It requires appraisal skills, and skills in communication.

We will look at the session structure, offer more detail on the genesis of the theory relevant to caregiving, and how we introduced this in the pilot at work. The structure for this session was:

Welcome

Centre – get in your seats – on your sitting bones – eyes open – attentive – this is transitional space – use a moment to arrive from wherever you have come from. To notice parts of you that might be lingering there or racing ahead and try to settle that and be here for the time we have together.

Outline of the session:

1   Over-time reflections, clarifications, subject intro, discussion, surprises learning satisfactions etc.
2   Feedback and reflections (not homework) from session 2 – the word "care" – any further thoughts.
3   Various clarifications and feedback from me.
4   Introduce the caregiving subject – but I will draw it out as well – when we come to it. Explain more about defensive caregiving concept.
5   Any questions?
6   Surprises, learnings, satisfactions and dissatisfactions.
7   Next session.

Welcome and reflections

The welcome and reflections gives the returning participants a chance to arrive in the session with me and with each other. I had met one of them in between the sessions; as this participant had not been able to attend the last session on care-seeking, the one-to-one time was offered as a means to bring them up to date with the theory and how the participants were applying it to their work situations, from the previous session. These meetings and checking in allows them all to arrive prepared to work and explore this subject together in this session. This was also an example of interest-sharing in action.

They all arrived able to join in by sharing observations they had made. Their individual observations contribute to embedding new understandings for them-selves individually and formed a part of the collaborative learning experience of the group. Additionally, someone else's insight might help progress a growing concep-tual breakthrough or aspect of learning being teetered on by another, but also might normalise a learning being formulated by another. It's a collective collaborative learning experience. Hill helped us understand this way of working is also known as using "threshold concepts" (Meyer and Land, 2003). These are pedagogical tech-niques which embrace a transformational, integrative, and re-constructional nature of learning. This is similar to the hierarchy of learning, conscious competence model or "four stages for learning any new skill"[1] with a greater consideration for a dialectic and organic aspect of learning. The theory suggests we move from uncon-scious incompetence (I don't know what I don't know) to conscious incompetence (I know what I don't know) to conscious competence (I am very aware of whatever skill, behaviour I am learning to use) to unconscious competence (it has become a body learnt, second nature, order of things). Essentially when I learn some things, I am changed by them. It might conjoin concepts or ideas I have, it might shine a new light on my perceptions, it might truly transform the phenomenological way in which I experience the world.

It also reinforces the notion that each participant has value in giving or receiv-ing this information. This model reinforces competence in all participants, as each has value in giving or receiving information. My attunement was playing its role in gently picking up any hesitation or worry and allowing their reflections to be expressed and met by me and by my care and interest. This also means we can recap on any aspects of the theory, that anyone might find themselves confused by – helping me address teaching shortfalls and using those questions to develop the learning of both myself and the whole group. It was in this session that their issue with the word "care" really began to come to light.

Introducing caregiving

I recapped on some of the major historical ideas that feed into the ideas of caregiv-ing by offering the following narrative together with a written summary. Darwin gave us his ideas about the evolution of humans and the various systems we have developed to deal with the world and hierarchical pecking orders. Then in the 1930s human ethology (Irenäus Eibl-Eibesfeldt) pursued this further with the study of human adaption, survival, character and its formation. William Ronald Dodds Fairbairn brought us notions that we can have innate tendencies to form relationships. His work brought to light the concepts that we are born with components of personality "hotwired in", as well as ideas on splitting, defence and repression from early hurts, including ego and self-to-self as well as self-to-other (object relations theory). John Macmurray joined this with his writings about the essentially relational nature of human beings. And of course, Bowlby deduced, from his observation of birds and from his colleagues in the field of ethology, that we have two biological instinctive complimentary goal corrected systems, which are all about affect regulation; managing what is going on inside myself, or and managing the impact of the external world upon me.

If we remember and agree that we have; firstly, an urge to attach – this is a pre-programmed, unlearnt behaviour of careseeking – the goal is to seek and get care. Secondly, we can have a capacity via a similar pre-programmed, unlearnt behaviour, to give care.

Caregiving can often be from an older and wiser other, with whom an affectionate bond has been established, but not just necessarily so. We then draw a conclusion that most infants are born with a capacity to attune to those around them.

When this careseeking and caregiving are working in a complimentary way (needs met) then both can carry on about their business whatever that might be, it is this accurate and required responsiveness that equals goal correction.

In other words, we are talking about an interpersonal system called attachment that contains two distinct and complimentary systems each with different goals, and when the goals of each are met we call this goal correction.

Ainsworth offered us the further insight that when these goals are met, our sense of security is also restored (a secure base), which is essential for survival and exploration and play. Exploration and play can also be what we call work! I mentioned earlier that Heard elaborated on this observation of Ainsworth's, to suggest that it was the quality and the nature of the interaction between the careseeker and caregiver that determined the level of quality exploration that can be returned to, this is clearly of major significance when we transpose these ideas to the workplace.

I reminded the group about Brian Lake, how he qualified in medicine, was interested in organisational dynamics and he worked in St James's University Hospital, in Leeds. I think this mattered on several counts, not only does it bring the theory in to the real world (and the external environment of these participants) but also connects the leadership ideas with medicine. It links the development of clinical practice for management, for work. Therefore, this theory and the developments offered by Heard, Lake and McCluskey connect to the organisation in which this pilot was taking place. Lake specifically explored ideas about interests, the importance of interests in people's lives and about the effect of interests and interest sharing on work-life, how it contributed to the development of ego strength through the acquisition of social and interpersonal competence. Lake's work helped us consider that interest sharing is linked to wellbeing and to a surge of vitality. Vitality is very connected with our energy to engage in work business and activity.

Therefore, I reconnect again this theory to our interest sharing together as a group and the wellbeing of my participants and of mine too.

***

McCluskey's research considers in great detail the minute aspects of the inter-actions of careseeking and caregiving and explores the nature of what happens when careseeking goals are met. It is in these minute studies that she discovers and coins the idea of GCEA, and identifies the process by which a caregiver (manager) can enable goal correction.

Heard, Lake and McCluskey explore further the idea of a restorative process which works to enable as much wellbeing as possible given the actual state of the instinctive systems within the person. Clearly if all the systems are reaching their goals a person's sense of wellbeing will be in very good working order. That person is likely to be in a position to take a creative exploratory attitude to their life-times and work. They are likely to be better placed to achieve and maintain their wellbeing (actualisation). Having then drawn a frame of reference for the systems and for the careseeking/caregiving relationship, Heard, Lake and McCluskey con-clude that we have the opportunity to identify these systems within the person and work with them (if they are interested) to enable them to reach the goals of that particular system thus contributing to not only increased sense of well being but competence to manage alone when a caregiver is not to hand.

I also nudge the group back to remember ideas about dominant and submis-sive behaviours – suggesting that if we haven't been met as a person – if we don't meet others as people, we are likely to move into dominant/submissive ways of relating. We do so because our fear system gets activated, and fear is about survival. I will dominate to take charge of my situation if I think others aren't capable, or represent a threat which I need to conquer. Or I go submissive because I either fear the other person or believe I don't have skills, talent, health to do anything else. The task as said before using McCluskey's words, "is to work on how we ease off the fear and work in non-competitive ways – delighting in our own skills and experience, sharing competition not threatening each other with competition".

***

Caregiving is the human version of feeding the open beak, an instinctive, hot-wired tendency for most humans' active from birth, to have a biological urge to respond to the request for assistance. Caregiving isn't just supplying the open beak though, it's about helping the other to explore having attended to the needs and noticed what going on helps them to acquire the necessary skills to help deal with these needs in the future and encourages them to find their peers.

Because we now know that an unfulfilled need fills us, or the other person, with fear (see Chapter 2) – caregiving is also fraught with danger. So, fear and needs are again linked together.

Caregiving when effective, (goal corrected) is having some skills/tools/language to discern their needs, explore what satisfaction might be like. It's complex.

These skills are learnt as a baby, a child in relation to others. Experiences of purposeful mis-attunements, maybe a part of our own learning cycles, are going to form key parts in our own caregiving behaviours. We might replicate what we experienced, or we might compensate for whatever we either ineffectively or self defensively experienced. I may have been taught to caregive to adults appropriately or inappropriately. I may have received rewards for these behaviours or it may have been risky. I may have consequently developed a fear that if I didn't do it right I might be abandoned or attacked by my own, crucial, caregivers.

I reminded the group of the careseeking presentations that form patterns which McCluskey (2005) had identified:

1   The careseeker wants to discuss feelings, conflicts and concerns.
2   The careseeker is reluctant to discuss feelings, conflicts and concerns.
3   The careseeker brings in issues which tangle and confuse the caregiver as they try to help.
4   The careseeker brings in issues they are concerned about but dismiss the caregiver when they try to help.
5   The careseeker is overwhelmed, incoherent, and disorganised in presentation of feelings, conflicts and concerns.

***

Goal correction in caregiving

Thinking back to Chapter 2 and learning styles, I invite the group to pause a moment and consider and discuss what goal correction looks and feels like in caregiving. I ask them to observe any examples in the room so far. This brings the theory again into the here and now, developing their competence to spot the ideas and reflect upon them.

To further their work application of the theory I recap on why I believe it matters at work. Each of them (each of you out there) will have others careseeking (needing care, time, solutions) from them, from you – these emotional requests (and they are emotional even if they appear transactional) prompt the firing up and down of our biological attachment systems. This is therefore physiological; it uses energy, if we can tune into this, observe it, we might then notice when our energy or capacity for attention-giving is getting depleted. Sometimes it is completely depleted.

Imagine the range of possibilities; one system firing up in one person, but another in another person, one who notices very little, one who notices everything. Somehow, we have to navigate across the variety of responses in ourselves and in others.

If we hone our skill at this we might gain the choice to give care and attention even when we are depleted, however doing so consciously, recognising the risks to take action or to withdraw perhaps, and find ways to restore ourselves; noticing this could be a trigger to use the technique of centering.

If those who are careseeking from us have become anxious, a pause before we respond might afford us an opportunity to better discern what they need. Then and only then, may we decide if we or someone else might be better to give what they need. We might even be better resourced to help them get help elsewhere. So this noticing, tuning in, centering (getting back inside ourselves), really can help us access very useful information to manage the motivation (and energy) required to give effective care. Of course, all of this depends upon our ability to tune in to ourselves, our emotional, psychological, and physiological wellbeing. Effective care is effective management. By allowing a pause we allow for the moment of centering (real focus) in management, leadership and peer support at work (and at home).

If we just crash on, though, being reactive, giving care whenever it is required regardless of the cost to us, we are most likely to become ill. We are very likely to resent or even start attacking the people who seek care from us. As managers, leaders, or carers, this is a dangerous and unhealthy state to be in.

We discuss again how effective caregiving needs to remain exploratory. Being able to identify your own individual and organisational (team) needs first requires separating out who is carrying various responsibilities. You may even be able to identify their skills and competence at giving care. This may lead to delegating the care giving, or even nurturing new caregiving talent, so beyond becoming more aware of the resources around you, it enriches them for the benefit of everyone. We explore how sometimes giving good care is about giving time and attention, not solutions. We notice how hard it can be to resist the temptation to pile in with a solution and inadvertently leave the other person without the very thing they needed from us, without a relational exchange. Could this be a new learning point (LP8), what would it be like to have caregivers assigned in a team, for a certain period of time say? To use it overtly? My colleague Butler notes how this could be aligned to coaching approaches to leadership. Approaches aimed at giving skills to, and developing the talent of, teams by identifying and managing what they might need to learn and practise until that skill has become theirs.

Identifying how we might replenish ourselves after the care has been given becomes a very important aspect of working with this system. Burn-out is such a worrying feature of the modern workplace. McCluskey has written separately about this with Gunn (McCluskey and Gunn, 2015). Burn-out is not just tiredness, it's not temporary depletion, it is an organic breakdown in the system. Looking for our enablers and our sources of empowerment and how to do that for others is just one way we might ameliorate the risks of professional burn-out. This session regularly goes back to the ideas of careseeking, recognising that careseeking patterns are based on learnt behaviour and are designed to influence others to get what we want – I want to have an effect on the other person, in order to regulate an affect in me.

***

This particular form of modulation is similar to the description and motivation of the ego state "Little Professor" in transactional analysis (TA). Interestingly TA emerged out of the Freudian field of psychoanalysis. TA is a system of social psychology developed by Eric Berne. Berne's theory consists of "certain key concepts that practitioners use to help clients, students, and systems analyze and change patterns of interaction that interfere with achieving life aspirations". (see http://www.itaaworld.org/what-transactional-analysis). The notion of an ego state was described by Eric Berne (1961) as "a consistent pattern of feeling and experience directly related to a corresponding consistent pattern of behavior". A sufficiently consistent phenomenological experience of a certain way of feeling and being that becomes particularly evident when we are interacting with others. A persona if you like; a coherent mini constellation within the larger whole. The little professor ego state is described as being creative, intuitive and manipulative. It is that part of ourselves that can work hard (and often imaginatively) to get others to do our bidding for us.

Within the McCluskey model there is great potential to notice when one is becoming contaminated by the affect in the other person, such as their fear or anxiety. If careseeking is blocked the careseeker is unmet, likely to remain in some state of distress, not having their needs met (goals not corrected), this is likely to lead them to increase their careseeking behaviour.

I then show my group a second elephant video – careful to explain that all the videos or supplementary material will not always be about elephants. The video (https://youtu.be/ItpItaMpN20) this time shows a herd of elephants crossing a swollen river, the youngest calf gets swept downstream with the strong water flow. The mother crashes through the water to rescue her calf but is unable to bring the infant up stream on her own. The rest of the herd become perturbed and move towards the struggling pair and then move away clearly confused and agitated about what to do. An extrapolation here to managing team crisis became apparent – any of us might find ourselves overwhelmed in a work flood, swept away or witnessing a colleague being swept away by some difficulty. The careseeking of the struggling pair becomes apparent. It isn't until a larger (wiser, more experienced caregiving?) elephant joins the drama and clearly recognises both the limits and dilemma of the two in the water, the inability of those who rushed to help and then gets into the water with the struggling pair; does a rescue actually take place. Placing itself in front of the infant alongside the mother, stemming the flow a little, makes it possible for mother and infant to clamber out of the river. Effective caregiving; it affords the survival of the baby, but also perhaps teaches or modeling a strategy for getting out of the torrent. Good attuned leadership, exploratory, not taking over, coming in to help and facilitating the growth of competence.

I model exploratory caregiving too, by allowing myself to respond positively with the group and how they like these videos to engage in the theory in another, possibly crucially non-cognitive but kinaesthetic and visual way.

To keep them applying these ideas to themselves and to their work I ask them to go back to their homework answers. You may remember I asked them to reflect upon their own patterns of behaving. My colleague Hill observed here how I continually switched back and forth between the home environment and the work environment allowing the participants to join up their experiences as an emotional "whole" to see these patterns.

Session 2 homework for Session 3: think about how you caregive at work

1   Where/how might you have learnt to do this?
2   When is it effective?
3   When is it ineffective and might that be described as dominant/ submissive
4   Is there a particular caregiving culture in your team that you can describe?

Furthermore, I pose these questions to them.

• How do you know you are in caregiving mode? Is there a biological body sensation?
• How do you know when your caregiving has met the goal of the other person?
• What might remaining exploratory in caregiving look like?'
• What might becoming defensive in caregiving look like?'
• What might intrusive caregiving look like?
• Is your caregiving a re-enactment of what you experienced in your past?
• Do you notice compulsive caregiving? (the other person loses the chance to explore themselves)
• What modes of caregiving do you notice in others – like or dislike?
• How might caregiving help other access their other systems?

These questions arose from my training with McCluskey and my considerations of how I might help my participants notice how patterns from their early years might inform them in the present. Helping them to tune into some of the emotional and biological nuances of their experiences.

I then encouraged them to look for examples of McCluskey's (2005) caregiving responses within the group discussions:

1   Caregiver remains attuned and regulates careseekers arousal.
2   Caregiver avoids the affect and attempts to deflect careseeker from exploring it.
3   The caregiver avoids engaging with affect and become disorganised – then responds to careseekers affect (the new one not original).
4   The caregiver avoids and becomes immobilised.
5   Caregiver mis-attunes and becomes disorganised.

***

Surprises, learning, satisfactions and dissatisfactions

What became super evident is that the notion of caregiving at work seems perfectly acceptable to participants. Using the word care is even acceptable. The previous session on careseeking was still resonating with the group in many ways. We clarify in discussion that they believed (thought and felt) giving care was okay, asking for it for was not okay. I resolve with them to raise the dilemma of using the phrase careseeking for themselves with McCluskey for discussion. Which I did do, as you will see the next chapter.

To everyone's credit they all get the incongruity, they understand they can't knowingly expect their teams and colleagues to seek effective care if they aren't prepared to do it themselves, but perhaps as leaders in particular – having safe and reliable places where they can seek care is crucial for their wellbeing, and therefore their performance? There is also some slight and interesting hesitation around whether or not care can be sought from a hierarchical junior, while at the same time also knowing they often give care to their seniors. It is a wonderful discovery of the way we tie ourselves up in knots at work. Fear came to the foreground and the group have some delightful anticipation in embracing the next system.

Here is a reflection of caregiving from one of the participants.

Caregiving was something I had always prided myself upon. Previous jobs (such as in an advice centre) involved helping and assisting others (a more obvious definition of care). I saw myself as a caring person who helped others, but by undertaking this work I realised that this sometimes spilled over into a dominant/submissive position in two ways; firstly, by always wanting to help, even if the person may not have needed or wanted it (i.e., my assumptions were incorrect); secondly, by my striving to care give taking precedence and overriding my ability to care seek. Following on from this, I have tried to remain caring, open and approachable to giving care but have placed the onus more on being approached than doing the approaching.

Course participant 3

Perhaps the exposition here and the discussion we had in the session could be used as evidence supporting the argument for large or demanding organisations to provide forms of accessible support and help. Could organisations formalise caregiving as a standard work process, and support staff to understand it as a skill? Drury asks here how we might formalise this as a skill, can we support people to learn how caregiving works within (self-to-self), as well how caregiving works without (self-to-other)? More good questions.

***

The homework and heads up for the next session

This included the questions below on a reflective grid handout (see handouts at the back of this book) and I also emailed these to them for those who might wish to work online.

Session 3 homework for Session 4: think about how self-defence or fear impacts you at work

1   Where/how might you have learnt to do this?
2   When is it effective?
3   When is it ineffective, and might that be described as dominant/submissive?
4   Is there a particular self-defence or fear culture in your team that you can describe?

Note

1 There is debate as to who first came up with this formulation of learning. It is variously attributed to Noel Burch in 1970 an employee of the American organisation Gordon Training International: in 1974 to W Lewis Robinson an industrial training executive; and to Martin M Broadwell, 1969, in writings he submitted through The Gospel Guardian, an American Christian periodical published from the 1950s–1970s.

Chapter 6

Self-defence and fear

In this chapter I will cover the fourth session which introduced the idea of the defence of self, as a discreet system that is inter-personally goal corrected or intra-personally goal corrected. The system of self-defence includes the fear system. It is a complex system that functions to manage threat; including managing threats derived through the arousal of attachment dynamics of careseeking, caregiving in securely or insecurely attached relationships, real physical threat, and threats incurred through internal supportive or unsupportive environments.

This is one of the three instinctive biological systems added to Bowlby's two of careseeking and caregiving. We will look at the session structure, offer more detail on the genesis of the theory relevant to self-defence, and how we introduced this in the pilot at work.

**

Clarifications first

The clarifications part of the sessions, was always important – by thanking and honouring participants for their questions I modelled the approach of one-for-all, meaning one persons' question is relevant for everyone. For example, one person's question has the potential for learning for others, and, as this is a relational experience, their contact and enquiries with me matter greatly to the effectiveness of the group's work.

Some participants had asked to get a sense of travel with the course, where we had started, how far we had managed to get, and where we might be heading. So, we looked back at the programme outline provided at the beginning of the course to reiterate what we had already covered and what comes next. As Hill (Chapter 3) was particularly good at highlighting for me, this is important for orientating people to their course of learning.

Others asked what the centering was about and why I was evoking repetitions of it. I was also interested if anyone was using the centering in their work at all. I was curious to know what if any of the ideas and practices were filtering into participants ways of working and being. Centering is especially relevant when considering the system for personal self-defence, which includes the two systems of: one fear (responding alone) and, two careseeking (engaging another to help). The behaviour activated by the fear system is to manage things by oneself, and the behaviour activated by the careseeking system is to seek help from others.

Centering regulates one physically, so their queries about centering here were particularly relevant.[1]Through centering we can learn to notice the arousal of the fear system (by attention to our behaviour) we may not experience the emotion of fear, and can develop skills to regulate physiological effects. If we can regulate and manage the impingement of these physiological effects, we are likely to be more available to consider how to respond, and be less at the mercy of our panic response. Practise and ability at doing this may also reduce the actual impact of the threat responses upon our overall wellbeing.

***

Care at work

It was in the previous session that the whole issue of using the word care at work had caused a valuable learning kerfuffle. One of the main outcomes participants reported from taking the course was how they were starting to bring the notion of care, and even use the word care, in how they perceived themselves at work. Therefore, one of the chief ways that people were affected by engaging in the course was to allow for and bring the word "care" into the idea of professional interpersonal relationships at work. A few of my participants struggled with another notion that it might be acceptable to consider how they got care at work. It was as though the word care needed to be put in the context of work in order for it to be legitimately (i.e, professionally) engaged with at work – the actual experience is familiar but the use of the word is usually associated with personal life outside of work. Most, if not all, recognised the legitimacy of their role as caregivers to their colleagues and teams. However, it seemed only acceptable to consider it as a one-way transaction. This highlighted one of the dangers of work for us, without a sound experience and notion of our own wellbeing we may easily find ourselves giving far more than we ever replenish or expect and need back from others. Yet there may be various behaviours that elicit, one way or another, some form of care, response and attention (attendance) by our colleagues. Through exploring how our careseeking and caregiving patterns formed in early childhood, the pilot was able to broaden (through exploration of the model and the terms) the notion of what care was, to really bring those original notions of attention, attunement, and goal correction in relational value for work.

A rejection of the word "care" wasn't wholesale but I decided we needed to spend some time looking at why the word care aroused such turbulence, and what that meant for the group. I chose to take the group through this together, so that the range of experiences from those who didn't get or like an idea, were as available for learning, as were experiences of those who had embraced an idea. I believe that blocks, aversions, and resistance to learning are important to consider. It is, of course, the therapist in me. Not only might someone wish to be autonomous and disagree with an idea, but sometimes there may be some important part of a conversation, learning or experience that hasn't yet been accessed which could be really helpful for everyone. Carl Jung used the phrase "gold in the shadows" (from Chapter 3) and I can honestly say I have had more personal and professional moments of learning around blocks. A block or resistance to an idea is information, therefore why not spend some time seeing if the information is useful, a habit or some kind of defence? If we can discover in a kindly way, it is an avoidant defence we might unhook a hindrance. If we discover it is an appropriate defence we can keep it in the skills toolbox.

McCluskey and I talked about the implications of using the word care in a work context and McCluskey suggested I offer the group the alternative to think rather in terms of 'affect identification' instead of careseek, and 'affect modulation or regulation' instead of caregive. I was rather pleased with my meeting of their need to be able to reject the words. I encouraged the group to take the new words away and try them out for themselves and in their workplace applications – they brought their findings back in the subsequent session covered in Chapter 7.

After clarification and the discussion about the word 'care', the session structure was:

- Over-time reflections: here I offered the opening that we'd been looking at caregiving and careseeking so far, and asked them if they had any narrative about that at that moment. I explained "blank is OK". It is especially important to attend to the experience of being blank in this session. Blank as we will see can be an indication of our state at the time. Blank is always important – but with fear it is even more important than normal. Blank might indicate the fear system is active. Because fear (and the spontaneous production of adrenaline, the effect of the vagal nerve) deactivates the pre frontal cortex, blank indicates occluded absence). The mind and body working together in some form of defence. This will be explained in more detail in this chapter.
- I asked them to look at their system for self-defence and their experience of fear in the workplace – to see where they were, and to do that, they all really needed to be present in the room – so we centred again. I was aware that even introducing the word fear that was likely to evoke an emotional arousal therefore, centering twice, was good practise of using it for emotional arousal.
- I had previously sent out the reflective grid handout – and I wanted to know what was it like sending it back to me?

From Session 4 they had been set the following questions.

Session 3 homework for Session 4: think about how self-defence or fear impacts you at work

1   Where/how might you have learnt to do this?
2   When is it effective?
3   When is it ineffective and might that be described as dominant/ submissive?
4   Is there a particular self-defence or fear culture in your team that you can describe?

This session was an important one to deliver because we had highlighted how fear permeates careseeking and indeed caregiving. Before I got into the theory of the subject I was really keen to hear what they had found out about their fear. The whole business of this pilot course is fear-free exploratory interest sharing. Creating a fear-free (fear being acknowledged, accepted and managed, not eliminated from natural experience) work environment will most probably reduce conflict; burn-out, wasted time, unhelpful defensive behaviours. Therefore, I wanted them to have an immediate opportunity to say what they had found out about their fear, so they didn't have to sit on their discoveries, as that in itself (holding on to the discoveries, anticipating saying it out loud) that can increase an experience of fear.

Fear affects us all; it affects our health, our sleep, our relationships with each other.

To embark on this, getting them to centre and settle and using McCluskey's opening practise was important to help them settle any fear or anxiety about themselves or in their bodies.

- **Centre – get in your seats – on your sitting bones – eyes open – attentive**
- **Find the tension and let it go – lets go very slowly today**

In centering on this occasion, I worked steadily through the process. I invited the group to observe any places of tension in their bodies – asking if this was information they might need to do something about? Could they adjust our bodies, and when ready perhaps you can check in with each other? Checking in with each other is getting a bit of eye contact with everyone else in the room. McCluskey uses this approach of encouraging people working in groups to get eye contact both at the beginning of a session after people have arrived in their seats or after a significant piece of work has been done. This reconnecting with the rest of the group is both acknowledging the group and the group process, recognising that we are working with others, and about not being left on our own to manage whatever emotions and content there might be to manage.

Eye contact helps to move the behaviour from the isolation of the self to the relational interpersonal caregiving/careseeking dynamic. This can be especially important if a group hasn't been together for a little while.

Some of the group reflected upon how they have noticed they have learnt to keep their experiences of fear hidden at work, to avoid being seen as fearful, to avoid attracting unwelcome responses in others. In Chapter 4 of the 2012 book Heard, Lake and McCluskey have described that as a defensive strategy, a strategy which might have been useful once but is being brought out habitually. I would describe that as a maladaptive coping mechanism. I am certain that will be familiar to some of you reading this. The problem of avoiding our fear is that it can truly become overwhelming, it can make us feel angry and frustrated. It can certainly affect our sleep. If there is a colleague who is able to manage fear in a team, it might work but only in so far as that colleague is available to manage everyone's fear. It doesn't increase the competence of the team. Furthermore, unmanaged, unassuaged fear leads to worry. There is a classic thinking habit called catastrophising. Those who catastrophise tell themselves if they can anticipate every difficult possibility they can prepare for it and not be taken by surprise. It's a neat idea but doesn't really work. Because we can't actually anticipate how we will phenomenologically feel under certain circumstances, so instead all we do is delude our bodies into a fear state in the present. Consequently, this doubles the fear experience! Worrying or catastrophising can make people very ill. Of course we should prepare, and anticipate up and coming difficulties, but these preparations need to be manageable.

The other very real aspect for the group is (lived) reality based fear responses. Some participants have difficult work situations, have experienced bullying in the past, some have been left with ineffective leaders and managers in previous jobs. This situation may arise for a variety of reasons, to name a few such as: there aren't enough staff; there aren't enough skilled staff; the work itself may be frightening; people may feel under attack in their jobs; and indeed those managers and leaders may themselves not be in a good state to do the jobs they are required to do. These kinds of experiences, can provide a person with evidence and reasons to be vigilant around certain behaviours in others. However, these comparable behaviours could have entirely different signification. In the McCluskey model these responses can be termed as look-a-likes to the past Some of the group also noticed in their reflections how the unassuaged fear really messes with their mental competence-this easily feeds into self-critical attack. Critical thinking and sometimes critical attack can be very pernicious especially in a knowledge economy, where smart, defensive or innovative thinking are a part of the day job.

The group also made some very interesting observations about defensive caregiving and defensive careseeking behaviours that emerged in these fear-ridden states. Some observed how they hoped their fear *was* noticed by others to be managed by others, even when it is kept under wraps. A fantastical world view of please know what I need even though I hide it. Or even – please know what I need even when I don't! (This harks back to those early moments of being tended by our caregivers, who were supposed to tune into our needs). Sound familiar? I know I do it sometimes, especially when I am tired or frightened. They also noticed they sometimes withdrew, wishing to conceal their fear, or even realising it was changing what and how they were communicating. The withdrawing behaviour aimed to avoid, understandably, any unprofessional appearance or seeming incompetence. If some of these behaviours could be perceived by colleagues as dominant submissive (bully or victim), they could perhaps also be perceived as stubborn or avoidant. Have you experienced these behaviours in yourself or in others?

Can you imagine how freeing it might be to be able to understand and work with these behaviours in the workplace and liberate ourselves from them? But instead we entangle ourselves over and over again, fighting against our very own nature, and if that isn't further fear-inducing, what is?

***

The theory

We could write a book just about the impact of fear on our bodies, about our wonderful autonomous responses that sometimes save our lives and other times seem to get in the way of going about our business. How fear responses are both innate and learnt. So please forgive us if this doesn't nail the subject completely.

The fear component (a system in its own right) in this model is located within the self defence (ancient) system, which also includes attachment.

Self-defence is a system that is a part of us which includes the mechanism and processes we have built up through relations with others and reminds us of our competence. It enables us to refute challenges that don't belong us. Our past experiences of fear impact us at work, and past examples are very likely to interfere with how we might manage in the present.

Self-defence and fear can be split into two – primitive (instinctive) and new mammalian (learnt as you experience life) – can you detect the difference?

Primitive: this is our hotwired, instinctive system that is designed to get us out of trouble, play dead, go sleepy, run, kill the attacker, dodge the danger, go into stasis, hide, defecate, vomit, attack physically, psychologically, or emotionally.

One of the important features of this system is that in the main, it is not cognitive; it is instinctive, natural unfettered animal behaviour. We can absolutely learn to work with it, around it, even exacerbate it. But it is very active. This primitive system is the one that activates in a nano-second when you knock a glass off a counter, when a small child heads precariously towards danger, when a loud bang makes your heart beat just that tiny bit faster. When you realise a misplaced email has aroused hurt or fury in a colleague. It's biological cellular heat.

An incredible characteristic of this system, which never ceases to interest me, is it can prompt us to respond in four different ways – towards (attack, save, action), away, avoid (run), freeze stock still, or freeze floppy (shut down, play dead in a way which really feels like dead or sleepy). To demonstrate this system in its full natural force I showed the following video.

Baboons Save Impala From lion and Hyena (https://youtu.be/Ul92zX45CbQ).

If this remarkable video still exists and should you look for it, you will see not only the real swapping of dominant submissive positions in the animal kingdom. But the amazing almost mind-boggling power of freeze (shut down) and the incredible power of the biological system to reset and restart. An impala caught by a leopard looks to all intents and purposes to be dead, but after the leopard is chased away, the impala appears to come back to life. But no gentle reboot, this is a violent and powerful restart. The lungs, apparently motionless, begin to expand and contract with such vigor the impala's entire abdomen swells and contracts violently, the expansion and contraction eventually pushes air through the impalas mouth; I assume the heart starts first to beat with greater vigor but that is impossible to know for sure. The violent beating and breathing eventually leads to the impala sitting up but shaking violently, a bit like the shaking you may have seen with anyone going into shock or maybe we should say coming out of shock. This shaking eventually passes, the impala gets up and runs away. It's utterly amazing. This is an example of full system reset. This resetting and shaking process is sometimes used therapeutically by therapists working with traumatised clients.

This primitive system is in us, but remember it is not primarily cognitive – our pre-frontal cortex gets switched off. We compute – but we compute very differently. This is one of my very favourite descriptions of what goes on:

Fight/Flight Response

'To our cave-dwelling ancestors, the fight/flight response was an essential tool for survival, evolved over many thousands of years living in wild and dangerous places. To us, living in today's technological twenty-first century, it is often an ineffective response, which can actively prevent us from responding usefully to a problem situation. This response to anything which is perceived as a threat, or potential threat begins when certain primitive parts of the brain send a message to the adrenal glands. These begin a process involving a number of hormones including adrenaline, whose purpose is to prepare the body for vigorous emergency action. The main changes that follow are below. Non-essential processes are immediately switched off. In particular, if the body is digesting food, that is stopped immediately, and people notice a feeling of churning or 'butterflies' in the stomach, or feeling nauseous or sick. A number of other changes follow, to make the muscles as strong as possible. The liver releases glucose into the bloodstream. Fats are released into the bloodstream from the fat stores in the body. These are fuel for the muscles, so oxygen is needed to burn them-so the breathing increases, and those under stress may notice feeling breathless. Having fuel and oxygen in the bloodstream, the body needs to get it to the muscles as soon as possible – (remember, the body thinks this is a life or death emergency). So to pump the blood quickly, the heart begins beating far faster – and some people notice palpitations. Blood pressure rises, and some people notice feeling hot or cold – even breaking into a sweat, as the body seeks to dissipate the heat that will be generated by the vigorous muscular activity for which the body is preparing. Becoming ready for instant action, muscle tension increases, and a person may notice shaking, or becoming restless – fidgeting. If the pattern in continued for long enough, chronic headaches or backache may result. As all this is happening in the body, there are two important changes in the neurology. First, reflexes are speeded up. At the same time, so is the thinking, and some notice racing thoughts. Second, the blood supply to the frontal parts of the brain, responsible for higher levels of reasoning are reduced, while the blood supply to the more primitive parts, near the brain stem, is increased. These parts are responsible for automatic, or instinctive, or impulsive decision making and behaviour, and a person undergoing a stress response may be prone to impulsive thinking and behaviour – which they may thoroughly regret later'.[2]

The new mammalian

The second aspect of our self-defence system is the one formed as you experience life. These are the fear behaviours that are learnt through our rather most marvellous mirror neurons and through watching, copying and being trained to exhibit certain responses by our primary caregivers. Part of the biological system deployed to help us copy, emulate and adopt survival behaviours from our peers and family. The copying of family patterns are learnt and adopted through social induction, repetition, and via experiencing and witnessing shocks. These responses become embedded socially as acceptable or non-acceptable and are therefore reinforced emotionally through our attachment systems. Some of these responses may also become maladaptive, built up through repetitions of failed careseeking/caregiving patterns.

The visual cliff experiments of the 1980s (Sorce, et al., 1985) show the power of these reinforcements very well. The experiments were actually designed to identify development stages of an infant's perceptual fields by seeing what an infant does when faced with an apparent void (a glass top) to cross to get to their mothers. The scientists observed that not only might the infant try to identify a path forward by banging the apparently invisible surface, but crucial to their progress was also the cues offered by their mother. If the mother smiled, was encouraging, the child progressed forward; its safety placed in the positive signals of the mother. However, if the mother frowns, looks angry or away, the infants hesitate. They might even cry. The absence of social reference causes confusion, fear. No information is available as to what is acceptable. Imagine the myriad of times these encouragements, blocks or absences occur as we develop. Imagine the many times an unintentional or intentionally inattentive parent inadvertently prompts a biological emotional pattern in the infant. These patterns then feed into our ability to know fear, take risks (move toward new experiences) or avoid risks (move away from new experiences). These encounters also feed into what we learn to rely on and the evidence that we can get (and interpret) from our own environment. However, since we can't go back in time and change these responses perhaps we can learn to feel them biologically, forgive ourselves for the hesitations, and if we are in a supportive group, explore how they manifest at work (and at home) and develop new skills to manage the biological and emotional impact of them. Manage and resource our experience of crossing endless apparent voids, places where we simply have not been before. After all, I can honestly say I have never been in this day of my life before; I am endlessly cutting new territory just being me.

We could say that both of these feed into what is described as the hypothesis of somatic markers (Damasio, 2006) in Chapter 2. Neural biological reflexes and pathways built up through different experiences and responses to the world outside of us.

You might notice it through some of your internal scripts (messages absorbed as a child). You may have overcome some of them.

I offered a personal example of a conflation of the primitive and mammalian fear systems in action. Arachnophobes may wish to skip this description. My mother used to leap up on sofas in response to seeing spiders and I watched and phenomenologically experienced this behaviour from being a small child. At the beginning, I copied what she did, however, another trusted relative once asked me if I was afraid of spiders. In our discussion, I realised that I was frightened by my mom's panic, and the sudden movement of the spiders, especially the dash, it made me jump, but I was not actually alarmed by the spiders as creatures. In fact, I found (and still find) them rather intriguing. From this point, I became more interested and even amused by my mom's response. At the point I could distinguish the difference between my experience and hers, her terror of the spiders transformed into anger at me and my response. I hear the words even now "get it Nicola, don't just sit there and laugh!

You may observe here the way in which one person can put pressure on another to attune their emotional state and regulate them, even when it might not be helpful to the other person, for example, in my mom's anger when I wouldn't attune to her fear. i.e., one person wants their emotion regulated, another person wants to be joined. The joiner risks losing their own sense of self and their own autonomy in the situation. This pattern can emerge many years later in work, where I might find myself being vulnerable to join a colleagues aroused emotional state, even though a large part of me can see what going on and even though this is not my state. Therefore, I may become depleted in managing others fears, regulating at the expense of my own needs. A better response will be to be a resource for them and help them learn to regulate themselves.

However, learning not just to copy mom's behaviour meant that I had the opportunity to find an alternative response which I got from a nan and an aunty who caught and freed the spiders in the garden. I unwittingly used my neuroplasticity to do something different.

Though I might still to this day feel the urge to leap when spiders dash because they still make me jump, and biologically I instantly recall the effect my mom's panic in me. Now, however, I register the adrenal jolt, as I believe I should; it is a survival response, but my flight inclination is now reasonably tamed into a managed behaviour of catch and displace.

I offered a subsequent example of a fear response set up in me but this time not through my attachments: the fear of flying. I had no lived external social references for being frightened to fly. This time, perhaps, some tuning into wider social notions of fears and fantasies of flying (maybe too much exposure to films with plane crashes). We must remember that fiction is still a stimulus to the body, and my primitive self is still likely to learn something in watching a film about a plane crash. Think here of what we are doing to ourselves with computer games and huge exposure to trauma via social media?

Anyway, in one trip to Australia I had to take in excess of six flights to get me to and from the various beautiful and exciting places I wanted to be. I simply couldn't sustain the fear responses in the face of so many sufficiently okay experiences of flying; to the degree that I managed to get on a helicopter without doors to do a fly-over a historic site called the Bungle Bungles in Purnululu National Park (though I can't say that flight was without any anxiety!). Therapeutically we might call this exposure treatment, but to be honest I think I became bored with being anxious and have never looked back with flying! Either way my body learnt to feel it differently.

***

Having delivered these large quantities of information I then invited the group to consider any instinctive fear responses that they have experienced. This change in pace allowed the group to bring their focus and attention back to themselves and to each other and away from what may have become, even if interesting, too much didactic input from me. This also felt like a good opportunity for them to exchange moments of competence (and therefore endorse it) with and for each other.

Remember this pilot was about developing their skills of curiosity in themselves and about themselves, and their encounters with others, but it was also about developing their competencies and their awareness of their competences. So, this is why I offered them the chance to consider a learned fear that they had discovered and have overcome? The group shared some of these with each other in pairs and then some also with the wider group. They were sharing skills and competencies, and were able to receive the support and encouragement of their peers.

Noticing our competence in overcoming fears really matters when thinking about fear at work. The group knew from previous sessions, that unmet careseeking arouses fear and consequently defensive strategies to deal with the unregulated emotion. One of the participants really came to grips with the notion, in his words:

> The self-defence/fear system was very interesting, and somewhat revelatory, in that it built on things I had learnt through CBT about my coping strategies and mechanisms. I could see how these affected me from short-term to long-term in terms of becoming more frantic, fractious, and obsessed with controlling and completing the things I could do to still feel effective, even though I wasn't actually being.
>
> Course participant 3

We have seen from the biological explanations that fear interrupts our cognitions, and interrupts acceptable social norms. It will therefore play havoc with professional exchanges. Because our fear system can kick in so rapidly, small failed careseeking attempts or clumsy exchanges can arouse this system for self-defence. Offering them the chance to consider their fear responses led to much discussion about the fear responses of those careseeking around them.

I then supplied the following ideas and strategies on a handout for them to consider when working with others:

***

Why centering helps managing the fear in ourselves and in others.

Centering as we have said, helps us slow the body down. It uses the redirection of the focus of our attention and gentle breath work to signal to the body that we are back in charge. The autonomic system powers back down when we can regulate our breath work because breathing is so heavily affected by the autonomic reflex. Centering does not try to ignore unhelpful stimulus, but it is an opportunity, a moment of prescencing when we can park the troublesome experiences for a moment, soothe the body, and then allow our cognitive minds to make some choices. It's about slowing down, easing off the accelerator (a phrase much used by McCluskey) and noticing what it going on in the body.

I offered them some information to take away to help embed this as a practice should they wish to explore the ideas away from the sessions.

Notice

Do you notice this in your body – if so where? How? What might you do if you think your fear system has taken over?

Learning to tune in to our bodies better and faster means that we might notice when fear has crept in. If we can use our meta-awareness at these points we may be able to make conscious choices on whether the fear response is needed or indeed if an alternative response might be available to us.

Have you or the other person deployed some defensive strategies?

Further exploration of the fear response could be done by following with these questions:

Is there a deadening? Is there sleepiness?
This could highlight the impala response at large.

Watch out for decoys or lookalikes from the past.

Again, one of the key features of McCluskey's model is to pay proper tribute to the impact of our past upon us. It could be that something or someone in the here and now is bearing a coincidental likeness to something we experienced with fear as children, or indeed as a sufficiently scary experience as an adult. This might be noticeable with such phrases as "I've been here before it didn't go at all well".

Assess

In terms of action, what might you do for the other person if their fear system has been aroused?

Keeping fear down by orientating people to the task

The McCluskey model also employs the strategy of regularly orienting people to the task in hand. You might liken it to coaxing a child by reassuring them the new experience will be alright. This take us very neatly back to the virtual cliff test and the importance of having good social clues and encouragers around us.

Understand

If the attachment/careseeking fear system is up we need to get back to careseeking and caregiving and see what might be restored first. The primitive fear system can be resolved alone but the attachment/careseeking system needs to be resolved with a relationship with another. To be:

> " . . . in contact with effective trustworthy and protective caregivers, whose behaviour towards a careseeker ought to be such that it enables the goal of careseeking to be reached"
>
> (Heard, Lake and McCluskey, 2012, p. 58).

In either instance, we stop being exploratory and therefore stop being productive, effective, collaborative.

Do you need to think about caregiving as an aspect of affect identification, regulation, and modulation? Or can the word care be used?

How might we become curious about fear and self-defence?

Review

What has worked what hasn't worked? How is your competence, and how is their competence now?

I really enjoyed this session, and the discussions about the subtlety of the fear system has been one of the most enduring impacts of the pilot course.

Heads up for the next subject

Session 4 homework for Session 5: to think about what interest and interest sharing has to do with the workplace?

1   What interests and where/how might you share any interests at work?
2   When is it effective – how do you know?

3   What happens to you if you can't interest-share?
4   What happens to other if they can't interest share?
5   Is there a particular interest sharing culture in your team that you can describe?
6   Reflective grid handout – they can email it back to me optional this time.

Notes

1 It also fitted with the organisational application of mindfulness practise which Rose had brought into the organisation.
2 Originally accessed in March 2012 From: http://www.helpishere.co.uk/fightflight.html but this website is now unavailable. The text is now also printed in Cumbrian Partnership booklet on "Manage Your Mind Overcoming Worry – An Introduction" A Self help Pack. Attributed to Martin Groom, Accredited Cognitive Behavioural Psychotherapist, Leeds Community Healthcare NHS Trust, 2013.

Chapter 7

Interests and interest-sharing with peers

In this chapter I will cover the sixth session that introduced the systems for interests and interest sharing with peers. This is the second of the three instinctive interpersonal biological systems added to Bowlby's two of careseeking and caregiving. We will look at the session structure, offer more detail on the genesis of the theory relevant to interests and interest-sharing with peers.

Reflections over time

What do you remember about what we have looked at so far? How has it been for you thinking about affect identification, modulation and regulation?

Remember from the last chapter, McCluskey had offered my group the alternative words of "affect identification" instead of careseeking, and "affect modulation or regulation" instead of caregiving. I had invited my group to take the new words away and think about them. Unexpectedly for me, their own reflections on the discussion and perhaps my willingness to reject the word "care" actually led them to want it back! It seemed to allow them to reclaim the word in some way, own it again and reframe what it meant for them. It was as though some of them had shocked themselves in the discussion of the word "care", realising that they had an embedded view that giving or receiving care had not felt synonymous with work. They recognised they were holding the notion of believing they were employed at work for their intellect; their minds only, and not their bodies and emotions. They had ignored themselves and their own careseeking needs. When the group finally conceded the word and notion "care" was ok, they began to open themselves up to more specific ideas of what their own care needs might be, and also to what the dangers might be of any low self-care behaviours they might practise. Consequently, they could also consider the effect of the way they sought care, might have on those around them. They became curious what different members of their teams might want in terms of care from them. They gained some indications into exploring further what their teams might be wishing to get in their ways of careseeking from them.

This was a vitality raising experience for me. Not only had it been a rewarding experience to take their query away to McCluskey as a real relevant concern about the application of the word "care" to the workplace, but also it highlighted the way in which working with this model had a trickle-down effect, a permeation quality to it. Time to reflect and choose how this model could work for them was a crucial aspect to getting their feelings and their beliefs of how this model transferred to the workplace.

To recap, as I put it to them, the task was to:

> Look at your systems for interests and interest-sharing and your experience of them in the workplace – let's see where you are, and to do that we all really need to be in the room – so we centred again.

Centre – get in your seats – on your sitting bones – eyes open – attentive
Find the tension and let it go – can we get curious?

What did they find out about their interests and interest sharing?

I had by this stage in the pilot recognised that I really needed to keep my contributions to the sessions down to a minimum. My group had interest and energy for discussion and if I spent too long talking at the beginning it kept them and their contributions at bay. The power of interests and sharing in real live process, perhaps. Imagine the impact on you of a person who may have taught you to do something but only ever by doing it themselves and making you watch. Whilst this teaching approach may be appropriate sometimes, it runs the risk of squashing the energy and learning of those you teach. Therefore, for this session, more than any of the others, it was essential I let them express themselves and their findings without intervention from me but with my unconditional positive regard and attention: that was very easy to do for them but I did have to manage my own excitement about the subject matter – balancing my needs to join in, with their needs to learn together and express themselves. I confess this is an ongoing professional challenge for me.

What they found incredible was just how deep interests and interest sharing seemed to go for them. They recognised that in seeking out shared interests with others, they were also searching for indicators of the values and beliefs of the other people. In other words, very quickly my interests say something about me as a person. In some ways my interests are signposts and indicators of the kind of person I am. This gives clues to others about whether or not I am the kind of person they may wish to consort with and even trust. There can be a very personal quality to interests – these might be something that I keep out of my professional life, or indeed only a select few may be allowed to enter this personal world of my interests. So interest-sharing includes vulnerability, it becomes a way we connect with others in potentially quite a deep and personal level. When they felt comfortable with their interest sharing they observed of themselves that work was easy, they felt relaxed, engaged, they noticed that good interest sharing creates enjoyment and pleasure in the work tasks. There is a saying, sometimes attributed to Confucius, "Do what you love and you'll never work a day in your life". It is criticised for over simplifying the challenges and difficulties of work, inferring that all work tasks can be rewarding, which is probably unlikely. It can be legitimately criticised, as not all of us, or all the time, have the luxury to work at what we like to do. It might never happen, or it might take years to happen. But for sure, when work is connected to our interests it certainly is easier and more pleasurable to do. Like anything however, there has to be balance; interests and hobbies outside of work contribute to our wellbeing considerably whether we enjoy our work or not. We were also examining the system of goal correction as it applies to pursuing an interest or sharing an interest with others, as a concept relevant to the workplace.

The group expressed the way they explored their interests outside of work, the effect of having these interests upon them, and the effect of having people to share them with. They observed how sharing these external interests with colleagues involves vulnerability, has the potential to cement connections across disciplines, work areas, hierarchies. A buddy in another department you can go to. Then we have interest as work, being interested in your work – anyone else in your team sharing your particular interest, equally too these others might be in another department or area – so you might find them at a conference or event. My group further observed that if the business of work can be the interest-shared it can have impact on group dynamics. If a team is newly formed, or going through a process together, then having the time to explore this together helps to form the fabric of their collegiality with each other. Therefore, all these different layers are vitally import for our wellbeing.

Two of the limits observed by my group were the limits of time and the requirements that workload would take us away from sharing our interests with others. Consequently, we have a paradox; if we know that sharing interests at work can join us relationally to others, and if we know that being in meaningful relations with others can help us improve the experience of work and perhaps also our mastery of it – why don't we prioritise these connections above the business of business?

It was a jolt for some of the participants to realise that when they were unable to interest-share with others they noticed they were inclined to write those others off, feel flat in themselves, feel alienated, overlooked, subdued; and whilst a job may still be do-able it became functional, lacked vitality. One of the group reported an ill effect upon themselves when they were unable to companionably share their particular interest (focus) in their work with their colleagues, who they knew had the same interest (focus). In this case shared interest introduced competition rather than collaboration. The group discussion led us all to deduce how the triggered response was a defensive one, and how the participant had gone into fear filled caregiving (see previous chapter) in response to their colleague being competitive. Wishing to defensively illicit a positive responsive by attending to the other persons needs and subjugating their own competence in order to get connected. Not the desired outcome.

They also observed how they could very quickly tune into the times when others were unable to interest share with them. The noticeable effects left these colleagues feeling short-tempered, anxious about how much they are able to share (some needing to interest share as a form of careseeking and validation from my group members). They observed failed interest sharing left these other colleagues less motivated. The terms interests and interest-sharing as an idea for work were perhaps less intuitive than some of the others, and as a consequence it was a new way of thinking for the group to consider, especially as we might often separate our interests outside of work with what we do as work. As we can see from the comments of one group member here:

> Interests and interest-sharing was difficult for me, as I never defined myself by my job, so struggled to see that [work]as a shared interest with colleagues. My interests are things I do away from work, which are not shared by most colleagues, much like theirs are not by me, so this helped me look at how this view could be tweaked to develop a more efficient working relationship, such as building on the interest in doing our jobs well and effectively.
>
> Course participant 4

Consider this, if my sense of my self could be (and I say is) so very tied up with my interests, and my colleagues fail to join in or even at least listen to my interests my self (me) is being rejected. See the interconnection here of the model and the different systems. Although we haven't come yet to the internal environment we can see it in action here. With someone to interest-share with I experience competence, mastery, pleasure, my careseeking system happily regulating, my ability to caregive equally stable and available to give care (attention, attunement) to my interest sharing colleague, my fear system generally in neutral. Interestingly my sexual system might get aroused (but more on that later) because this can be an intoxicating mix. But with no one willing to share interests with me, my sense of competence, mastery, skill, is reliant on just my own interest in what I am doing. Without support and validation, it may be enough to carry on, but it doesn't have the same buzz as being with another person or a team of people who are engaged in spontaneous creative work, who are engaged in a shared interest. So again, my fear system is very likely to arouse, careseeking to power up, caregiving at a low point or acting out defensively. What fabulous argument for the value of active interest sharing at work! This is a key facet in good leadership: to be able to identify and amplify common interests with a team so they can come together and collaborate.

The richness of their findings here were most extraordinary. This session itself felt like a real example of exploratory interest sharing.

***

Before the group got into the discussion further I offered them the innovative ideas of a colleague of mine, Joanna Stevens (2015). Stevens and I trained together, in exploring interest sharing she discovered multiple layers to the quality of the interests we may share with others. These she describes as:

- First generation interests (those interests we discover for ourselves).
- Second generation interests (those interests that are linked to the interests of others we grew up around).
- Work generated interests, and the idea that work may be a form of interest sharing.
- Generic interests (© Joanna Stevens, 2015, 7th International Conference. Exploratory Goal Corrected Psychotherapy (EGCP)©).

Stevens' typography of interest and interest sharing really resonated with my group. Two of the members further observed how their interests had formed; how in some circumstances these interests not only spoke of their own values and preferences but also of their personal histories. Whether we knit because our grandparent did, the knitting binds us to the memory of that grandparent – it takes its significant place in our attachment world. This was one of the systems where some of my group had found it very hard to separate out a personal self to a professional self. Stevens' description gave them a way to make sense of this and I was grateful for her thinking to do so.

It could look like interest and interest-sharing have no place in the regulation of the self and in our emotional expression – that could not be further from the truth.

The danger we notice as authors by following the flow of what happened in the session here is that the one thing which maybe be missed out is the concept that developing ones own interest and delighting in that competence can be something one does on ones own and can be of great value to my wellbeing. I can sit with a book, tinker with a car, can solve mathematical problems, take a walk with my dog and experience great satisfaction in my ability to do these things by myself. This self-affirmation is equally as powerful as peer validation and affirmation.

Some theory

Heard and Lake believed that our capacity to interest share starts at about the age of three. But McCluskey has some evidence of it starting much earlier from a video clip of a four-month-old sharing the experience of enjoying a piano piece that her mother was playing. Interest sharing develops as we begin to explore ourselves and our world with all the senses we have at our disposal. Think about how you were cheered on for success in motor skills as a child, think about how you might cheer on a child now, or how might you applaud your colleagues in their endeavours, and how important it be they applaud you and join you in your pleasures and successes. We cannot interest-share if we are careseeking (because our careseeking must be attended to before we give our energies to play again) or caregiving (managing someone else need for care). Can we explore, or reflect upon, what might have stopped or become a barrier to interest-sharing with others if that has happened?

We cannot interest-share if we are frightened. According to Heard, Lake and McCluskey (2012) p.87, interest sharing performs three functions, to gain ". . . new levels of understanding in the world . . . to attain new achievements in skill . . . and to experience others doing the same or appreciating your skills . . ." With the process of interest sharing "we experience an increase in our vitality and an increase in the sense of wellbeing". At work this links to peer validation, companionable mutual interest-sharing, peer support in acquiring new skills. And just for information this doesn't include gossiping – gossiping belongs to the world of non-exploratory interest sharing. Defensive, almost always.

Having a peer at work doesn't always happen, and finding someone who you can share with matters, and this has implications for lone working. This is especially relevant as the modern work environment, now often involves working from home, but also relevant for those who travel for their work, those who run their own business. Interests and interest-sharing, like the other systems, affect the other systems. Participant 4 noticed that "interest-sharing aids the development of resilience to negativity both at work and personally".

Heard and Lake developed their ideas on interest sharing from 1986, through their work we can see that it is not just a case of having peers to share our interest with, we also need those peers to have the same stamina and intelligence.

The overarching concept of this pilot course was based upon fear-free exploratory interest sharing. Creating a fear-free work environment (where fear is acknowledged and managed) where people can interest-share is going to probably increase the creativity and productivity of those at work, as we see above. If we can enjoy our skills, and share and develop our workforce competence not only might we enrich the experience of those at work but we might also increase the sustainability and flexibility of the organisations that we work for. Having interests gives us a sense of mastery, there is nothing like the sense of acquiring a skill especially if we've had to work at it a bit. It feels good, it might even be a relief; indeed my internal environment might be very connected to my belief about how I should be able to develop a skill. We experience this as competence and ability and then the pleasure can be increased by sharing this competence with others, if our mode of being is social and relational.

Ineffective interest-sharing, or an absence of opportunities to interest-share, can very quickly lead to anxiety. One way to identify these would be to look for repetitions of requests from others (or by you to others). This may take the form of reframing or saying the same thing until the comment lands effectively with a suitably attuned fellow interest sharer or caregiver. Are there any of these repetitions around you, with your teams? Is there some potential interest that could be explored to increase the vitality (sense of self, of value) of a team member or colleague? Can you offer the time? It would need to be done genuinely though, we know when someone is faking an interest in us.

The Rowntree family famously used these ideas:

> Joseph [Rowntree] was an active philanthropist. He worked to improve adult literacy, and to safeguard democracy and political fair play. Acutely aware of the social conditions many of his factory workers lived in, he was keen to improve the quality of life for all through the provision of affordable, decent housing, recreational facilities and opportunities for self-improvement (See http://www.jrct.org.uk/history-and-heritage [accessed 04/12/2016])

Rowntree's work underpins our own understanding of the poverty trap:

> particular emphasis on the cycle of poverty . . . 'Each study showed the relative poverty of young single men, the way that it increased when children arrived, was relieved a little when the children left home, and returned with a vengeance in old age'. The work was hugely important in developing the concept of the poverty trap and the wishful thinking of those who argued that hard work and a little extra effort were the solutions (See https://www.theguardian.com/society/2010/apr/08/seebohm-rowntree-slides-york-university).

In addition to understanding how workers needed an all-round good environment to support their wellbeing, and people needed skills and work to help them keep out of the poverty trap, Rowntree also recognised how skills (interest-sharing) help support the wellbeing of employees and encourage the disaffected youth. Butler suggests for us here that if we agree interest-sharing is equivalent to skills, and we think it is, then perhaps interest sharing can be seen as secular fellowship. A very interesting idea indeed. And evident in the 1950s Rowntree work, as various volunteers undertook to offer skills such as carpentry techniques to young men, in particular, who had found themselves on the wrong side of the law (http://www.yorkpress.co.uk/features/features/10843968. Memories_of_Rowntrees/)

In helping young people develop their competency they offered them an opportunity to develop skills, interests, which might flow into a value system to live by. As well as having practical application, skills help us have self-respect, self-worth.

We may recognise when we are off work for even a very short amount of time we can start to become very anxious about our skills and our value to society. Without this value, fear creeps in, anxiety, stress and depression are not far away.

So, when Dame Carol Black concluded for the Government in 2008 (Black, 2008) that work is good for us, she was really on to something. Sharing interests with others also brings us into the community and relationship of others. For instance, a team in conflict will often cohere and rally to fight a common enemy. This may end their rifts forever with the new experience in common, or ancient tribal disgruntlements will resume after the battle has been won. Either way more is known and shared between them – relationally changed from whatever it was. If we can notice, prize and support "secular fellowship" perhaps we can have considerable benefit from the work.

Without competence and some sharing of those competences with others, fear creeps in again. It's really important to create a culture of work where individuals are noticed and validated for their particular competences, this simple act of validation would change the whole culture and work environment. Remember not being seen for the value we contribute to work [life] can induce anxiety. This anxiety (fear) affects us all; and it affects our health, our sleep, our relationships with each other as we saw in the previous chapter.

***

Another training peer of mine, Eliane Meyer, generously brought to my attention of the importance of interest sharing when retired from work. This was not something we raised in the pilot but absolutely worth the time and space here and I thank and credit her for the insight. If work has been a chief expression of our interests, skills and competence, and if it is through work we feel value, we feel good, then how dangerous can it be to go into retirement without having strategies and ways to further those interests or develop new ones? How many times might you have heard of a colleague or friend who may have gone into a decline after retirement? How might an elderly person's world become so reduced because the opportunities for healthy interest sharing just aren't available? We know this can lead to mental and physical decline. So perhaps interest sharing is a huge component for a life lived well at every single stage. Organisations that make provision for this exploration prior to retirement perhaps make a most valuable contribution to the employee's life after their interests have been used for the organisation's benefit. Might this also be something we can think of for mentoring in organisations, but in society too? We don't leave the need for interests and our desire to develop our skills when we stop work, so it is important that we attend to these needs in retirement. Can we carry on contributing and enjoying value for ourselves by continuing our interest and skills sharing in retirement? Isn't there also much that communities would get from this expertise? Butler again notices this could be especially relevant to government policy for the wellbeing of the over 70s, as this wellbeing even now is a very current and expanding issue of societal and financial national pressure.

To deepen their considerations of interest sharing at work I invited the group into two exercises in the session. The first exercise was pair-work to discuss the following questions: what interests them about their work? Is there is anyone in their work environment who is aware of their particular interests? Who makes you feel competent in that or those interests?

The other task was to consider the impact on oneself when the interest in the job is not validated. Do you have a work interest that you can't share with others? What is the impact?

To take away my group were offered a handout that included these questions for interest sharing alone and with peers.

Observe

- How do you feel when you share interests, is there an uplift in vitality?

Assess

- Has the interest been thwarted or supported?

Understand

- Without competence and some sharing of interests with others fear creeps in. Remember that fear affects us all, it affects our health our sleep our relationships with each other.

Review

- What has worked what hasn't worked – how is your competence and how is their competence?

We finished the session with surprises, learnings, satisfactions and dissatisfactions, and really felt we had only just begun to mine the depths of interests and interest sharing for the workplace.

Heads up for the next subject

Session 6 homework for Session 7: think about the impact of sex and sexuality with the workplace.

1 How might sex/sexuality affect you at work?
2 When is it helpful – how do you know?
3 When is it unhelpful – how do you know?
4 What might be the problems about not talking about it?
5 Is there a particular sex/sexuality culture in your team that you can describe?

Chapter 8

Sex and sexuality in the workplace

In this chapter I will cover the sixth session that introduced the system of sex and sexuality in the workplace. This is the third of the three instinctive biological (also motivational relational) systems added to Bowlby's two of careseeking and caregiving. We will look at the session structure, offer more detail on the genesis relevant to sex and sexuality in the workplace.

As you will see from the questions at the end of Chapter 7, I asked my group to consider their experience of their system for sex and sexuality in the workplace. This was a highly anticipated session for some of the group, some were excited, some were wary, and a little frightened. Very fitting, because this seemed, and perhaps is, the most overtly personal, in a private way, of all the systems. It was more important than ever I supported the group and encouraged them to centre and settle as well as possible. My job here was to really help the group explore this subject without fear of attack or shame. It helped that this was the sixth session; this positioning meant they had good time to build up knowledge of each other, safety in the group and experience of working together.

The theory

Sex and sexuality in the workplace

Like any of the systems, the sexual system emerges and becomes fully functional in its own time, as we are, in most cases, born explorers in the world and sex is part of this exploration. For some it also plays a creative and procreative role. In a positive way, it can be an expression of our self, very connected to careseeking and caregiving, and interest-sharing. In a negative way, it may be connected to self-defence and fear. If the latter, then an overactive system of self-defence expressed in this way, may lead to great vulnerability, ill health and for some danger, or predatory behaviour toward others. We consider defensive sexuality to be primarily a closed system where the person uses sexual arousal relief or release, to manage difficult interpersonal situations which they are experiencing now or have experienced in the past. The aim in the defensive case, which may be occluded from consciousness, is to avoid bringing all of oneself into relationship

with another person, and without taking full account of the need and vulnera-
bilities of the other person. The primary aim instead is the survival of the self
and regulation of one's emotional self. We are aware that for some people their
desire or intention may well be to move from a situation of a defensive expression
of their sexuality, to a more companionable form of relating. Some people will
sometimes use their sexuality defensively, although they may also be capable of
being in highly affectionate relationships. We are also aware some start from a
level of extreme violence, where a person's sexuality is used in an abusive way.
It's complex, a huge area in itself, and as authors we are aware it needs much
more exploration and development.

In brief then, if we find ourselves treating others as sexual objects, relating as
objects rather than as complex people, we are most likely going to negate all those
other systems and complexities, and easily become hurt, or hurt others emotionally, psychologically or physiologically. Sex in this objectified way can be an
intoxicating distraction, an obsession, even feel like a compulsion, but is most
likely to be a symptom of something else. It may be an expression of hurt or
anger. It might be a learnt response to sexual relationships. It might be a defence
against getting hurt. If we have felt powerless, been shamed, have an absence of
peers to share with, then sex might be a place to feel powerful again, to gain peers
even briefly, and to experience some form of vitality. However, the more inappropriate the sexual relations, the more isolating they may be. Specifically, transient
sexual relations maybe easy to gain but in this ease, we may miss the danger and
isolation they bring. This is not to say that as authors we believe only long term
monogamous relations are okay; the sexual world is vast, and rich and should be
diverse, so long as we understand what we are doing and have good sight of the
risks we might be taking.

Notions of love and attractiveness sometimes cause us to become confused or
ashamed of our feelings and connections with others. However, if we deny our
sexuality or our impact sexually on each other, we may become confused or we
may become frightened by some of the responses we receive. Drury has suggested
here that our confusion could either be because we hadn't expected the responses
either in ourselves or the other, or we become confused because we don't understand them – or both. We become fearful of the power of our feelings or the feelings of the other.

The sexual system is described as goal corrected and having three functions
"affectional sexuality that has an interpersonal goal, the defensive form of sexuality that has an intrapersonal goal, and the third function, which is the reproductive
function of sexuality" (Heard, Lake and McCluskey, 2012. p. 95).

The sexual system activates other systems including caregiving, careseeking,
interest-sharing, and the external and internal environments.

As the group considered this subject I was aware they were keen to be sensitive
to the way sexuality was expressed in the workplace, especially about colleagues
being in relationships with other colleagues. And whilst tentative my group also
expressed a relief this aspect of life could be explored on this pilot at work as a

part of our life and a part of our life at work. Further thought could also be given to those not in any relationships at all. We recognise the attitudes to sexual relationships has evolved, but could it now be the case though that the last prejudice might be held against people who have never been in a sexual relationship, who are single by choice or circumstance. Although not raised as a part of this pilot, the absence of this discussion itself perhaps raises interesting questions about what we might assume to be the case for the relationship status of our colleagues, and what that means for us in teams.

We can keep in mind this pilot took place in an organisation that held values of diversity and equality. The group's sensitivity to consider negative and positive connotations of sexuality could have been very different if we had been different, or if we had been in a different organisation, or even if there had been less shared values amongst the group.

Dominant/submissive

When thinking about the sexual system, ideas of dominant or submissive behaviours take on a whole new quality and can work well or badly in either way depending upon the consent of the parties. We might find we are coming in to contact with, or working with, past sexual experiences of all kinds, including trauma for ourselves or for others if we inadvertently trigger any past look-alikes in how we relate or connect with each other at work. Transference and counter-transference (see Chapters Two and Three) can be very powerful in these encounters though not maybe apparent to those involved.

Historians, scholars of literature and art, and sociologists will have plenty to add in to our thinking about what happened in the seventeenth, eighteenth and nineteenth centuries in the UK, often typified by Queen Victoria and Victorian values. Was it connected to the growth of the Commonwealth; a response to our experiences of meeting other cultures (often then described as bestial or tribal) as we explored, engaged with, or debased and conquered others? We encountered other cultural ideas that celebrated or abhorred the body, rejoiced in or suppressed any notions of biology; accepting and inviting new ideas had to have an impact on thinking about sexuality. Was it the growth and dominance of Christian values? Who knows? It will have been a combination of these and other factors, but it seems to have left us with a shame-based notion of sex, where some expressions of sexual encounters became off limits, risky, for behind closed doors. This stigmatisation suppresses the very natural, out into obscure references – underground – not to be spoken about: a very held and contained zeitgeist. We aren't quite out of the zeitgeist yet, although there have always been visible differences in the arts that typify a more open stance towards sex. We might know we are sexual, but we are still a little frightened to talk about it.

My colleague, Drury, asked me here, how do you match our not wanting to talk about it with the proliferation of sexual material in the media and social media? For instance, there was widespread talk about *Fifty Shades of Grey* and the fact that women specifically were reading it openly. How does this fit with the ideas we are exploring here? Do we mean we still don't want to talk about it at work? On three separate occasions Drury had experienced group discussion at work on issues on transgender and non-binary identification – is this unusual? Just where are we in this zeitgeist? Is there something to be said for the idea that this apparent openness in media, and in discussions puts a mask over the fact that we still find it a hard subject to talk about in context where we are not sure that everyone shares our opinions and values, real, human interaction and relationships? Or is it that our reluctance to be open has just moved along the spectrum of discussions? And is it okay that the discussions were about openly predatory aggressive sexual behaviour? Are these conversations happening in every culture, every religious group, does every young person get a chance to explore this without vilification?

And yet sexual relationships are not only helpful for procreation, they are biological and physiological, pleasurable ways of being relational human beings and being met by each other. The importance of sex and sexual identity evolves as we develop as people, and without doubt certainly belongs in the model. It was this system, amongst the systems for the internal and external environments, which especially attracted me to the model in the first place, and inclined me to wish to use it for the workplace. How many relationships form at work, through work or run along in tandem whilst we work? How many successes and failures in relationships or healthy singledoms happen whilst we work? Now perhaps we are finally able to really start thinking about sexual biology, gender definitions, non-binary genders, pansexuality, trans, or genetic fluidity. It's an exciting time for us to change the zeitgeist and open ourselves to exploring a whole new paradigm. Of course, the workplace is going to be a huge arena to explore the emergence of sexuality, because whether or not our work is of interest to us, we are very likely to find people, at work, who are of interest to us. You might like to refer back to Figure 3.3 here.

Influences

By looking at the wheel again we can see some of the influences upon how we might develop healthy affectionate exploratory sexual relationships and experiences.

As with all the systems, sexuality is primarily informed by the cultures and practises of our immediate family and peers and by our local society and culture, our role models. It is informed by the media, by the creation of idolatry and artificial (photoshopped images of the human body, for instance) sexual standards. It is based in (or limited by) the language we are allowed to use within the confines of these religious, cultural and familial and social structures. It is now influenced by social media and teenage culture. Of all the systems, this is perhaps the most underrated, under explored aspect of ourselves especially at work. In this current climate when hundreds, thousands of people, of all gender forms, are coming forward paying brave testament to sexual exploitation, it remains crucial that we learn to look at and talk about this in society. This current climate includes a huge increase in social media use, unfortunately aside from the positive connectivity, adults, teenagers and children are also using this medium to abuse, shame and control each other. This has led to the rise in access to pornography for children and young teenagers. This evolution in technology, widespread access, has influenced and affected the culture and cultural expression of sexual expression in the workplace. This area has many layers of depth that go across all of generations. A TUC survey of 1,500 women in 2016 (TUC, 2016) found that over 51% of women surveyed said they had been sexually harassed at work, and whilst the survey reports most of the perpetrators are male we know this happens to men as well. The full scale of the problem remains unknown, this survey focussed upon women – consequently we perpetuate the paradox and limits to what we are willing to know. The scale of this awful revelation is only beginning to come to light as evidenced in campaigns such as "Me Too", covering all workplaces and all forms of abuse.

We need to manage the fear or shame to speak out, we need to understand what prompts perpetrators to act in aggressive and violent ways, and we have to enable those who have been abused to come forward and bring an end to these cycles of oppression. Clearly there are a lot more issues with sex and sexuality at work at an organisational level which we may still feel ill-equipped to deal with. Learning the skills to manage the volume of revelations that are emerging is going to take some psychosocial and emotional care, as well as considerable sophistication. We need to get some balance between natural justice for the people who have experienced the abuse at work and those who are charged with this abuse. Add into this all the perils that are arising through internet access, internet stalking, entrapping for children as well as adults, this is a vast and important area to be considered. At a basic economic level, there has to be an effect on productivity – how does one keep focussed on ones work when one might be subject to sexual debasement of any kind? Or when one might find oneself accused unjustifiably.

Development

Different theories draw different conclusions on when sexual maturity actually happens in relation to one's chronological maturity. It may be reasonable to say that sexual maturity is reached in our twenties but that all depends on the caregiving, careseeking, management of fear and attachment experiences in the years before. You might even say sexual maturity changes again much later on in life post-40s. By sexual maturity we mean we have the ability to understand ourselves sexually, what we like, what we can do and what we can ask of others. It is real careseeking and caregiving and interest-sharing in a sexual sphere. Fear may play a part of the sexual frisson, excitement, and this fear ideally should be managed and assuaged in ways that are shared and safe enough.

The Baobab Centre in York runs a parenting course. Part of this course explores the different stages of sexual development. Table 8.1 is a part of a grid they provide,

Table 8.1 Stages of sexual development

	Stage 1	Stage 2	Stage 3	Stage 4	Stage 5
Sigmund Freud (Psychiatrist) 1856–1939 Psychosexual development	Birth – 18 months **Oral stage** Fixated on mouth for food and pleasure	18 months – 3 years **Anal stage** Focus on retaining or eliminating faeces	3–6 years **Phallic stage** Focus on unconscious sexual desire. Oedipus/ Electra complexes (castration anxiety and penis envy)	6–12 years **Latency stage** Focus on school and friends	12 years onwards **Genital stage** Focus on sexual needs and forming sexual relationships
Arlene Harder (Child psychologist) Psychological development				13–19 years Learning about identity, sexuality and separating	19-death Learning to integrate the rest of life's lessons

Source: © The Baobab Centre, 2008

it offers an excellent overview to thinking about how this side of ourselves develops and matures.

The pre-work for this session was for my group to think about what sex and sexuality has to do with their workplace:

What do you know about sex and sexuality at work?

The challenges of talking about our sexual system are highlighted here, without a given cause; we perhaps don't feel it is acceptable to consider this as a part of our work world.

> Consideration of sexuality in the workplace was difficult, especially relating it to my current job. However, I had previously worked in sexual health, and the culture of that organisation and the people who worked there was much more open (sometimes this was useful, sometimes not), so reflecting on this aided my understanding. Your personal attitude to sex and your sexuality/personal identity helps to define who you are and who you think you are. So the natural instincts, thoughts and feelings linked to this play a role for you (and others) in the workplace and it is important to understand this.
>
> Group participant 3

The group were able to identify that notions of sex and sexuality had changed in the last 20–40 years. Lewd and provocative images were, in the main, a thing from the past and no longer seen as acceptable ways to decorate workplaces. They noticed that when people work and collaborate closely, sometimes in challenging work situations, strong bonds can grow. Those bonds can be, or can seem to be, sexual with a high level of interest-sharing, as well as being biologically highly chemical. However, given a still predominantly reserved cultural back drop, talking about these bonds remains difficult and awkward. Further evidence perhaps of how much work there might be to do around the issue of sex.

Our discussion covered how it is possible to see how any of us might become confused about what might count as a joke or light hearted double entendres, or abusive or offensive behaviours. Cultural diversity broadens our understanding of different ways to live, and may also call into question ways of being which one may have accepted as okay and another as not okay in a different cultural light. There is such a debate, for instance, around the hijab; these are very important discussions for us to engage with and without arousing fear. These types of discussions should be especially pertinent in a diverse workplace.

The group observed how some of them, or colleagues with whom they worked, had been in, or were in sexual relationships with others in their workplaces. The workplace is one of the key areas where we meet partners and lovers as we spend a lot of time there. A further layer of complication identified was the issue of having managers and leaders in relationships, having relationships that cross organisational hierarchies; or across partner organisations, they noticed how this could engender a culture of fear around the couple. What would their pillow talk cover, what could be said safely to one without the partner finding out? Thinking about an educational setting meant there was great discussion over how staff/student relationships were approached, and how staff had to recognise the vulnerability of students and also respond appropriately to these students as adults.

Is it unusual that a charismatic, well versed lecturer has sexual appeal to their students (or vice versa)? How do we help both sides manage these interactions without falling into unhealthy dominant/submissive pairings? Organisations might have a policy on close personal relationships with students based around an approach of transparency and ensuring the member of staff is removed from any supervisory, for example, PhD role for that student. This recognises the difficulty in telling a student, who is a grown adult, who they are allowed to form relationships with. It might be easier to say a *carte blanche* no, but this would not reflect the reality of the social and human situation. It is of course important to say that this does not mean this can't happen in many forms of organisation. Bonds and relationships will form in a multitude of ways, and may be completely easy to navigate, or may form and become incredibly hard to navigate. In some cases, the requirement to declare sexual relationships does make it easier for colleagues to manage. There may also be issues of safety with emergency services for instance too. Would you wish mother and daughter, brother and father to be on the same dangerous shift if it could be avoided? The same concern might apply to lovers and partners too. But also for congruence sake, it means we have transparency about who we are talking to when we might need to. If I am letting off steam to my director's lover, I think I would like to know that before I begin my tirade!

Furthermore, different members of the organisation may have very different beliefs about their sexual boundaries; these boundaries might be family, age or culturally-based, and navigating across these differences is no straightforward matter. Sometimes we might be tempted to avoid it altogether, but that really doesn't make the situation any easier to manage. This takes us right back to the paradox of the overt/covert sociological traits written most particularly about in the Victorian epoch.

And what about rules around what one gender might find is acceptable to say to each other, or assume so, and what might not be acceptable across different genders and sexual forms? How do we manage our clothing, our smells, our attractions or repulsions with each other if we can't talk about them?

The group had an open discussion about gender, about how gender-neutral toilets were perhaps some of the first, and very welcome, visual indications that the work environment was beginning to reflect a non-binary way of seeing ourselves as sexual beings.

My group discovered in this discussion just how unsexy it was to talk about sex, and how vast a subject it is.

It is one of the considerable values of the model, as it invites us to consider these matters in a supportive and collaborative way. We are all in a real world full of these sexual ambiguities, considerations and moral dilemmas, so we can get at least more skillful in having the conversations.

Even as I write this now I can feel a hesitation, I am aware of several concerns: I might offend one of you as readers, I might have misrepresented the excellent and brave discussions within my group, or someone will infer some lewd or unprofessional aspect for the organisation just because we talked about it reasonably and openly.

Clearly there is some work to do here, perhaps for me as much as anyone else, to help the participants reflect and note their competence in taking this subject on; heralding their bravery felt very important at the end of session.

In a note to myself I wondered afterwards if I could have pushed the subject further with them, but upon reflection just bringing it in was an excellent first step; to openly recognise the relevance of talking about this in work time. Drawing only on policies around inappropriate behaviour and sexual misconduct as guidelines fails to deal with the complexities and nuances of sexuality. It's a very black and white approach. Policies help but we need the skills to be able to talk about sex and sexuality in a more nuanced way.

To conclude I offered them a handout with a few questions and ideas to take away.

Observe

- How do you feel when your sexual self is nourished?
- How do you feel when your sexual self is not nourished or feels under threat?
- Are there colleagues who might be struggling with their intimate relations?

Assess

- How you might take care of yourself? What might colleagues need?

Understand

- Without some sense of positive body image, or affectionate sexual possibilities, a defensive sense of self and therefore fear can creep in. Remember fear affects us all, it affects our health our sleep our personal and professional relationships with each other.

Review

- What has worked what hasn't worked? How is your competence and how is their competence now?

Heads up for the next session

Session 6 homework for Session 7: think about what your internal environment is like. The internal environment is not goal corrected (like most of the others); it's fluid and ever-changing. It is the furniture on the inside.

1   Is your internal environment supportive (compassionate) or unsupportive (overly critical)? Or something in between? Can you identify some things you ought or should do?
2   How has your past contributed to your internal environment (or internal working model IWM)?
3   What is your internal environment like at work?
4   Is your internal environment different outside of work?
5   Can you identify any statements and rules that you or your team might try to live/work by?
6   How do you know your internal environment is troubled or agitated?

Chapter 9

The internal environment

In this chapter I will cover the seventh session that introduced the idea of the "internal environment" for consideration in the workplace. As said earlier, the model contains seven systems, five of which are interpersonal. Two of these systems (the personally created internal and external environments) differed in the following ways; both are designed to enable a person to function with as much wellbeing as possible without access to a caregiver, another person who can support their wellbeing, but only one is goal-corrected. The system for the internal environment, however, is not goal corrected because as we will see it is under constant construction.

The session had the now normal structure: welcome, centre, theory and discussion.

Welcome

I welcomed the group to a different room, as we had now experienced the familiarity of one room a few times. Perhaps this movement between the familiar and new is a bit like our internal environment? Aspects of our inner world that are familiar; we sit in the same place, having the same perspective, expecting and having a familiar view on ourselves and the world. Or we might sit metaphorically in a different place in the same general area, experiencing and exploring a slightly altered view on ourselves and the world. Or, as life happens, find ourselves in altogether new territory, discovering it may confirm what we have deduced so far about ourselves and the world or discovering instead, it contradicts or transforms us in some way.

To centre everyone I concentrated on guiding them to get present in the session, actively noticing they are in their seats, in a metaphysical as well as physical way. This concentration on arrival, being present, recognises the transition from whatever previous activity they may have been engaged in, acknowledges the movement into a different space; it highlights the opportunity they had accessed to be in this session for two hours. I encourage them to notice posture, breath, tension, eyes open – to be attentive. To continue starting with this arrival ritual, to find any tension in their minds or bodies, it helps them really get into the habit of asking themselves if this was information they needed to notice or to do something about? We then adjust our bodies, and are really ready to start.

I wonder as I write this, how, for you the reader, this is probably even more important than it was for my group, if you are reading more than one chapter in a sitting. Are you taking a break? Are you checking your body posture? Are you observing any inner content – even chunter against anything you may have read so far? It all counts, it all matters, it's all information, and if we don't pay some notice, we might find we aren't really paying attention to what is in front of us, and, well the body has to bear the brunt – so if you haven't shifted position for a while – maybe this is a good time to do just that.

The theory

The system for the internal environment is different to the other systems in that it is not goal corrected – it influences the other systems as they all do. It is one of two systems "whose function is to support the self when no caregiver is available" (the personally created external is the other) (Heard, Lake and McCluskey, 2012, p. 5). The internal and external systems either support the systems for caregiving, careseeking, self-defence, interest sharing, sexuality, or, impair them.

There is philosophically a much longer legacy to a theory of an inner self originating in the works of Socrates, Plato, and Kant. Various ontologies are available for study; many religious ideas of self or consciousness, conscience, and psychological theories (i.e., from Freud, Jung, Maslow, Rogers), of meta-awareness. These all flow around the notion, idea, of an internal construction of the self that can know something of itself. Inherently problematic because we have as yet not been able to see the "self" in a microscope, grow a bit of one in a culture dish, we haven't managed to photograph it, listen to it, watch its energy outside of our own private inner experience of it. The best I can do is use my words to convey mine to you. However, some (not all) believe there is something going on in our bodies that might be described as "me". It might emerge in our relations with others. It becomes consistent or coherent as a process over time so in spite of the ways we change, we can still recognise ourselves (Emde, 1983).

The internal environment is as biologically physiological as any of the other systems – it may evoke stronger notions of the bio-physiological "milieu intérieur" as Bernard described or it may be more noticeable as a sense of self (Stern, 1985; 2002).

Bowlby referred to it as the "working models of oneself relating by interacting with specific parts of one's world (the people, the animals, the terrain, and its climate conditions) in which one lives and interacts" (Heard, Lake and McCluskey, 2012, p. 112). Bowlby used, and we will also use, the expression "internal working model" (IWM). For our purpose here the expression "IWM" and the internal environment are referring to more or less the same thing; an entity, or phenomenon, with the important addition of our phenomenological encounter and experience of such internal model. Heard and Lake, however were more precise in this understanding of the internal environment and coined the term "internal model of the experience of relationships".

Most interestingly he regarded the function of the IWM to help us make plans for any project we wanted to undertake and rehearse them in our heads. So, Bowlby's assertion was that the IWM is primarily about planning and prediction, and making use of past experience.

Heard, Lake and McCluskey observed and concluded that our internal environment is:

1   Important as a psychological model to have knowledge that one is competent or incompetent in specific situations; and
2   Whether we have enough persistence (motivation) to carry out a plan (Heard, Lake and McCluskey, 2012, pp. 112–114).

The internal environment (or IWM) is a combination of our experiences of the past, the present and a developed skill of anticipating (imagining) a future. Therefore, my internal environment is constantly analysing and phenomenologically synthesising whatever I have experienced before (consciously or unconsciously) with whatever is going on now. I also euphemistically call it my back brain (holistic mind/body) absorbing and processing data and stimulus to help me navigate in the present, decode my world, make choices, understand and know what I need to know at any one given time. It is never "off", it is a marvel, a source of survival, creativity, wonder, confusion, review and planning as Bowlby has said. Heard contributed the idea that we internalise as fact, the characteristics that become attributed to us both negative and positive over a lifetime and that these are highly if unconsciously influential in defining our identity. In making any decision we utilise this system, and without driving ourselves mad with introspection, probably have little awareness of all that is going on.

Imagining different kinds of futures is surely one of the core competencies of any leader or manager. Having enough inner security to hold various concepts in mind of self, self-to-colleagues, self-to-organisation in order to construct and engage in operationalising and planning takes a lot of the self and mind. This cannot be under estimated in terms of significance for leadership. Planning and conceptualising is hard to do – a skill to develop, especially with so many different considerations that may need to be held or conceptualised at the same time. Not only does this have to be done, as we can't plan, budget, set staffing levels, choose between competing agencies for funding, without some ideas about what we are planning for, but we must also have some way of knowing how our own experiences might be clarifying or clouding the futures we are imagining.

Another key aspect of our internal environment is a biological/neurological/phenomenological system that encapsulates memories and beliefs about our relationships with key attachment figures, our peers and children. These are aspects that develop from about the age of four. Significant moments, either very good or very bad, may have greater influence on how our internal environment works.

These may be very well-known or may have slipped into a more unconscious or bodily remembered "somatic markers" as Damasio (2006) might call them.

Therefore, the internal environment is under constant construction as it incorporates the here and now, aspects of it may become neurologically habituated. I can't always be cognitively aware of my internal environment.

Discussion

I recapped with the group that I had asked them to reflect upon their system of an internal environment following the last session. I had asked them to observe (as you will see in the grid) whether they could notice if their internal environment was supportive (compassionate) or unsupportive (overly critical) as they took up their roles in the workplace.

It seemed important to me that I supported my group to explore this topic with a keen focus on the workplace. This was one which could easily reach into their very personal selves, and whilst as a therapist I absolutely recognise the value of those explorations, I had a duty to keep this group focused, and not let the subject matter take them into a therapeutic group style of working, which they had not signed up for; but to keep them supportive, collaborative and work orientated. A McCluskey technique to keep people focused on the task in hand and not wander off into unchartered territory without some planning for it.

Again, I used an exercise to get them talking to each other. They had (and still have) developed such a genuine supportive learning environment that I wished to support and nourish these experiences by offering them frequent opportunities to talk to one another.

In pairs I asked them to consider why knowing about their internal environment might matter at work? And also, to think about how they might describe the internal environment of the organisation?

Through the discussions of this system my participants really started to grapple openly with notions of self-compassion and self-critical talk. I invited them to think of the manner of their internal ways of thinking about and talking to themselves. I referenced the ideas from Carl Rogers, of conditions of worth (Rogers, 1959). Conditions of worth can be found by reflecting upon internal "I should . . ." or "I ought to . . ." statements. Conditions of worth are formed in our early years as we take cues from our guardians about which behaviours we are rewarded or chastised for. In reflecting upon these notions, the group was able to bring into conscious awareness rules they may have swallowed or absorbed as children, but may not actually be sustainable as adult professionals. This helped them recognise aspects of their ways of being that contributed or hindered to what we might describe as work/life balance. If we can get hold of internal self-to-self-talk that attacks or criticises, and drives us from a habit, rather than supporting balance and kindness and healthy growth, we can do something about it. Left unconscious they might stalk our lives endlessly tugging away at any success or self-care.

The group wondered about notions of motivation here, in themselves, and it helped them reflect on the idea and implications of the internal environments of the people they work with. These hidden entities moving like "constellations of potential" as Kurt Lewin (1952), rather beautifully described them.

> The internal environment was, like the self-defence/fear system, something I had learnt about in CBT, and was something historically that had been very negative and damaging to me. I had a clear (but unrealistic) picture of who or what I was, especially in a work context, and when that picture wasn't fulfilled I was often very harsh on myself, and struggled to come out of a self-deprecating or negative spirals. Being more aware of this pattern has helped me be kinder to myself, and more realistic in who, or what, I am.
>
> Group participant 3

Some of their reflections included noticing how their families and upbringing had a real influence on these inner statements of self and how perhaps they had stopped observing how critical this internalised content could be. They also really noticed how very biological the impacts of these experiences are. They observed effects in their stomachs, their heads, shoulders and its impact upon sleep. I wonder now in summarising this, that with the exception of self-defence (which includes careseeking and fear system) this system, despite it's more ethereal qualities, might in fact be one, that is experienced most fully at a biological level.Perhaps it might be easier to recognise the arousal of this system? This reminds me of Bernard's idea of "milieu intérieur" and amplifies the powerful and physiological phenomenon of these systems? We can also see how maintaining our wellbeing through the systems can assist and strengthen our overall resilience. This might be the resilience to manage ourselves, our interactions with others, to enable our skills and competencies to develop and stabilise.

It was in this session that the group considered self-esteem. They explored the standards by which they judge themselves and others. They acknowledged how much their internal capacity for tolerance and empathy of others is massively impacted by the changing nature of their own internal environment. This capacity, they observed, could be affected by having a more benign attitude to the nature of what was going on inside themselves which was driven quite extensively by what had happened in previous work settings and formative past experiences and situations.

The workplace implicitly relies upon every person's internal environment being robust enough to manage their tasks, manage themselves, and be present and productive in the ways they are required to be. Sometimes this gets translated to feeling that we must all be busy and productive, and relate in mature and supportive ways with others all the time. But is that possible? And if it was possible would that even be desirable? If our internal environment is ever changing, processing aspects of our past, aspects of the present and conjuring those into some form that might help manage the future, perhaps more time reflecting on this content and less time dismissing it might make for a more stable settled self that could leave us free enough to attend to whatever might be in front of us? The capacity to bring something to fruition requires a secure sense of self, if we are overly critical we have to ameliorate the effects of the self-critical attack, in order to achieve or complete the plan. Or we have to work hard to quieten the inner attack enough to be a little present, and watchful that this inner struggle doesn't seep into the professional encounters we are having. A secure sense of self, a managed and reflective approach leaves more energy and attention available for the job in hand.

The group were also able to identify how this content of theirs, left unattended, unsupported, can easily take us in to the territory of unmanaged fear. And we now know unmanaged or unacknowledged fear is not the best emotional or physiological set up for work.

Perhaps this is why we must think about how competencies are brought into the workplace, how we review performance, how we enable staff to match themselves to their work, and to the development of themselves as people. Making room for the impact this has on a person's competence and sense of self-worth has huge implications for performance assessment in any work context.

I left them with questions to take away to use perhaps whenever they might note their internal environment was becoming overly critical.

Observe

- Is an aspect of your internal environment at play? How do you know – are there memories or associations of a previous experience?

Assess

- Is this previous information relevant and helpful now?
- What would it mean to follow it?
- What would it take to not heed it?

Understand

- Do you know why these feelings, thoughts, bodily sensations are evoked now?

Review

- What will help you?
- How can you compassionately review your experience here?

These questions are a structure for reflective practice, to help participants embed these as practises going forward if they chose to.

Heads up for the next session

Session 7 homework for Session 8: think about what your external environment is like.

1   What is your external environment like at work?
2   Is your external environment different outside of work?
3   How has your past contributed to how you construct or have expectations of your external environment?
4   Is your external environment supportive or unsupportive? Or something in between?
5   How do you know your external environment is agitating you?

Chapter 10

The external environment

In this chapter I will cover the eighth session that introduced the idea of the personally created External Environment for consideration in the workplace. This is the second of the supportive unsupportive systems that enable us to manage when no other caregiver is available. This system is goal corrected, but the goals are intrapersonal not interpersonal.

As with the last session, I had chosen a different location for this one. A room in one of the oldest buildings on campus, a building I imagine had previously been a home before the organisation had encompassed it in its growth across the years.

This room was airy and bright, it had more windows than any of the other rooms so far. It was a bright and sunny day, and this resonated with the group. I invited them to notice what this new room might mean for them – did it change their "affect" in any way – did it generate or promote any different needs in them. Did it affect their wellbeing? I wondered what they might notice.

I don't know whether it was the time of the year, the quality of the sunlight or a co-created humorous bonhomie, but there was an especially light and warm atmosphere within the group. We were on the last of the systems. They had been learning and growing together, and they had been applying the ideas and had formed a supportive learning association with each other. It felt lovely.

As always, we began with the invitation to centre and to consider this room and building as another different space. In centering, we focused on really settling on our seats, noticing how (and if) we were using our sitting bones to sit and support our bodies. Noticing any slumping forwards or backwards and finding a good posture to sit with. As before, I invited them to keep their eyes open, be attentive. Their task in this moment was just to find any tension and see if they could let it go. I reminded them, as the model supports, that if they find any tension in their bodies, this tension is information. They can decide if this is information they need to do something about. Their options might include adjusting their posture, a need to set aside a thought, take a few well-placed and deliberate breaths to really arrive. After this is done and when they were ready, I invited them to check in. To do this they can establish eye contact with each other, which is even more important when we hadn't all been together for a little while. It had been three weeks; a longer interval than on some of the other occasions.

The plan for this session followed on from the plans for the previous sessions with: overtime reflections, theory and a discussion about the implications of the theory for their context.

Overtime reflections

I reflected on how we'd been looking at various systems. I asked them if they had any narrative about this work, at that moment. What did they remember about what we've looked at so far? Were any clarifications needed? Progressing, I invited them to engage with any curiosity about their thoughts, emotions and ideas around this subject. I recapped that I had asked them to reflect on the kind of external environment that they had created for themselves in the workplace that they had found supportive?

To bring this system to life I had decided to prepare a very short PowerPoint which showed a variety of different workplaces from the internet. These images were offered to stimulate their thoughts and feelings about what an external environment, especially an external work environment, could be like.

The images were readily available on the internet, but not reproducible here in the book. To draw a few pictures for you now, they were shots of some of the modern offices of Yahoo, Coca-Cola London, Moshi Monsters, Canon and Co-op. These workplaces are vibrant, often shabby chic, bright, airy, with bold colours juxtaposed against striking design. In some, those you might imagine, there are strong actual and subliminal references to branding, words or colours. In fact, there was a very interesting use of brand colours. Some of the work spaces have big bold table tops, occupy large warehouse like airy spaces, and have snugs in different colours for more intimate meetings. One office even has a slide in it. The canteen areas wouldn't be out of place in New York, the art strong, distinctive. Each place looked creative, vibrant, if you like that kind of thing. The slideshow also included an image of a garden pod. These are either egg shaped or cubic glass structured designs to house seating or desks that are located outside in garden spaces as the name suggests. Also, a photo of the Pons and Huot office, housed in what used to be an industrial space, with ceilings that are high enough to accommodate the Ficus-Panda tree. Work spaces have glass or perspex coverings over them. This company have reversed the idea and brought the trees indoors rather than taking the office into the garden. If the images are still there you might find them online (see http://www.deeproot.com/blog/blog-entries/so-a-tree-walks-in-to-an-office). I also showed an image for White Mountain Office – Stockholm, Sweden, another amazing workspace of "A high-security data center run by one of Sweden's largest ISPs, located in an old nuclear bunker deep below the bedrock of Stockholm city, sealed off from the world by entrance doors 40 cm thick", well worth a look (see http://royal.pingdom.com/2008/11/14/the-worlds-most-super-designed-data-center-fit-for-a-james-bond-villain/).

I also included images of their organisation, its new library and an aerial shot from some years ago. Juxtaposed against these new world work environments were images of vast floors of less than modern call centres, rabbit hutches for humans crammed together, separated only by coloured baffles; an office with a desk with piles of paper toppling over; a car with files, food wrappers and rubbish strewn all over, and a view across a great valley stretching off into the distance. The images weren't me necessarily saying one is better than another – it was to contextualise the question which environment or what aspects of an external environment might resonate with them, and why? Which environment might support the work that needs to happen? And whether firms allow employees to fiddle with their given environment to fit their needs?

More and more people are now working from home. But working from home isn't particularly easy (or necessarily good for you) if you have to share your office space with the rest of the family. Which is why garden pods are becoming more popular. If you work from home do you think about the nature of the environment you are in? Do you notice what supports you? How much influence do you have on the work environment you might go to?

This was a good way to get the discussions going.

The theory

The external environment has an intrapersonal goal rather than one that is interpersonal, and it also influences how one experiences the other systems. It is one of the two systems "whose function is to support the self when no caregiver is available" (internal is the other) (Heard, Lake and McCluskey, 2012, p. 5). The internal and external systems either support caregiving, careseeking, self-defence (including fear), interest sharing, and sexuality, or impair them.

There is lots of talk about our external environment in terms of healthy workplaces, or say, Feng Shui, but what is our external environment really about? The McCluskey model indicates the:

> External environment is the home we have created for ourselves to live in, it may be a small as a one room, but it is created and fashioned in a way that is designed to provide support for the self as a whole or for a particularly specially valued part of the self. The external environment we create may serve to defend the self against the awareness of painful experiences, or may promote our wellbeing and creative potential.
>
> (McCluskey, 2010)

Earlier in the research:

> The concept of an external supportive/unsupportive system was introduced by Heard and Lake (1997) as a lifestyle, which everyone is always constructing, of an environment within which a particular person feels she or he can

live with comfort and safety. The function of the system is to maintain a life-style which constantly reminds one of the situations in which: (1) the goals of the five systems of the dynamics of attachment and interest sharing have been met to the highest degree so far experienced; (2) the natural phenom-enon and human artifacts, which currently produce a sense of wonder, awe, or delight, can be experienced; and (3) for some, religious experiences are available. The lifestyle is reached by one's own efforts and therefore has an intrapersonal goal rather than one that is interpersonal.

The system for the external environment covers different aspects of the way a person organises their life, it will therefore include

> . . . (1) the resources to engage activities they find congenial in regards to work, recreation, and life at home: (2) the personal routines, pace of life, and the organisation of belongings that are most enjoyed: (3) the kind of terrain and architecture of houses that one likes to live in; (4) the degree of light, colour, warmth, food, and physical comfort one enjoys; and most impor-tantly, (5) the interactions with peer companions, caregivers, and careseekers which are predominantly enjoyable and conflict free.
>
> (Heard, Lake, and McCluskey 2012, pp. 116–117)

How does this description of a personally created external environment relate to the workplace? If in order to function well we need to feel secure; the context around us needs to resonate with us, not cause constant disturbance. In order to be creative, our places of working and thinking need to be inspiring. For some this might mean lots of life relics around us, for others very little. This isn't to say some disturbance isn't helpful, I learn about other ways of living by changing my environment, exposing myself to different cultures, trying alternative ways to work, live and be. By explor-ing these I might find something that supports my wellbeing that I wouldn't have otherwise considered. However, a disruption to the norm can be difficult. For some it can be especially difficult. Disruption or disturbance in the external environment can impact negatively on our systems for caregiving, careseeking, interest sharing, systems for sex and internal environment and of course our system for self-defence. Thinking about our external environment can lead to us thinking about "belonging or not . . . of unease and isolation, of not being able to settle in any one particular place or country, and the accompanying expenditure of energy in trying to find the right place and the place one can feel at home" (Heard, Lake and McCluskey, 2012).

> The external environment – this has always been very supportive away from work, and is also very supportive within work, and this has been a great asset. The course helped me appreciate that.
>
> Group participant 3

If one feels one has difficulty belonging to a place, a town, or a city, because of being of a different culture, one can bring those anxieties to the workplace, which might emerge as one's responses to being given a designated space. For others – not having a designated space will not carry the same charge. Similarly, the fear of redundancy, of being pushed out, of not having a space, could resonate with early childhood experience, and may cause some considerable disturbance. We move between these two worlds of our intra and interpersonal selves all the time.

One of the group participants also reflected whether we could think about this system further and really consider and plan what we do to support and help manage people's stress around migration. Could this guide us on how we treat non-indigenous colleagues in any organisation, non-indigenous students? I wonder if there is a chance that we make assumptions that they are doing okay, often based around sharing a language or language skills, and missing the possibility that the loss of their own external environment as well as the new external environment might be causing stress. To count this in as factor to help people transpose themselves, even briefly into a different environment. Less stress in this system more energy for the others.

Belonging is such an interesting idea; what makes us feel we belong in a place, what is it out there that we attune to inside? Do you echo these in your office, do you take the same route, and have rituals, objects in certain places? If we know some of this – can we tell how it plays out in how we construct our external environment? How does that work when we are sharing our living or working spaces? Are we supporting our wellbeing at work through our external environment or is it unsupportive of our wellbeing at work? This system had particular resonance for one of participants, and she is kind enough to offer her thoughts here on the theory and a case study for your benefit.

External environment

Concept

> The external environment is also not goal corrected – it influences the other systems. It is one of the two systems whose function is to support the self when no caregiver is available (internal is the other)
>
> (Heard, Lake and McCluskey, 2012, p. 5).

The internal and external systems either support care giving, care seeking, self-defence, interest-sharing, sex or impair them.

We know that in order to be the best version of ourselves and to function effectively our external environment needs to enable this. Where and how we find ourselves has a direct influence on our ability to function. Every moment of our lives we are surrounded by some kind of external environment or another, be that our home environment, our work environment or any other place we find ourselves. How we behave in each of these will be determined by any previous experiences, and in fact the environments we chose to inhabit may well be an intentional choice in order to protect ourselves.

So what does this mean for us in the context of the workplace and today's way of working?

> The very nature of work is changing . . . The physical workplace is one of many factors in modern management and work that needs to adapt, with business leaders needing to continually innovate and challenge conventional wisdom about what drives performance and engagement
>
> (Peter Cheese, chief executive, CIPD).

We know of the importance and impact of environment. We also know that often too little time is spent considering how best to set up the workplace to ensure it is fit for the purpose of the work being carried out there, and the individuals doing the work. Open plan remains hugely popular due to the thinking that it facilitates better communication and removes some of the perceived or real hierarchy, and yet it is the worst nightmare for introverts. Hot-desking and shared work spaces are sometimes selected by organisations as a cost saving exercise without a consideration of the human cost of such a move both in terms of satisfaction and productivity. Some people see their desk as their territory, and if this is removed or changed feelings of being threatened can arise, thus invoking the fear system.

Understanding the needs and frustrations of the workforce by involving them is crucial, understanding what teams do each day and how the physical environment can support that is a key success factor in delivering successful, effective workplaces. Of course there isn't a one size fits all solution, but understanding the workforce and the ask of them will help create an environment that will foster productivity

Case study

Move to a new office space

Faced with the reality of re-locating 140 members of staff was an ideal opportunity to consider the impact of the external environment both in the lead up, during and after the move.

The previous office space was not conducive to collaborative working and by default encouraged people to work in silos. It was built as a Victorian villa and therefore was old and in desperate need of refurbishing, and yet it was perceived as safe and predictable. It was stifling creative potential and was beginning to have an impact on workplace wellbeing.

There was a familiarity to it as it had been "home" for some people for over eight years. It came as no surprise therefore that there was a mixed reaction to the announcement that there was a requirement for us to move. Whilst some embraced the opportunity others became fearful and started to demonstrate some quite negative behaviours. Those in favour were delighted at the thought of brand new purpose built premises equipped with the most up-to-date facilities, whilst the naysayers bemoaned the thought of an open plan space and in some cases became fixated with the minutiae of the move.

The move was delayed by nine months and whilst on the one hand that caused a certain amount of frustration it did allow those who were more anxious about the change of location the chance to work through some of their concerns.

As an organisation this was by no means the biggest change we had been through but it was a change nevertheless, and if we had learnt anything from previous change programmes, the success of the move would lie in getting our people involved. Giving them a voice and making sure that voice was listened to and acted upon was an approach that had worked for us in the past.

Due to the building schedule we were unable to visit the site, so we decided to bring the site to the people. Why was this important? We were expecting people to embrace the new space without having any concept of what it looked like; unintentionally we were fuelling their fear system! They were seeking care and we had an opportunity to give it. What we needed to do was create some interest-sharing.

We also knew that people interact with information in different ways, so using a spectrum of medium we brought the move to life. A team of "super movers" with a representative from each team became the voice of the move. A series of newsletters kept staff up to date with progress, informed them of key dates and actions. Forums enabled them to collectively describe the "house rules" – how we would operate in the new space, and to get a feel for the furnishings through mood boards and ask any questions they might have. Postcards and a postbox enabled those who had something to say but wanted a more private way to get involved. And the trump card was "21QS – the movie"! Filmed entirely on an iPhone it gave staff a sense of the space and facilities. It was so popular that a sequel was filmed. It lightened the mood, made people laugh and truly started to engage them in what was to be their new environment.

The interventions meant that when it came to move people were better prepared and as it turned out the reality was so much better than the thinking about it.

Course participant 2

These reflections give us a real-life insight into the application possibilities. Her reflections in the case study show how her considerations met the needs of the moving workforce to have a sense of where they were going to. To help them form new attachment to the new environment. If there had been no awareness of this, less caregiving, this force of 140 people could have had a much less supported move, and as a whole this part of the organisation could have lost its relationality, creativity and the move could have been the cause of much trouble at work. It could have ended up an authority issue with the hierarchy taking all their energy. The essential thing she did was to address the feelings of the workforce and take them seriously, exemplifying the findings in the McCluskey research that you have to address the affect you can't just jump over it. A brilliant example of how this system works and affects all of the others.

In addition to the PowerPoint and the discussion, I also devised an exercise for the participants to do in pairs. This exercise was introduced not only to bring them back into relationship with each other, to attune back to themselves, but also to reduce the risks of didactic monotony from me.

They were invited to choose a question or two from the list here below to apply at work.

1 How might your external environment defend the self against painful experiences?
2 How does your external environment promote your wellbeing and creative potential?
3 What are the parts of your external environment that you can influence here at work?
4 What is it like having parts that you can't?
5 What has your experience of the different environments for the course been like?
6 What would your experience have been like if we had stayed in one room?
7 Imagine if we had been indifferent rooms each time.
8 What if I had kept moving the chairs around?
9 In a new office environment what would you say are the key components you like to have around you, what's the minimum?
10 Do you know where you got these ideas from?
11 Is your external environment supportive or unsupportive for you in general?
12 How do you know?
13 What is it like for you?
14 What helps? What hinders?
15 How has your past contributed to your present construction of your external environment?
16 What is your external environment like at work?
17 Is your internal environment different outside of work? How?
18 How has your past contributed to how you construct or have expectations of your external environment?

19 Is your external environment supportive or unsupportive? Or something in between?
20 How do you know your external environment is agitating you?
21 Does the external environment support the work of your teams? How?
22 If not what is possible to change?
23 How do you know the external environment is agitating your teams?
24 What do you know about the external spaces requirements of the people around you?
25 If you have to share an environment what does that mean for you now?

A further refinement for another course would be to invite them to distinguish between a found environment and a sought environment, and then perhaps the personally created environment. What keeps us in a place? What helps us create an environment within the found or the sought environment?

This worked for me like this: Thinking about questions two and three above, I prefer to have books in sight somewhere; they have defined my space from others when I was a child. I had to share my space from a very early age. The books were essentially mine, and of my world at various stages, so they delineated an emotional and psychological space too. I replicate this delineation in my various work and home spaces.

I also prefer to have something living too, as that feels nurturing, echoes of my childhood garden, that was only ever a room away. To me perhaps it symbolizes the garden that meant freedom, no adults, no grief. So psychologically green living things feel like psychological space too, although maybe this is changing as I notice now that I am not great at keeping them alive. And of course, what we want from our environment changes, what I needed as a child, teenager, twenty-something is also different to me in my forties!

The group had lovely discussions both of the spaces they work in now and how they have been able to influence those spaces and bend them to be meaningfully representative of aspects of their selves. We could really think more about our external environments and consider how we commute, notice what has been put in places we shop or visit, to create a relationship with us, notice where these things echo with our childhood places, our cultural symbols or become new symbols for the epochs we are in and will form part of the story going forward. It is an incredibly interesting subject.

They were offered some questions to take away to reflect upon whenever needed.

Observe

- Is an aspect of your external environment a measure of how you are?
- How do you know – are there memories or associations of a previous place?

Assess

- Is the information from this previous relevant and helpful now?

Understand

- Do you know why these feelings, thoughts, bodily sensations are evoked now?

Review

- What will help you change your external environment if you can?
- How can you compassionately review your experience here?

We then reviewed our progress using the wheel image and observed the work we had done getting all the way through the systems. We considered then what they might like for the review and finish to the course. It was a big moment to have made it through all the systems. As have you made it through too!

Chapter 11

Final session, review and the application in practise

This last session was an opportunity to integrate their learning over the course and an opportunity for me to hear how they had got on. It was their chance to tell me about their experience of the pilot, their understanding of the systems and the theory, and any opportunities or applications they had made along the way. It was important for me that I heard how they understood the model, important to me they had a felt experience of how the systems work together as a single process to maintain wellbeing. All one body one mind.

The plan for this session was preceded by an introductory email I sent to them to prepare them for the elements that I might be looking for:

A   You are invited to contribute a question (or questions) to evaluate this pilot; so what would be the most important question(s) for you to ask/answer?
B   What are your overall satisfactions, dissatisfactions, surprises and learnings?
C   Please bring a (brief) case study of how you have seen, or been in, a situation differently because of this course (impact on you or others).
D   Do you have others in mind for a future course in its current or a revised state?

Welcome
   A different space (I had chosen a different room) to end in – notice what this might mean for you – does it effect you in any way – any different needs
   What do we do first – Centre – get in your seats – on your sitting bones – eyes open —attentive
   Find the tension and let it go.
   Catch places of tension in our bodies – is that information we need to do something about – adjust our bodies and when you are ready perhaps you can just check in with each other – get eye contact.
   Breathe out.

Outline of today's session:

- Over-time reflections: we've looked at all the systems now, is there anything you need to check in at this stage or can it wait for the review part? What do you remember about what we've looked at so far? Blank is okay.
- Any clarifications needed now?
- Case studies.
- Questions.
- Themes from feedback.
- Future courses.
- What are you over all satisfactions, dissatisfactions, surprises and learnings?

As a reminder, I had put the wheel and the fear to interest sharing diagrams plus a comment from Una on a whiteboard:

> If we haven't been met as a person, if we don't meet others as people, we are likely to move into dominant/submissive behaviours and activities.
> The job here is to work on how we ease off the fear and work in non (aggressive) competitive ways – delighting in our skills and experience and sharing competition and interest and careseeking and caregiving competently and compassionately.

I was delighted that most of the group had been able to attend. They offered extensive feedback, for which I am truly grateful. Amongst their ideas were the following thoughts, suggestions and learning points that will inform further applications of the theory and are offered here for inspiration and for their credit; great suggestions for the future use of the model to meet people at work.

LP9: Is it possible to use the wheel as a graphic plotter, diagnostic tool?

Others from McCluskey's trainings have raised this possibility too. Sometimes having a visual aid prompts us to return to a theory or a way of thinking, it acts as a reminder to access a different frame of view. Like a good learning acronym might take you to a formula, there is good evidence to suggest that using the diagram is an excellent way of reminding a person to use the model as a guide and get more familiar at using it. I have the wheel up on my notice board at work. I drew it out in every session of the pilot. Repetition and constant orientations to task keeps the fear system down and enables interest sharing and this is what the work is all about. It helps with that very permeable nature of the theory as mentioned in the testimony in the next chapter.

LP10: Could the wheel diagram be used as a check-in tool along the lines of where are you today? For instance, when checking wellbeing and progress when conducting staff reviews.

I think this is a lovely idea. The wheel could be used as a prompt to get a conversation going. If we agree that exploring ourselves at work through this model is a good way to get at issues of wellbeing, self-care, creativity and productivity then to use it as a frame for those conversations would perhaps normalise the terms, normalise the approach and raise the model as a standard of practise – not a just a one off.

LP11: Is there a way to create an abridged version of the course that might be deliverable in short bursts?

This is possibly the most problematic idea – although the terms are familiar, there is something irreplaceable in the embodied conscious competence experience of the model, possibly not attainable in shorter work. The training repetition creates familiarity through chewing it over and a benefit of trust is created over time to consider and apply it. Currently the experiential model offered by McCluskey to groups of caregivers is delivered over a three-day period, anything shorter than this would be hard pressed to actually give participants a chance to absorb the model. However, once inducted into the model it can be used in more intuitive ways. However, given my experience of introducing this work to an organisation I do believe it is better done over a period of months as it gives people time to try it out and come back together to talk it over, and this mirrors standard reflection learning practice. We know that people at work often wish to go faster, but that doesn't mean we should go faster

LP12: Can it be used as team building activity – a tool kit?
This is really good idea and we need to work out a way of doing it.

LP13: When one person misses a session, get another who attended to do the catch up – embedding the knowledge of the one who was there and fostering potential interest-sharing and mutual learning between the two.
This is a much better idea than me coaching and updating the participants each time. The benefit of the group cross-coaching certainly would embed the learning in the coach further, therefore developing their competency and forging greater links and networks across the organisation. It also fits with a model that shares knowledge across a wider cohort.

LP14: Consider catch-ups that could be run part way through the course.
This would be an alternative to the course mentoring, this could include two or three shorter consolidation sessions to allow the learning to consolidate and deepen and to keep bringing the cohort into a greater unity with their stages of learning.

LP15: Think about running it as a longer course.
Consequent to the pilot this group do still meet, they use the model to explore work situations they encounter and they use it to notice any unidentified needs. I would hope these meetings continue and when the next cohort are trained this skilled group could increase in size, offering again more opportunities for the most experienced to develop and coach those fresher to the model.

LP16: Think carefully about the timing of the sessions to 12–2, 10–12 was much more preferred.
This was especially useful feedback to receive, delivering the model at a good time of the day which allows them to really think about it as work and not conflate it with lunch. A good approach to wellbeing especially when so many desk based workers often eat their lunch at their desk rather than taking the time to take a break from work activities and move away from their desks to eat.

LP17: Think about how I clarify the pitch and articulate the pay-off to organisations. Align the course much more closely to wellbeing.
My group very quickly recognised the benefits to their wellbeing and they felt strongly these benefits should be evident in its early pitch going forward. It is reasonable that any course, pilot or otherwise, run within an organisation, is clear to the organisation and its internal stakeholders about the benefits to the organisation. Reflective practise has long been established in the world of therapy as a crucial component to managing the wellbeing of an individual practitioner but also to develop and increase the skills the practitioner brings to their clients. Aside from learning about the intricacies of this model, this model is encouraging reflective practise for managers and leaders too. Encouragement for them to attune to their inner content, recognise how this may be present in their exchanges with others and develop good techniques for managing themselves and their teams. In 2015/16, stress accounted for 37% of all work related ill health cases and 45% of all working days lost due to ill health (HSE, 2016). Stress has been in the top three reasons for staff to be off work in the UK for some years, so alleviating peoples experience of stress where it may be in their control, has national and organisational benefit. If we can say that this course may lead to greater levels of creative exploratory interest-sharing, this certainly supports the interests of an organisation.

They also noticed how it had a benefit for some in helping to demystify the behaviour of others. Sometimes it can be hard to understand what the behaviours, words, patterns of others might mean, and it isn't always possible to ask. This model gave some a framework to observe repetitions in patterns of those around them and consider alternative responses to see if they might resonate more appropriately supportive and creatively to their colleagues. Could it be a tool for HR managers?

LP18: Recognise the real value of group learning as opposed to tutor or didactic led learning.

The group was very good at supporting me to speak less. It was my fear system that led to an over active didactic input (well-intentioned but nevertheless dominant caregiving) at the beginning whilst being balanced with a requirement that some teaching take place of course. This was certainly one of my chief learning points.

LP19: It is ok to experience fear at work, and noticing this is a strength not a weakness.

Some participants as you see in their descriptions were indeed relieved to able to normalise feeling fear and anxiety at work, it doesn't mean the workplace is a bad place (although it could be) but rather that human being nature includes feeling fear. If I can recognise I am frightened I can do something about it. Sometimes the somatic activation of the fear system is much harder to grab, but if I can learn to observe those sensations, learn to catch the narrative (if there is one) there is a real strong possibility I can do something differently. Important here is the understanding of the biological nature of these systems; these are not failed cognitions, weaknesses, these reactions are strong highly evolved systems designed to protect me – occasionally gone awry. If we can really get a handle on the notion of goal correction we can tune to ourselves much better - notice when the agitation settles, notice when it increases. If I can recognise I need help I can ask more overtly and maybe get something that I need, this gets me back on track.

LP20: Noticing odd careseeking behaviour.

We probably all do it strangely sometimes, but if we can catch the pattern, certainly notice the failed attempts to support ourselves we might get exploratory again, we might just find another way to assuage our needs.

Chapter 12

Conclusion to the pilot

Introduction

This chapter was first produced for an OPUS conference presentation held in London, November 2016. The paper was written after the pilot and whilst this book was being written. It provides a summary of how the McCluskey model "Exploring the Dynamics of attachment in Adult Life" and the "Theory of Attachment-Based Exploratory Interest Sharing" (TABEIS) (Heard, Lake, and McCluskey, 2012) was used as an intervention to support staff in leadership and management positions for the benefit of the participants at the conference. The paper and this chapter summarises how I adapted the intervention used by McCluskey with people in caring roles, for an application in the workplace. It reflects how it was delivered, and what we all learned from it is described. The potential of the model to understand and work with interpersonal organisational dynamics is explored.

As a BACP accredited, humanistic psychotherapist, with a background in private and public-sector business systems, marketing and administration; and before then in campaign training, I have long held an interest in what influences how we relate, self to self, self to other, selves to society and to organisations. My therapeutic training featured a strong focus on Rogerian values (Carl Rogers 1902–1987), and person-centred principles. I then developed considerable interest in transactional analysis (Eric Berne, 1910–1970), and more recently in attachment theory (John Bowlby 1907–1990). I have the belief that people, generally speaking, are interested in themselves, in how they tick, and are interested in other people. Good, resonant concepts or frames of reference for understanding how we are and how we relate to each other can be vehicles for exploratory interest sharing. This exploratory interest sharing can be used to engage with matters that are otherwise difficult to discuss as working professionals. This in turn can lead to positive considerations about how we organise ourselves in our families, our communities and in our workplaces.

Part of McCluskey's model is the notion:

> that as a matter of course we all work in jobs that require us to respond to the needs of others, have our own needs, and often don't create the conditions to support our own personal and psychological development.
>
> (McCluskey and Gunn, 2015)

I had previously worked with The Baobab Centre in York, and not unlike Rose and McCluskey, they hold the belief that:

> by increasing the knowledge and understanding an individual or corporation may have about their ways of living and working, the more able they will be to make informed and effective choices and decisions about their lives and work.

They therefore work in a variety of ways to:

> promote an understanding of human processes, behaviours and interactions which is clearer and has more depth.
>
> (The Baobab Centre, 2016)

This pilot explored the notion that if we can understand how we are, how we feel, how we learn, how we interact in both intra and inter personal ways, we might better manage work, better manage ourselves and maximise the chances we have to thrive.

The models and the concepts

McCluskey, as we have covered in this book already, had written extensively on individuals, couples, and family systems, and developed her own model for exploring attachment dynamics in adult life. She joined forces with Brian Lake and Dorothy Heard, who, built upon what John Bowlby described as instinctive goal corrected systems of "careseeking and caregiving" (Bowlby, 1982, 1988). More recap on those later.

Heard, Lake and McCluskey deduced that the systems (careseeking, caregiving, interests and interest-sharing, self-defence, sexuality, the internal environment and the personally created external environment) work and interact as a restorative process for the self. A set of biological processes working together to maintain wellbeing and manage threat. Heard and Lake coined this theory, "the theory of attachment based exploratory interest sharing' (TABEIS). As the name implies, when the dynamics of attachment are assuaged, exploratory interest sharing with peers will take place. Clearly this has implications for work based organisations. TABEIS suggests experiences of careseeking and caregiving have their roots in infancy and shape our expectations and responses to careseeking and caregiving in adult life.

These experiences influence our internal working models. They shape our expectations, influence our responses and manifest themselves in our working patterns and professional relationships. Wellbeing, creativity, productivity all go together – this isn't to say inter and intra-relations need to be harmonious all the time, this isn't possible nor reasonable to expect – but if we can identify when they aren't okay, identify the cause, and what we might do about it, we might get back on track to feeling ok enough and when at work, support the organisation to deliver its goals.

McCluskey (2012) put together a model for "exploring the dynamics of attachment in adult life" which to date over 800 professional caregivers have attended (McCluskey and Gunn 2015). In addition, she developed and rated the concept of "goal corrected empathic attunement" (GCEA (2005). GCEA is a way of interacting with another which assuages careseeking and the fear component of the system of self-defence and enables exploration and interest sharing to resume.

McCluskey gives lectures, has talked to various organisations about systemic applications of this work, and offers three day experientials in the systems. These experientials are key to the McCluskey approach. The days involve taking one system at a time, exploring personal experience, narratives and consequences of these systems for each adult. It is McCluskey's expert practise of GCEA, which enables attendees to experience at a physiological, as well at an emotional and cognitive level, the impact an exploratory supportive enabling caregiver can have on innate instinctive systems. An outcome is positive effects on wellbeing and relations with others. One of the key elements is a developmental extension of Bowlby's safe base for exploration, this McCluskey encapsulates as fear-free exploratory caregiving. Working to notice fear (rather than act out of fear), manage it and talk about ourselves, and our selves, in relationships.

McCluskey has trained four cohorts of caregivers now immersed in her models and approach. These caregivers span the caregiving professions.

In my role as staff counsellor I saw the potential of bringing McCluskey's ideas into my work with staff. I could see how McCluskey's work could have considerable impact on the wellbeing of staff particularly on their effectiveness as team members and leaders, not to make them work harder but to help them work well and with self-competence. The application of this extended attachment theory for the workplace demonstrates how attachment theory, post-Bowlby, can be raised into a central place to understand relational dynamics in business and organisations and increase staff effectiveness and wellbeing.

The application

Following my encounters in the experientials and in the training, I decided to run a course introducing the theories and taking each system one at a time, with a group of colleagues. The course was to explore specifically how colleagues thought these systems manifested in their work experiences. The pilot to apply

McCluskey's innovation ran over nine sessions of two-hour group meetings between May and October 2015.

The McCluskey Model has a quality of permeation about it. You can't do it quickly. Whilst the terms may be familiar to us, understanding how the systems manifest in us at work and considering them for application at work takes time. Given this and given the nature of busy professional lives, in discussion with colleagues, we devised the nine session programme to pilot the model and its potential application at work. This meant the sessions could be delivered in two hour time slots, with time for reflection and application built in between the sessions. Attendance to the sessions was consequently high, enriching both the experience of the other group members and the feedback available to me of the efficacy of the theory for them at work.

Marcus Hill, Senior Staff Development Adviser in this organisation. was fundamental in recruiting the cohort of pilot course participants, in grasping the overall concept, he published the programme and the questions I set out to answer. These were:

- Is there any impact from the course on your interpersonal encounters with your colleagues?
- Is there any impact from the course to how effectively you think you might be working?
- Is there any impact from the course on how you regard yourself, and take care of your "self"?
- If so can you describe what these are?
- Can you imagine this working for other groups or members of staff?
- Any unexpected outcomes, surprises, learning, satisfactions, dissatisfactions?

I had no involvement in selection at this stage, thus avoiding any unconscious bias on my part on those who would join. Following their expression of interest, I met with, or talked at length to, all who were interested in the pilot, to cover its boundaries, its remit, my requirements for their participation and to air any assumptions or misconceptions before they were invited to join the programme. The dates and times were set for the first six sessions and the course began in May 2015.

The pilot course offered the participants a historical context with insight into the various contributors and ideologies which contributed to the formulation of this evolutionary approach to restorative practice. The formulation is built from the Bowlby notion of "the environment of evolutionary adaptedness" (Heard, Lake and McCluskey, 2012). It is evolutionary in that it has developed over the period of human development as part of our response for survival. This approach of offering historical context, also acknowledged I was working in a knowledge economy. I was working with colleagues who are interested in the genealogy and epistemology of ideas, and therefore also recognising their capacity for self-study and further exploration, if they were so inclined.

The first session introduced them to the process of the course, the history, and then the subsequent sessions took one of the seven systems in turn. The order of the sessions was careseeking, caregiving, the system for self defence (fear and attachment careseeking), the system for interests and interest sharing, the system for affectionate sexual relations, the system for the internal environment, and lastly the system for personally creating an external environment which is supportive of the self.

This organisational environment is akin to a small village. As the pilot developed I moved our meetings to different locations, this had the unintended consequence of offering the participants an opportunity to detach from their normal work environments, get out of their particular buildings, out into the fresh air, enjoy and gain mastery in finding the next location of the next session. This deliberately brought out a means of discussing the impact of our work environment, as our external environment, and highlighted how a sense of mastery and competence are key components to wellbeing.

McCluskey understands how work, and this exploratory work, in particular can invoke fear and trepidation, therefore she and I worked consistently in the background considering what ways we might support the participant's exploration of these models whilst remaining as fear-free as possible. One of the principle approaches here was to prevent the arousal of anxiety in participants by comparing rank. Instead of entering the programme as grades or with hierarchical status, they came as individuals, only invited to share their first names.

Each session began with a centering and settling, a little more explanation of this using ideas of both McCluskey and mindfulness to allow participants to arrive and be present, to make a choice to bring their attention and focus in the here and now, to engage with the work in hand. Arriving practice is now steeped in our training and group work approach.

As we have shown in the book the sessions had a range of didactic and discursive elements. Occasionally I used video or pictorial assets to complement the ideas being suggested. In between the sessions the participants were given a reflective sheet with questions to support their personal enquiries and reflections upon the ideas being introduced. I encouraged them to send these back to me to help support a process of reflection to embed through their learning.

A brief summary description of how the course considered the systems now follows.

Careseeking, caregiving and fear

Careseeking is part of our preprogrammed urge to signal to others to get what we need to survive. We become attached to those people we experience as most responsive and related and effective. It is an instinctive behaviour in most humans, the goal is to seek and get something. This is the human version of the open beak, a hotwired tendency for most human's active from birth, a biological need for assistance. Mary Ainsworth (1913–1999) who worked and developed attachment theory with Bowlby, described it as a biological dependency upon a vital care or health nourishment giver. An unfulfilled need fills us with fear; it's a threat to our survival. Fear and needs are inextricably linked together.

When an adult at work senses an occurrence, which presents as a threat to his or her sense of wellbeing, the attachment careseeking system and the system for personal defence are activated; after a suitably attuned empathic caregiver (a peer or line manager) has interacted with the careseeker in an appropriate manner, the experience of wellbeing is restored (as far as is possible, depending on how well attuned the caregiver has been). The need is satiated.

The effectiveness of careseeking is dependent upon having the skills and confidence and the language to discern my needs, ask for them and then seek satisfaction from an appropriately equipped caregiver. It's complex. These skills are learnt as a baby, as a child. Later Stern (Stern 1985; 2002) was to identify micro moments, and what was significant was that if the parent used purposeful mis-attunement maybe as a learning cycle, to up or down regulate the child, or due to problems with the caregiver - repetitions (and not many) of mis-attunements are going to key in different responses into the care seeking behaviour of the child. Imprinted if you like. If I never get what I want, I might give up, get angry, sad or try to get it by manipulation. On the other hand my caregiver might have over-whelmed me with their disorganisation as a child, and I may find a corollary of this happening at work. For instance this might play out as: me asking my peer to organise authorising my holiday; get them to do the asking for me, to receive a rejection if there might be one. However, they might not do it right, I might not get my holiday needs met, but I can blame my peer rather than improve my skills to do this myself. A replay of the early learnt attachment dynamic, causing conflict, distracting from the organisational goal of work.

Caregiving, to be effective, needs to remain exploratory. Persons in leadership positions at work, will either be natural caregivers or be with out great caregiving skills, either way they need to be clear about their nature and the limits of their responsibilities. Crucial to wellbeing is also identifying how we might replenish ourselves after the care has been given. Looking for our enablers and our sources of empowerment and how to enable and empower others. Caregiving can also be done defensively. I might over care to subdue another person with whom I am angry, to send them off-scent on a problem or as a response to an absence of having my own needs met. Giving care involves understanding what has been asked for and giving as good a match, to whatever it maybe, as possible, it could be just a smile. At work, it is also about making sure you are the right person to give the care, and the care is boundaried. Unfettered caregiving to colleagues is a quick route to burnout.

Self-defence

This system activates when we perceive an internal or external threat. That threat may be an unmet need – careseeking without a caregiver or with an ambivalent or inattentive caregiver. Fear is chemical – it fills us with adrenalin, it energises us but left unchecked it changes how our brains and our body's function. It's motivational. This is also a system that is a part of us which includes the processes we have built up through relations with others and reminds us of our competence to look after ourselves. It enables us to reject challenges which don't belong to us. But past examples of failed self-defence can interfere with how we might manage in the present. A moment of "xyz always happens to me".

Fear can be split into two – primitive (instinctive) and new mammalian (learnt as you experience life). If I am in a state of fear and self-defence, if I have unmet careseeking needs, my ability to interest share effectively (work) is deeply hindered. Creating a fear-free work environment could reduce conflict; burn-out, wasted time, unhelpful, and defensive behaviours within any organisation. A paper outlining this very subject was published in 2016 called "The dynamics of fear in the workplace: The contribution of attachment theory to leadership training and behaviour" (Brandão, Miguez, and McCluskey, 2016).

Interests and interest-sharing

The whole business of the pilot course was orientated around fear-free exploratory interest-sharing. Having interests gives us a sense of vitality, mastery (expertise), competence, ability. The Quaker organisations, such as Rowntree's, also famously used this as an approach to help disaffected youth. Sharing with others brings us into the community and relationship of other people. A team in conflict will rally to fight a common enemy. Without competence and some sharing of this competence and skill with others, fear creeps in again. Remember fear affects us all, it affects our health, our competence, our sleep, our relationships.

We cannot interest share if we are careseeking, or caregiving or if our system for self-defence is activated. But we can explore whatever might have stopped the interest; for example, shame, past hurts.

Interests and interest sharing in organisations is about peer validation, companionable mutual interest sharing (collaboration), peer support in acquiring new skills. Interest sharing can bring us back into professional relationship again. Interest and interest sharing should form the very fabric of an organisations values.

Sex and sexuality in the workplace

Like any of the systems, the sexual system emerges from the fact that we are in most cases born explorers in the world and sex is part of this exploration. For some it also plays a procreative role. The sexual system is the hub of it all, it's the powerhouse of our survival, it activates other systems (caregiving, interest sharing, external environment). In a positive way, it can be an expression of our self, very connected to careseeking and caregiving, interest sharing, in a negative way it may be connected to self-defence and fear. If the latter then an overactive system of self-defence in this way may lead to great vulnerability and ultimately burn-out. Work brings us into contact as sexual beings, many relationships form, thrive and fail in workplaces. One of the many gifts of the McCluskey model is an opportunity to discuss the implications of sexual relationships, gender, and power relations; and the play out of dominance and submissive dynamics at work.

The internal and external environments

The internal environment is not goal corrected as it is constantly under reconstruction based upon experience – it influences the other systems. It is one of two systems "whose function is to support the self when no caregiver is available" external is the other (Heard, Lake and McCluskey, 2012, p. 5). The internal and external systems either support caregiving, careseeking, self-defence, interest sharing, sexual systems or impair them.

Most interestingly for work, the internal environment is:

"1   The psychological knowledge that one is competent or incompetent in specific situations; and
2   Whether we have enough persistence (motivation) to carry out a plan."
(Heard, Lake and McCluskey, 2012, p. 114)

Therefore, the internal environment (or IWM) is a combination of our experiences of the past, the present and a developed skill of anticipating (imagining) a future. Planning for a future in an organisation could be a source of ambition and organisational success, planning for effective retirement, for change. The internal environments of the staff inform the potential for the organisation to thrive and adapt.

There is much talk about our external environment in terms of healthy workplaces or, say, Feng Shui, but what is our external environment at work really about?

External environment is the home we have created for ourselves to live in, it may be a small as one room, but it is created and fashioned in a way that is designed to provide support for the self as a whole or for a particularly specially valued part of the self. The external environment we create may serve to defend the self against the awareness of painful experiences, or may promote our wellbeing and creative potential.
(McCluskey, 2010)

The concept of an external supportive/unsupportive system was introduced by Heard and Lake (1986, 1997) as a lifestyle, which everyone is always constructing, of an environment within which a particular person feels she or he can live with comfort and safety. The function of the system is to maintain a lifestyle which constantly reminds one of the situations in which: (1) the goals of the five systems of the dynamics of attachment and interest-sharing have been met to the highest degree so far experienced; (2) the natural phenomenon and human artifacts, which currently produce a sense of wonder, awe, or delight, can be experienced; and (3) for some, religious experiences are available. The lifestyle is reached by one's own efforts and therefore has an intrapersonal goal rather than one that is interpersonal.

(Heard, Lake and McCluskey, 2012, pp. 116–117)

Thinking about our external environment at work can help us consider the motifs around us which join us to the organisational system, and connect us to our own histories and life experiences. Logos, spaces, ways to be attached to the wider organisational world, its values, whilst having enough to remind us of who we are, supports the self to thrive. De-personalised work spaces surely have the potential to cause some considerable negative effect in our systems for wellbeing.

Benefits to staff wellbeing of applying this model in work setting

One of the chief ways that people were affected by engaging in the course was to allow for and bring the word "care" into the idea of professional interpersonal relationships at work. It caused some controversy at the beginning as my participants struggled with the notion it might be acceptable to consider how they got care at work. It is as though it needed to be put in the context of work in order for it to be engaged with – the actual experience is familiar but the use of the word is usually associated with personal life outside of work. Most, if not all, recognised their role as caregivers to their colleagues and teams. However, it seemed only acceptable to consider it as a one-way transaction. This highlighted one of the dangers of work for us, that without a sound notion of our own wellbeing we may easily find ourselves giving far more than we ever replenish or expect and need back from others. Yet there may be various behaviours which illicit, one way or another, some form of care, response, and attendance by our colleagues. Through exploring how our careseeking and caregiving patterns formed in early childhood, the pilot was able to broaden through exploration of the model and the terms and the notion of what care was, to really bring those original notions of attention, attunement, and goal correction in relational value for work. The rejection of the word care wasn't wholesale but we needed to spend some time on it and what this meant for the group. McCluskey and I talked about the implications and McCluskey offered them the alternative to think rather in terms of affect identification instead of careseek, and affect regulation instead of caregive. This meeting of their need to be able to reject the words, allowed them actually to own them again and reframe what it meant for them. It was as though they shocked themselves in the discussion, realising they had in the notion of believing they were employed at work for their intellect, their minds only, and not their bodies and emotions; they had in fact ignored themselves and their own careseeking needs. When the group finally conceded that "care" was ok, they began to open themselves up to not only more specific ideas of what their own care needs might be, what the dangers might be of any low self-care behaviours they might practise and the effect that might have on those around them. They also gained some indications into exploring further what their teams might be wishing to get in their ways of careseeking from them.

The second and maybe even more powerful aspect to the pilot was through our consideration of what fear does to us at work, and how fear can arise from the failure to meet the needs of a careseeker. McCluskey (2005) details the experience of unmet needs diagrammatically, her descriptions show how if a careseeker approaches a supposed caregiver and does not have their need met, their system for self-defence arouses. The system for self-defence does not support interest and interest-sharing. Interest-sharing is work. Therefore, if our fear system gets in the way, work and creativity stop. Throughout the pilot the exploration of fear, continued within the discussion of all the other systems.

Fear alters the way our brains work. Fear triggers our autonomic nervous systems, these primitive responses impact on how we are with our colleagues. Fear interferes with my attachment patterns. I might want more or less of a person. I might want to hide, to attack, I might freeze. If we can learn to tell the difference between healthy stimulation and unhelpful fear responses we can perhaps reduce the negative personal and professional impact it has upon us at work.

The pilot enabled me to further pursue my belief that our childhood experiences form and shape us in the here and now.

The application of these attachment based models fits neatly into the approach my service espouses, which is to bring psychological theory into the workplace to offer staff ways to consider how they are and how they work. Like transactional analysis (TA) (Berne, 1964), which allows us to think of the idea of an inner self. TA has enriched our understanding of interpersonal exchanges; it offers a frame in which we might understand why we might be drawn to, or away from, certain behaviours in others. TA also recognises that there are small units of content which are exchanged between us which have relational impact. And whilst TA may pay less attention to the biological formation of these ways of being, it gives a means for us to rationalise the times we get scared by others. Similarly, the work of Carl Rogers (Rogers, 1951) gives substantial recognition of the impact of the childhood situation to the formation of the inner world of the child to become adult. His work on "conditions of worth" and the "locus of evaluation" have been crucial in my formulations at work.

Attachment theory is rich in the consideration of the relationship between the child and parent/guardian. It invites us to consider moments of child to adult contact, the impact of these going well or not going well. It shows how these experiences form the personality and influence the behaviour of the adult. Looking at this at work, offers us a rich opportunity to see these attachment behaviours in our professional relationship and understand how our biological selves, are also our professional selves and behaviours. All of these theories help us consider the impact of those who gave us care, attention or mis-attuned to us in our formative years.

With these theories in our context, it felt possible to encourage my participants to reflect upon their early years in the spirit of enquiry, not to blame but to wonder about the experiences which may influence how they react with others at work. This exploration helps them find what McCluskey describes as look-alikes, people, situations or circumstances which resonant historically for them if not initially consciously. The encouragement of the work is to spot the feeling, to tune into it gently and see where it might lead. To recognise, therefore, where their past might be hindering them in the here and now.

Conclusion

The whole experience was an example of the models in action. The possibility of the pilot was initiated because of the positive attachment dynamic I enjoy with my boss Sally Rose; this flowed into and provided potential for us to share interest in supporting the work of culture change and psycho-education and psychological support. If Rose and Hill hadn't responded to my interests and careseeking with caregiving (support and encouragement) I would not have been able to explore the potential for the application of the model. This meant I was also able to explore and develop my competence. I needed to have some substance in my internal environment which was a sufficiently robust internal working model that afforded me enough confidence to give it a go. I sought care from McCluskey to support me in the enterprise, she met my need with enthusiasm and we interest-shared throughout the application – we still do. In turn when we advertised the programme we were seeking careseekers, staff who knew they might need something, we were offering care, even though we had the dance around the word for some time. I gave care by inducting them safely into the course, they gave me care by attending the course. We played with the impact of the external environment all the way through the course by moving around in different spaces. Fear danced in and out of the process; I was anxious at the beginning, and so were they, but rather than pretend, we talked about it. I invited my participants to look to their histories and stories and discover themselves in them – the more they allowed themselves these reflections the more they appeared to find. I could have pushed a little harder on the session for the sexual system, but do you know what, Rome wasn't built in a day and the discussions they did have were amazing. The coupling of the model and group was perhaps sexy enough on this occasion.

The pilot course is being followed up by the cohort coming together to form a work group to use the model as a reflective tool to shine a new light on their dilemmas, within themselves with others, and with their wellbeing at the forefront.

The predominance of open discussions about fear, exploratory interest sharing, careseeking and caregiving made it possible for us to consider all these biological systems, to catch their attachment dynamics, to start looking at the attachment dynamics around them. And the most important outcome for me, to think about how they looked after themselves, that it mattered for their wellbeing and it absolutely related to the wellbeing of the organisation.

Chapter 13

Feedback from participants and what happened next

We must say how utterly amazed we are, and remain so, by the commitment my group showed to the course and to the ideas presented through it. It was with considerable joy that I welcomed the opportunity to carry on meeting with them, to apply these ideas, to explore applications of the understandings on an ongoing basis. The effect of their learning continues to inspire McCluskey and I, and supported us to write this book.

Here are three further examples of their experiences in their own words.

A view of a participant about the impact of the course

I lead one of the largest academic libraries in the UK. I have responsibility for over 200 FTE staff and a multi-million-pound budget. Academic colleagues as well as library staff look to me to ensure access to information crucial to research as well as to student learning. As a leader, I have to manage myself as well as a myriad of sometimes complex personal relationships. Over the past three and a half years I have experienced a series of family tragedies including the loss of my son. Counselling, meditation and work itself have helped maintain my mental wellbeing. However, I have been aware of the difference my grief has made to several relationships. I joined the TABEIS programme to gain a deeper understanding of the dynamics of these relationships. I hoped that by understanding more I would be able to develop strategies to help me manage them and perhaps heal them while I am experiencing extreme stress.

I was particularly struck by the relevance of the caregiving/careseeking model to the relationship between manager and direct report. The course allowed me the opportunity to reflect on what happens when that relationship is disrupted for example when the caregiver (me) is severely unsettled. I had seen in my own team, individuals behaving in ways I had not seen before, becoming agitated at issues which previously would have been easily agreed. I interpreted this behaviour as fearful responses to perceived instabilities in the caregiver and I made a positive effort to reassure my direct reports through my behaviour; that although I might not be singing from the rooftops I could still lead them effectively and I was still very concerned to support their needs for guidance and leadership. It worked; arguments and irritation subsided and we remain a high-performing group focused on quality service.

I have also tried to get senior staff to think of themselves as caregivers. This has been helpful as we have gone through organisational change which often makes people fearful. The McCluskey model has been useful here. I have encouraged senior managers to think about and explore the motivations behind behaviours when staff are resistant to change. Why do staff come to work? Recognising, say, a commitment to providing a quality student experience, enables the manager to convince staff of changing roles or structures by focusing on the student benefits of the changes. This is a form of "interest-sharing" and has proved effective in getting staff to agree to proposals which initially seem unattractive to them.

I did also try sharing some of the theory behind the McCluskey Model with my senior team. I tried explaining an overview in one afternoon session. I concluded that it had not been a wise move – the ideas, ultimately simple but initially quite involved need to be assimilated over a period of weeks and months, allowing as it did for me a period of reflection and discussion.

Course participant 4

Not only can we see here, just how an application of the model led to insight for this leader and consequently for their team, but also how some learning just can't be delivered in a shorter period of time (LP21). The resonances of caregiving and careseeking are immediately evident both on the intra- and interpersonal encounters of the writer. A bravery in the powerful recognition of the implications of exploring these notions and an understanding of how we need time to see what it means for us. Although the terms are all familiar, it takes time for us to notice what is going on, what systems are triggered in us such as careseeking, caregiving or fear.

Here is another participant's experience of the course – his words also permeate this book in summary experiences for each system.

In the couple of years prior to partaking in the TABEIS pilot group I had left a job through a stress-induced breakdown, consequently receiving counselling, and I had also undergone a later course of CBT. I initially became aware of the TABEIS pilot via a colleague who I met on a series of leadership and management training modules provided by the organisation. We shared an interest in development of the self, and in our experience of CBT. I had previously done some work linked to mental health with students and I wanted to continue to develop my ability and skills as a manager and a person. I also had an understanding of attachment theory due to my partner and I following an "evolutionary parenting" model for our young son.

Much like my experiences of counselling and CBT, the work in the TABEIS group, like any sort of introspection, was challenging – emotionally, mentally and physically. That being said, I saw the value in it very early as my interest was piqued, and it was a challenge I embraced. For the first few sessions I struggled to relate the theory to me at work, instead of my personal life. I had come to define myself by who I was outside of work, not within it. As I came to understand the systems more, the more they related and fitted with issues I was facing in work (during the pilot I took a new job internally with extra managerial responsibilities and inherited a pre-existing team, while my department had undergone a challenging review of performance).

Via the programme, I have learnt a lot about myself and why/how I do things (or don't do things), and I feel that this insight can be used to work with colleagues. I feel it helps me understand the reasons for certain behaviours, effectively framing my conversations and methods when working/dealing with staff and colleagues. I continue to see the value in the TABEIS group, as we are currently functioning akin to an "action learning set", and this kind of group support and understanding I find greatly beneficial, especially with like-minded people who see the value in the approach. I think the experience has improved my awareness of my feelings at work, or at least, my understanding of my reactions (potential or actual) to situations. Continuing on from the work I had done with myself prior to the course, I think it has aided my understanding of myself and my patterns, and assisted my ability to prevent negative spirals of behaviour, by heightening my awareness of my cues for things like stress, excessive worry etc.

Believing in the principles of basic attachment theory anyway, the ideas contained within this work truly make sense to me, and I see their worth. I truly feel they could be an asset to other colleagues, teams and organisations by enabling them to better understand where people are coming from, and how best to work with them, as well as oneself.

Particular challenges existed when addressing each of the individual systems, often linked to terminology, varying degrees of awareness of them in oneself, and level of comfort in considering aspects of the system.

Like a lot of group work, the experiences and insights of another can often aid your own understanding of similar situations in yourself.

Group participant 3

Hill, who has contributed elsewhere to the book, also offers us his summary of his evaluation of the theory in the workplace.

What do you believe are the organisational benefits and organisational challenges for the theory?

By surfacing the mechanics of dynamics within an organisational context, TABEIS puts key issues on the table for discussion. It isn't a judgemental system – so provides topics for discussion, to which everyone can relate. To demonstrate this; take any workplace interpersonal conflict or awkwardness – it will map onto TABEIS. For example:

A member of staff keeps secret a health concern in case the boss uses the information to stall career progression. This may be seen as a method of avoidant self-defence, in association with a fear system. Thus, to unfreeze this behaviour, TABEIS would suggest the individual seeks care, perhaps by discussing with a colleague, and through the caregiving, they may both enter exploratory interest sharing which can reduce the fear.

I think the extent to which the theory may cause discomfort within a host organisation depends upon that organisation's culture. For example, if not used to speaking from the heart at work, participants will need to overcome their inhibitions to talk plainly in front of colleagues. On our programme the programme facilitator skillfully used the model to point out difficulties which arose, in real time. "What systems are at play here?", "What do you need from the group right now? (careseeking)". This reinforced the learning and meant we could see the systems being acted out in the sessions, which was very powerful.

What was it like thinking of people to select?

Because I wasn't quite sure what kind of experience the TABEIS programme would offer, it was difficult identifying possible attendees. In the end I opted for colleagues who I knew were open to taking a few risks and had previously shown their interest in personal self-development. I found it hard inviting senior managers as I thought they would dismiss the offer out of hand due to the duration and commitment required (they would be too busy). I overcame my fear system and invited them anyway(!) I was very happy when they accepted.

What was it like being the only other person who knew everyone else?

I am used to leading sessions where I know all the participants but they don't know each other. However, with TABEIS I was more aware than usual that I could be seen as one of the leaders' of the programme rather than a participant myself. This often led me to feel like I had an awkward dual role – caring that others were getting value out of the programme; wanting the programme leader to feel the programme was a success, and bringing the real me to participate. I don't think I achieved the balance I would have liked and so often found myself floating between these identities.

What are the lasting impacts?

A vocabulary amongst the programme alumni which can be used to signal needs and pinpoint/discuss difficulties in the workplace.

What did you wish for that didn't happen?

Nothing.

Would you do it again?

Yes, definitely.

How would you recommend it for others if you would?

A programme of events using a model which will help you tune in to relational and situational aspects of coming to work. It helps explain the interactions which take place, the situations you can find yourself in, and why they might have developed that way (LP22).

Which system contains the gold for you?

The fear system and how it can be soothed via a process of careseeking and caregiving leading to exploratory interest-sharing leading to decreased fear and more rewarding relationships with others.

Which system did you get instinctively?

The internal and external systems because I feel I am quite self-aware and also am aware of how important my work surroundings are in relation to my mood and effectiveness.

Notes on fear-driven caregiving

The TABEIS programme helped me plot the timeline of events which can transform a desire to help others into dominant caregiving behaviours.

I learnt that when caregiving is motivated by fear then it is not provided in service of the recipient. For example, if a colleague is making a presentation in a team meeting at work, and stops to allow silence and reflection for the group. But a colleague who is listening finds the silence unbearable, in the fear of the unknown (for example, "What's happening here? Or what may happen here – everyone has gone quiet? I can't bear this uncertainty!!") Then this fear may lead the colleague to try and rescue the presenter (for example, "Do you want me to give you some ideas?") – even though the presenter doesn't need rescuing! This can be very irritating for the person receiving the fear-driven care.

This awareness has helped me notice when my caregiving is motivated by my own fears at work. Although not always a comfortable thing to become aware of, this helps me avoid overbearing others in my need to calm my fears. I have found the benefit of this to be a calmer me at work, instead of being in a cycle of dominant caregiving followed by regret ("I wish I hadn't said that") I find that less is more.

Notes on fear-driven careseeking

The programme has helped me come to know the difference between ineffective and effective careseeking. In my words this depends upon whether I own, and ask for care in plain sight (e.g., "I need your help please!") as opposed to seeking it through the back door (e.g., "I think we all need a greater explanation of that don't we?") The act of shaking hands is a way of saying "look I carry no weapons" – and similarly I am aiming for careseeking which is out in the open. I find this hard in the workplace because my programming says that asking for help is tantamount to showing my weakness. TABEIS has encouraged me to reframe that belief and ask for help from colleagues more regularly. In particular, in email subject lines to colleagues who attended the programme, for example, I now write, "I am careseeking!"

Course participant 1

I wasn't expecting such detailed feedback. We remain amazed at the impact on the participants, especially to what could be described as a really quite compact management and leadership intervention.

The group continues to meet to explore their own experiences of the systems and develop their fluency with the terms and the interplay of the systems. They share their learning openly with each other and therefore continue to learn from each other. The learning alliance that formed in the pilot is still ongoing two years later; the learning point is that a good learning alliance will stand the test of time (LP23). I believe this to be the result of a combination of the effect of the pilot implementation and their spirit and characters. Delightfully and expertly they are very able to move from personal introspection to consideration of how the model applies to themselves and their teams, the nature of their inter-actions with colleagues, and, they are now showing sophistication in applying the model to understand the nature and form of the organisation itself. They are becoming interested in using the model to think about exploring which of the systems are triggered in other parts of organisation, as it responds to the changing wider external work environment in the UK. They transpose their understandings to consider how the organisation meets it's people as people, offers care, asks for care, enables and actively shares interests within its various parts or indeed with other organisations locally, nationally or internationally. They wonder about the internal environment of the organisation like a microcosm of a person, basing its identity on its knowledge and experiences from the past and making plans for its sustainability in the future. They observe the constant changing external pre-sentation of the organisation seeing the competing needs of the systems as they manifest in planning, budgeting, and decision making. They identify how fear plays an inevitable part of any organisation managing its parts and trying to hold on to its integral personality, its character, indeed its reputation. This thinking and continued application of the model really helps us also wonder about future appli-cations. This pilot couldn't have run, and this book couldn't have been written, if it hadn't been for the willingness of the cohort on the pilot to give it a real go.

Does the model have to be delivered in this way? The ongoing work might really be to see if future applications will require someone to be as immersed in the model as I have been to facilitate the experience, or can the model be refined and distilled to enable others to access it in a different way.

At the moment, we recommend that for anyone interested they should first take the opportunity to attend a three-day experiential in the model. At the very least this facilitates an emotional and personal phenomenological understanding of the biological systems and how these grow with our life experiences. The "train the trainer" programme gives the skills and a safe place to rehearse an application with experts and learning colleagues developing with you. Perhaps after that, and with the descriptions of the pilot from here it might be possible to apply the model in other ways to other workplaces.

It isn't clear to us though, whether we need the full encounter to have a trans-formative experiential paradigm (Kuhnian) shift and a narrative shift. We are cer-tain this work is essentially relational and anyone thinking of moving it forward will need supportive access to a good caregiver, supervisor or consultant.

Throughout that pilot, and in the writing process, McCluskey and I have been meeting and digesting the experience; and working together to formulate this narrative and explore this application. The nature of the attachment between us was tried and tested in the length of our professional relationship and interest in the work and this provided a secure base in which to initiate this experimental project. A quality of the model seems to encourage generosity between peers and interest-sharing in peers exploring the work. We see a progression with the transposition of the theory and application of the practise; starting with Heard and Lake, McCluskey took their work on and in addition to her own saw its application to caregivers. I have now taken the work in to organisations.

I rely upon the professional learning alliance with her and with my initial training cohort. We all embarked upon a voyage of discovery which includes supervision with my training cohort. The success of this group actively involves all the systems, we careseek and caregive to each other. We observe the impact of the places we meet and our personal work and private environments. We enjoy loving affectionate and close relationships with each other, and observe the impact upon our families. We regularly frighten the heck out of each other and use the systems to restore our equilibrium and relationships with each other. This invariably involves a change to ourselves, our internal environment.

Moving forwards will certainly involve further rupture and repair, this is the very fabric of the model, of sound resilient professional relationships, the secure base from which these explorations could have been made.

Chapter 14

The integrated person
Theories of people at work

If we can agree that work is good for us (Black, 2008), then creating conditions for working well, surely go without question. We might disagree on which approaches support appropriate wellbeing and growth, but perhaps we can conclude that understanding how we are, and how we are in relation to our colleagues, and workplaces, is worth taking some time over. This pilot was by no means an easy thing to embark upon. It involved much thinking, planning, agonising, reviewing and discussing, let alone some courage and active management of my own fear system on a regular basis. The pilot served to introduce the theory of the restorative process (Heard and Lake) and McCluskey's concept of GCEA and her model of group facilitation in a workplace setting. It combined didactic presentation, structured and unstructured opportunities for reflection inside and outside of the sessions, interactive discussion, visual imagery on white boards, short film clips from the internet, photos, and hundreds of reflective questions (see Appendix Two). It had its experiential components and there were handouts to support the retention of learning. The incremental and iterative approach I believe, were essential to the success of the application. This chapter reflects upon some of the key features and learning points; and briefly considers this model and approach alongside transactional analysis and person centred theory, as other theories that can be used in a workplace setting to aid an understanding of how we are, for the benefit of how we are, at work.

***

Key features

Some of the key features I will repeat in subsequent applications would include: use names not roles to prevent hierarchical positioning creeping in; if one person is working they are working for everyone (all for one); work alongside, if one person is considering something consider what that might mean for you; don't get into fixing each other's problems; and enact a real parallel process of doing it and talking about it at the same time.

These features support an environment where participants might develop a greater sense of competence in being themselves, and can use this as a framework to grow and support themselves at work.

I was not analysing or assessing them, I was a fellow explorer. The participants remained expert in relation to themselves, gaining insight where it might be had, rejecting whatever didn't work for them, keeping their autonomy intact, for example: "How is this for me?" is a question that I can answer for myself. My job was to help participants learn the terms and theory and use it as a guide in their work. As an approach it can't be, nor needed to be, useful for everyone all the time. We created a context where they could make their discoveries. They were all able to use the idea of the biological systems (thinking about biology rather than intellectual successes or failures) in a workgroup which was established to explore their experiences without shame. Consequently, fostering an atmosphere of trust and intimacy, with less risk of feeling vulnerable, and therefore offering them a place where they might be more inclined to uncover themselves and their work encounters with the supportive exploratory workgroup.

Coming from a department within the organisation which is designed to support staff, it was fairly normal for me to be asking: 'What do you need? What are your needs? How do you get care? How do you avoid being depleted by excessive (defensive or otherwise) caregiving to your colleagues? How might natural fear interfere with your work and work relationships? What interests you and how do you know?'

The consecutive and iterative nature of the pilot allowed these questions and the ideas of the model to permeate through so a practise of reflecting upon themselves in their work became normal and habitual. This was not just my observation as you will see from the contributions of the participants themselves.

I was introducing participants to the idea that interpersonal relationships at work are instinct-based. We constantly have particular biological goals we need to reach in order for us to be free to use our faculties to deal with work. For the workplace, this approach is a way of perceiving if some of these systems were reaching their goals or alternatively interrupting the business of working creatively. For instance, one might consider whether a person was careseeking from their manager, and to see, not only if the subsequent response was effective, but also *how* to detect whether the response was effective. Furthermore, given the scale of instances of burn-out at work, can we take this evolutionary theory to help us look at workplaces in the twenty-first century, and how we might prevent burn-out and fatigue at work?

***

Emotional intelligence for work

I am a person at work, in my being is the combination of all the factors that make me, me. The notion of emotional intelligence for work has been around for

50 years or so, made popular by Daniel Goleman (1995). There are numerous forms of emotional intelligence tests; ways to rate personality; diagnostic tools to assess our preferences, leanings and aversions. There is a growing number of articles, books and presentations which link emotional intelligence to work performance, some making explicit the consequent link to organisational benefit, such as the writings of Bar-on and Parker, 2000; Brandão, Miguez, and McCluskey, 2016; Druskat, 2005; Schutte and Loi, 2014; Wheeler, 2016, to name only a few. There is a growing body exploring work through the biological and neurological (Damasio, 2006; Rock, 2009). And whilst some of these explorations, studies and methodologies might incorporate an exploratory self-diagnostic element, not all do. I wonder then if some miss a key point, that we are the best diagnosticians of our own experience and encounters. If we can be offered ways to understand how we have formed biologically, emotionally, relationally and how all these systems interconnect, we might bring this intelligence, this information and data, into use with how we are working and if we are managing our professional encounters and wellbeing. Maybe we are talking about emotional literacy here, and the key aspect of this is access to an exploratory caregiver. There is something very important about the sense making of any theory that draws conclusions about who and how we are, that is not judgemental or limiting in its meaning and application. This exploratory model seems to me to allow this sense making to be made in non-judgmental and empowering ways. A model that can perhaps sit very well with other theories of self and emotional intelligence at work.

For the last part of this book, then, we wish to consider the McCluskey approach against two other theories which can be applied to how we are in a work context.

***

Transactional analysis and person centred theory

As an integrative practitioner, bringing in and using multiple theories is a part of the way I work, and of course there are other theories which might help us think about how we lead, how we influence others, and how our interpersonal professional relationships at work are affected by our individual life experiences. The two which I use most often and which are perhaps most familiar in terms of use in workplaces are transactional analysis and person centred theory. We have mentioned them earlier in the book but here we are going to look at them alongside TABEIS and the McCluskey approach to explore any connections or similarities especially for use in a workplace setting.

The beginning of integration starts with me. As a person, psychotherapist, philosopher, explorer, I like ideas that help me conceptualise my world. I especially like ideas that seem to help others conceptualise their worlds, and help them know themselves in a compassionate way, know something of their emotions, motivations and urges, and perhaps lead to changes that suit them. I am interested if theories contradict each other, when theories change, and when evidence points to their limitations. I like making a sense that is meaningful for myself and others. However, I know that however interested and excited I can get by theories I am bound by my own experience and conceptual encounter of the world, and can believe that is all there is. Sometimes things make sense to me because I think and feel them. If I experience sufficient repetitions of the sensation, emotion, the thought, it becomes a belief, organically located in me – something I know. It becomes so familiar it seems to me to be truth. However, if we reflect back to Kuhn (1962) we remember that we become locked in a paradigm until it stops working for us. So whilst I recognise that the theory and models presented here all seem relevant for me, I know and appreciate there may be alternatives outside of my experience that might be just as effective.

As already mentioned in Chapters 2, 5 and 12, I have valued the theory of transactional analysis (TA) written by Eric Berne (1961, 1964, 1975) ever since I first came across it in my psychotherapy training years ago. I liked the terms, they made sense to me. Like TABEIS the language is accessible and recognisable. My experience is that organisational learners start applying and reflecting upon themselves and their interactions, quite quickly through the lens of the theory. Although it exists I don't yet understand systemic TA theory well enough to write about it here, this is ongoing work. I have over ten years of experience of using the earlier ego models developed by Berne, and the further theories of the "drama triangle" developed by Stephen Karpman in 1968, published in 2014, and the "Quinby durable" developed by Lewis Quinby in 1994, in my work with organisations, to good effect.

I can see how the theory of TA and TABEIS complement each other, and like McCluskey, Berne encouraged others to develop his thinking and apply it in different settings.

Berne posited that we have three primary ego states: parent, adult, and child. Two of these split further, I will talk about that shortly. These ego states are collections of neuro-biological emotions, cognitions, behaviours, characteristics, and ways of being which are sufficiently coherent to be grouped and distinguishable as a set.

The parent ego state is one born mainly from scripts and narratives which we imitate, copy – swallow, if you like – from our primary caregivers. This is learnt behaviour; repetition and duplication often without mindful conscious understanding, biological training. You may even say to a child as a parent "copy me". However, not only will the child observe the behaviour and imitate the emotions they are instructed to observe they will be observing and copying everything they witness: being bossy, being kind when others are in distress, being knowledgeable, being a leader, being in charge, fussing over poorly others, as well as being avoidant, anxious, fearful and insecure. Much early play will be about testing some of these emotions and behaviours out on each other, and on the parents too.

Some nurturing or useful leadership could be seen as caregiving to others, but where there may be a desperation to be in charge or look after others, it could be viewed as fearful and based upon an impulse to be in control, or as careseeking through the veil of defensive caregiving. When a group of children play mummies and daddies, these emotions and behaviours are being developed through their play and interest sharing – the collective job may be to look after the babies. We can notice here how in play children will naturally construct an external environment to reflect the activity going on. They may form relationships and partnerships; they may also play and act out angry or fearful responses. All the time this play and rehearsing has biological impact on the self – I like being so and so, I don't like being (acting) like this but can try it out, I can behave one way but think another thing.

These ego developments don't stop in childhood; as we move in to work roles we carry on rehearsing the behaviours of being team leader, a parent, or an expert in something, managers, moving with age into positions of wisdom, acquired or otherwise. Through all these developments each of the systems will be triggering and responding, interrelating and acting to restore balance when things get 'hairy' – when you experience a fear response in some way. Remember the first time you took on a responsibility in the family or in a job. How you gave and asked for care may have changed, your interests developed, your self-talk, self-regard is likely to have altered – you may have positioned, even dressed yourself differently – your experience of fear may well have had a completely different aspect to it. As we develop so do these traits of parent ego quality, the ego state reflecting both the here and now encounters but also all the information and data that our body has collected across the time of our lives, stored ready to be used if needed. One of the particularly helpful cues from Berne is the encouragement to look at our phrases to help detect an ego state, in *Games People Play* (1964), he offers phrases to help us identify certain aspects of the theory at play, and calls these scripts and games. We might notice this when we find ourselves repeating those phrases we may well have hated when we heard our parents mutter them to us. Equally so we might notice hearing ourselves repeating anything a previous manager or boss may have uttered to us at some point too?

Berne described the parent ego state as being either controlling or nurturing, depending upon the behaviour a person has experienced. TABEIS would describe parenting as having a nurturing and development aspects and in its defensive form having a controlling dominant aspect; it separates out the caregiving and care-seeking systems. So where Berne's theory helps us notice we have moved into a role or entanglement with someone at work and offers a route to communicating differently, which may help combat the consequences of being contaminated or caught in crossed transactions, TABEIS gives us another dimension for thinking about how we might restore our own and the others equilibrium. TABEIS theory explains that effective caregiving is attuned and exploratory (see Chapter 5). If we are talking about defensive caregiving we are really talking about self-defence or the infiltration of caregiving with careseeking, or it might suggest if the behaviour was controlling it could rather and helpfully be seen as behaviour that is infiltrated by fear. Therefore, it gives us the opportunity to manage the fear or careseeking needs first. This isn't to say the TA wouldn't enable us to make this discovery, but you may need to work a little harder to get there.

The adult ego state is one that emerges through understanding and problem solving as we go along. This is our pragmatic self, figuring things out and identifying resources. In terms of the instinctive systems of Heard and Lake the adult ego state may well develop from successful experiences in interest-sharing, learning new skills, and acquiring competencies. This may extend to competencies in caregiving and careseeking, such as, knowing I need to ask for help, and who to go to for help, for example, I don't know how to do complex formulas on spreadsheets, John is expert in spreadsheets, I will ask him. I have a need and I rationally find resources and people to satisfy those needs. John may well attune to my need and offer both the care and the interest sharing with me. The adult ego state is likely to be very good at creating the right external environment to match the needs of the self and situation. The adult ego state might meet other people's needs very practically. The adult ego state may pass on skills in a tried and tested mechanistic way. An adult ego state may very well see the formulaic notions of the restorative process of TABEIS and the McCluskey model as a useful way to consider personal and professional relationships.

The child ego state is based around the present and how we feel, our needs in the moment. The child ego state is described in three different formations. The "free or natural" child, engaged in play, here and now satisfaction, fun, creative, instinctive and unthreatened exploring – the adventuresome moments of life. From kicking up a pile of leaves, jumping in puddles just for the fun of it, to going to the theatre, the pub, pushing our feet into the sand when we sit on the beach on holiday. Really well attuned in the here and now.

'Pleasing or tantruming adaptive' child, a state of using one's emotions to attract the attention of someone we perceive to be in the position of parent – careseeking through sometimes covert ways to get our needs attuned to. In TABEIS the appeal for attention, which in that framework would be called careseeking, might be paralleled to the TA notion of exhibiting either pleasing adaptive or tantruming behaviours, doing something to gain attention, connection (a requirement for attunement to a need) from someone they perceive to be in the parent ego state or as an identified potential caregiver.

The theory of interaction for caregiving (TIFC) (2001) that McCluskey developed and which we have been describing so far as the 'McCluskey Model' then helps us see the biological nuance in these requests. It isn't just my head or mind (not that these are separate) that require something but in fact my entire body might crave it. If we can learn to detect what has aroused our careseeking, or indeed caregiving, we can, as we might with figuring out what we need from someone in adult ego state, learn to develop our competencies to assuage our own needs, or get more competent at finding the people with the skills or competencies to assuage those needs at work and elsewhere. In TA we might call that developing our own internal parent as well. Another parallel between the two models is the perceived parent (caregiver) in the transaction may not know they have been defined as such, may be oblivious to the appeals from the tantruming or pleasing adaptive child (careseeker).

Berne (1964) identified transactions, exchanges between people, Heard, Lake and McCluskey (2012, p. 28) talked about "non verbal signals" which contain information about emotions and which get picked up accurately or inaccurately by the people concerned. McCluskey analysed these interactions in great detail in her 2005 book and conceptualised the concept of, and the process for, effective communication as GCEA. Where there is no GCEA we could perhaps also describe this as a TA crossed transaction (Berne 1964).

A later addition to TA was that of 'little professor', a child ego state which is skilled at identifying our needs and then using our expertise in others, and their foibles, to get them to give us what we want or do something for us. Social change is based on the creative use of this ego position. Here you could say that the attachment pattern is perhaps ambivalent therefore the request for careseeking cannot be made directly for some fear of failure. The manipulation is driven by defence, but can also be a really useful means to an end.

A further parallel between these two models could be drawn between the effects of the quality of caregiving upon the careseeker. The suitably attuned and effective caregiver gives what is needed and the careseeker returns to interest share, (remember all the systems are inter related) so that when one system is assuaged, such as careseeking, other systems are also affected. The effect of the parent oscillating between controlling and nurturing stimulates growth in the child, however misattuned nurturing or limiting a child's exploration stifles the child's development. In attachment terms the caregiving system is expressed through two forms, a) support and nurturing, and b) support for exploration along with helping the child, adolescent or adult access the skills necessary along with the support of their peers. Therefore, in attachment terms, the likeness is the defensive caregiver would stifle the careseeker, have a restrictive effect on the development of the child (or colleague) regardless of their careseeking patterns.

I consider these to be very interesting connections between the two theories. Interesting especially because I have found many workplaces very open to the TA ideas. There is something useful about understanding how our work relationships stem from all our experience of life and that we can repeat patterns that have been developed in childhood. Anything that catches unhelpful (conscious or unconscious) patterns can help us get out of fearful, dominant or submissive relationships and is likely to be a good thing, to lead to greater fulfillment and creativity – very good for every organisation.

I further believe the flow of the McCluskey model chimes with the drama triangle and the Quinby durable. I have utilised these two models many times in working with organisations. As above they appear to make sense to staff, and allow colleagues to consider in a non-judgmental and exploratory way, how they are relating to others.

In brief, the drama triangle in its simplest form is a description of the codependence of the three emotional (can be actual or habitual) conditions of victim,

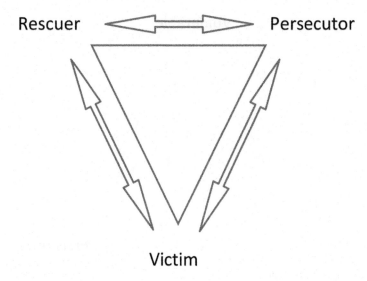

Rescuer   Persecutor

Victim

Figure 14.1 Drama triangle

persecutor and rescuer. In an unhelpful version of the scenario these three lock themselves into a state of relating.

The victim becomes pinpointed so because of the persecutor or the rescuer, the rescuer because of the victim or persecutor, the persecutor because of the victim and so on. All get their condition from the existence of the others. It is a power struggle: plenty of dominance and submission going on. One of the chief ways we can tell we are in a drama triangle is when something changes but rather than there being resolution everyone just switches position.

What I wonder and is still up for exploration is how these states might work when lined up with the McCluskey's theory of interaction for caregiving (TIFC) – could we consider with a work triad how a poorly attuned caregiver, whose caregiving system was infiltrated by their system for self-defence so that they become harsh or worse (persecutor) might make victims of colleagues by, say, micromanaging. In this scenario a defensive caregiver, whose own fear system becomes aroused observing this (rescuer) might rush in to give care to appease the situation and communicate displease at the persecutor, without considering what was being triggered for themselves and for the others. Might the models work to help colleagues recognise something might be amiss? And perhaps it doesn't matter which of the two models you use to identify a problematic situation. If a workplace can offer more than one option perhaps it is more likely to meet the needs of its diverse workplace.

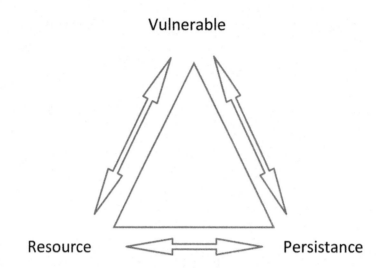

Figure 14.2 Quinby durable

Might then the Quinby durable diagram (below) be one you use to consider how you are resourcing yourself within the McCluskey model at any one point in time? Could you use this as a frame to consider if your internal environment say is supportive or unsupportive? Could you use these as diagnostic tools to review your work resilience or work sustainability? Perhaps this would be an interesting development to explore further?

The Quinby Durable shifts the descriptions of the roles and by doing so removes the power struggle – rather than gaining power from the other roles – each one here is empowered, has self-determined clarity and boundaries. Here we have a chance to attune to our needs and seek care or interest share with clear sight of our needs and skills in the situation.

TA also suggests that our early lives may have inclined us to develop a greater fluency in one ego state. I have a sense that my fluent state is that of 'pleasing adaptive child'. I have to resist what feels like my instincts to please others in denial of my own real needs. While I have highly developed skills as a caregiver in reality, I am also aware that it has a defensive under structure (it contains a hidden careseeking component) as it allays my fears of separation. I am aware that this state in me has its roots in the habituation of my childhood to be a conscientious and attentive child. Whilst I may have had a biological predilection to this state (possibly based around the fear of what would happen if I didn't follow suit, survival) the conditions of growing up certainly exacerbated the tendency – and this behaviour was actively rewarded. Therefore, as an adult I have to be cautious around acquiescence to others and allow myself sufficient time to think through my responses to others. It also means I have to manage the biological howl my body still makes when I don't just do overtly what others want me to do.

McCluskey has just recently began to consider how any one of the systems may be in what she has coined as a "keystone position" (McCluskey, 2017): a perfect description for this discovery, especially with the diagrammatic form of the wheel. A system of particular significance to the self because of holding within it some particular aspect of the self, or some particular data from the past that proves crucial in the restorative process. So, the 'keystone system' for me would have to be caregiving. It is the one with most data in it, most work for me to do. And it is the one that has defined my professional life. Clearly the possibility is that my "self" and my personally created system of the internal environment has been hijacked by external pulls on my caregiving systems and this has affected my biology'. It begins to look like the McCluskey model has another dimension with this new conceptualisation – I can see how that will work in my clinical work, and I can also see how it will work with groups and with the organisational clients too. This also furthers a notion from both models that we can work with our preferences for the benefit of wellbeing in work, once we understand more about them from whichever theory resonates at that time.

If we can agree that we have inclinations, whether they are organic or psycho-emotional then it would figure these preferences could play out in all the systems. You may be more prone to the subtle changes in your opportunities for working with others (interest sharing), if in some way a part of you has become very located in interest-sharing. Professionals who really become absorbed in their work could have interest sharing as their "keystone system". If you know that you really need attuned caregivers around you, perhaps a part of you is uniquely held in the system for careseeking. If you know that fear completely stifles you then perhaps something significant has become lodged in the system for self-defence. If your internal world is constantly knowable to you, is it overly critical? Perhaps your personally created internal environment is your "keystone system"? Could we dare to wonder if depression might be linked to the systems for the personally created internal environment, anxiety to the fear system, even agoraphobia to the system for the personally created external environment and so on – another piece of research to conduct? It would be interesting to find out.

***

Person centred theory

One of the elements that instantly struck me about the McCluskey approach was its likeness in manner to person centred theory – especially its use of advanced empathy.

McCluskey's theory of interaction for caregiving (TIFC) brings another dimension to our understanding of empathy in its depiction and description of the shift in vitality affect (what we feel and how we are in our bodies) in ourselves when the goal of careseeking or caregiving has been reached. This shift is noticeable, can be caught on camera and in addition is subject to reliable ratings by the participants themselves or an observer (2005). Concentrating on this we use sophisticated empathic attunement. An understanding on the one person's part that they have really attuned into the nuance of what is going on for the careseeker. Here perhaps we might parallel the role of empathy and unconditional regard, to goal correction and exploration.

Where Rogers (1980) see also Chapter 3, talked about the condition a helper needed to be in, in order to help, this model is talking about the caregiver being in sufficient state to give exploratory care to the careseeker. There are dangers for both if the helper (Rogerian) or caregiver is really unable to help or give non-defensive exploratory care, the client or colleague may be negatively affected and the helper/caregiver may become unwell. We know from the work of McCluskey that professional caregivers often burn-out because they pay insufficient heed to their own needs and indeed their caregiving may be defensive, and left unchecked, potentially dangerous (McCluskey and Gunn, 2015).

There are clear parallels between the two, and these differences appear in the tracking of the process and the focus on enabling an instinctive system to reach its biological goal, and when that happens it has a profound effect on the self, in the sense that once a system has met its goal the self is free to plan and execute decisions with all its available resources. Where the Rogerian person centred emphasis is placed upon the helper communicating an understanding to the other person and of course the therapeutic alliance, no reference is made the nature of the interaction between the two persons (McCluskey, 2001) or to instinctive systems or a biological resolution. However, Rogers was onto the notion of a biological experience of it, he described it as the "phenomenal field . . . this private world of experience of the individual, only a portion of that experience, and probably a very small portion, is consciously experienced. Many of our sensory and visceral sensations are not symbolised" (Rogers, 1951, p. 483). It was the rating work of McCluskey that helps us to know these experiences are not only knowable they are also visible. When Heard, Lake and McCluskey (Heard, Lake and McCluskey, 2012) observe that Bowlby considers the careseeker has their own "set goals to reach" might we compare this to Rogerian conditions of worth, an inner biological system working to establish some sense of regulation and normality. He was perhaps describing the same thing; his catches however are in the narrative and the attentional skills of the helper, not in a biological attunement. I imagine many person centred practitioners, will be very able to attest to the biological component of it. It is reasonable Rogers didn't describe it in these terms, considering at the time he did not have access to the kind of data and means of recording that we have now.

When Heard, Lake and McCluskey discuss the inner language associated with the IWM in considering the unsupportive "I ought to be able to manage" or "if I don't no one will like me" (2012, p. 119), these Rogerian conditions of worth like thoughts are indeed the very aspects that staff can find themselves in great tangles over. How does our childhood, our childhood rules, assumptions, IWM, really prepare us for the workplace? Probably not terribly well. So, becoming more sophisticated at knowing this, and knowing our biological responses to threats to ourselves (personal or professional) might be clues for new action needed rather than a sense of failure.

As an integrative psychotherapist and trainer, I find it almost impossible not to see how these theories work together, offering a different language and different perspectives on the person. The common ground is all of these theories seek some form of sense making for how we manage what we experience, learn, adapt or resist; and how these emotions and behaviours locate themselves in our here and now experiences with ourselves and with our colleagues. Therefore, for making sense of our professional lives they all have something useful to offer. The McCluskey model is the only one, however, that works with the fact that we have these built in biological systems and makes explicit a consideration of our sexual self and our external environment and these for the workplace are perhaps crucial additions.

This work could be perhaps part of the new wave of being human at work, a new wave of psychotherapy and training for work. Non-judgmental, exploratory, enlightening and opening up potential to know more about ourselves and our relationships with others. It can help us become more sophisticated careseekers and caregivers at work, knowing that becoming effective careseekers and effective caregivers not only enhances our sense of ourselves, it actually leads to exploratory creative work which has got to be good for any organisation. It can help us know how to respond to and manage our fear, understand our internal world, inform and affect our external world and think about our most personal relationships, share our knowledge, interest share, make more opportunities to restore ourselves and each other. It can foster a way for being met as a person at work.

Appendices

Appendix One – Lists of abbreviations

CBT   cognitive behavioural therapy
EGCP   exploratory goal corrected psychotherapy
GCEA   goal corrected empathic attunement
IWM   internal working model
SCGT   systems centred group therapy
TA   transactional analysis
TABEIS   theory of attachment cased exploratory interest sharing
TIFC   theory of interaction for caregiving

Appendix Two – Reflective questions used for before, within and after the sessions

General

Do you have any ideas what could be done differently in a situation?

How does it feel different for you now?

Are you the same or different as someone else, if so how, what might this mean for you?

What does it feel like to be a member of this team, this group, this organisation?

Is there any impact from the course on your interpersonal encounters with your colleagues? If so can you describe what they are?

Is there any impact from the course to how effectively you think you might be working? If so can you describe what it is?

Is there any impact from the course to how you regard yourself, and take care of your "self"? If so can you describe what it is?

Can you imagine this working for other groups or members of staff?

Any unexpected outcomes, surprises, learnings, satisfactions, dissatisfactions?

As you start to become conversant with the systems, as you learn to tune into yourself, notice which of the systems is being aroused and by what exactly?

Can you notice the activation of the systems, careseeking etc., and then if the system is goal corrected could they tune into the sensation of assuagement?

Can you observe any places of tension in your body – is this information you might need to do something about?

Careseeking

How do you careseek at work?

Where/how might you have learnt to do this?

When is it effective?

When is it ineffective and might be described as dominant/submissive?

Is there a particular careseeking culture in your team that you can describe?

Is the caregiver, able to attune, are they attentive, do they have any capacity to offer care?

Can the caregiver endeavour to understand and handle any defensive behaviour of the fear ridden seeker?

Caregiving

How do you give care at work?

Where/how might you have learnt to do this?

When is it effective?

When is it ineffective and might that be described as dominant/submissive?

Is there a particular caregiving culture in your team that you can describe?

How do you know you are in caregiving mode? Is there a biological body sensation?

How do you know when caregiving has met the goal of the other person?

What does remaining exploratory in caregiving look like – what does becoming defensive in caregiving look like and what about curious caregiving?

What might intrusive caregiving look like?

Is your caregiving a re-enactment?

Do you notice compulsive caregiving? (Where the other person loses the chance to explore themselves.)

What modes of caregiving do you notice in others – like or dislike?

How might caregiving help other access their other systems?

Self-defence

Think about how self-defence or fear impacts you at work:

Where/how might you have learnt to do this?

When is it effective?

When is it ineffective and might that be described as dominant/submissive?

Is there a particular self-defence or fear culture in your team that you can describe?

Do you notice this in your body – if so where? How? What might you do if you think your fear system has taken over?

Have you or the other person deployed some defensive strategies?

Further exploration of the fear response could be done by following with these questions:

Is there a deadening? Is there sleepiness?

How might we become curious about fear and self-defence?

What has worked what hasn't worked – how is your competence and how is their competence now?

Interest-sharing

What do you think about interests and interest sharing has to do with the workplace?

What interests and where/how might you share any interests at work?

When is it effective – how do you know?

What happens to you if you can't interest share?

What happens to others if they can't interest share?

Is there a particular interest sharing culture in your team that you can describe?

Can we explore, or reflect upon, what might have stopped or become a barrier to interest sharing with other if that has happened?

Are there any of these repetitions around you, with your teams?

Can you offer the time?

How do you feel when you share interests is there an uplift in vitality?

Has the interest been thwarted or supported?

Sex and sexuality

How might sex/sexuality affect you at work?

When is it helpful – how do you know?

When is it unhelpful – how do you know?

What might be the problems about not talking about it?

Is there a particular sex/sexuality culture in your team that you can describe?

How do you feel when your sexual self is nourished?

How do you feel when your sexual self is not nourished or feels under threat?

Are there colleagues who might be struggling with their intimate relations?

How you might take care of yourself?

What might colleagues need?

What has worked what hasn't worked – how is your competence and how is their competence now?

Internal Environment

What is your internal environment like?

Is your internal environment supportive (compassionate) or unsupportive (overly critical)? Or something in between? Can you identify some oughts and shoulds?

How has your past contributed to your internal environment (or internal working model IWM)?

What is your internal environment like at work?

Is your internal environment different outside of work?

Can you identify any statements and rules that you or your team might try to live/ work by?

How do you know your internal environment is troubled or agitated?

Are you taking a break?

Are you checking your body posture?

Why mighty knowing about your internal environment might matter at work? And also to think about how might you describe the internal environment of the organisation?

Is an aspect of your internal environment at play? How do you know – are there memories or associations of a previous experience?

Is this previous information relevant and helpful now?

What would it mean to follow it?

What would it take to not heed it?

Do you know why these feelings, thoughts, bodily sensations are evoked now?

What will help you?

How can you compassionately review your experience here?

External environment

What is your external environment like at work?

Is your external environment different outside of work?

How has your past contributed to how you construct or have expectations of your external environment?

Is your external environment supportive or unsupportive? Or something in between?

How do you know your external environment is agitating you?

Can you reflect on the kind of external environment that you have created for yourself in the workplace that you have found supportive?

If you work from home do you think about the nature of the environment you are in? Do you notice what supports you? How much influence do you have on the work environment you might go to?

Do you favour the same in your office, do you take the same route, have rituals, objects in certain places?

If we know some of this – can we tell how it plays out in how we construct our external environment?

How does that work when we are sharing our living or working spaces?

Are we supporting our wellbeing at work through our external environment or is it unsupportive of our wellbeing at work?

Supplementary questions about the external environment:

- How might your external environment defend the self against painful experiences?
- How does your external environment promote your wellbeing and creative potential?
- What are the parts of your external environment that you can influence here at work?
- What is it like having parts that you can't?
- What has your experience of the different environments for the course been like?
- Imagine if we had stayed in one room?
- Imagine if we had been indifferent rooms each time.
- What if I had kept moving the chairs around?
- In a new office environment what would you say are the key components you like to have around you, what's the minimum?
- Do you know where you got these ideas from?
- Is your external environment supportive or unsupportive for you in general?
- How do you know?
- What is it like for you?
- What helps? What hinders?
- How has your past contributed to your present construction of your external environment?
- What is your external environment like at work?
- Is your internal environment different outside of work? How?
- How has your past contributed to how you construct or have expectations of your external environment?
- Is your external environment supportive or unsupportive? Or something in between?
- How do you know your external environment is agitating you?
- Does the external environment support the work of your teams? How?
- If not what is possible to change?
- How do you know the external environment is agitating your teams?
- What do you know about the external spaces requirements of the people around you?
- If you have to share an environment what does that mean for you now?
- Is an aspect of your external environment a measure of how you are?

- How do you know – are there memories or associations of a previous place?
- Is the information from this previous relevant and helpful now?
- Do you know why these feelings, thoughts, bodily sensations are evoked now?
- What will help you change your external environment if you can?
- How can you compassionately review your experience here?

Summary questions

Is there any impact from the course on your interpersonal encounters with your colleagues?

Is there any impact from the course to how effectively you think you might be working?

Is there any impact from the course to how you regard yourself, and take care of your "self"?

If so can you describe what these are?

Can you imagine this working for other groups or members of staff?

Any unexpected outcomes, surprises, learning, satisfactions, dissatisfactions?

What do you need? What are your needs? How do you get care?

How do you avoid being depleted by excessive (defensive or otherwise) caregiving to your colleagues? How might natural fear interfere with your work and work relationships? What interests you and how do you know?

Could you use these as diagnostic tools to review your work resilience or work sustainability?

How has it been thinking about affect identification, modulation and regulation?

Looking at various systems, do you have got any narrative about this work, at this moment?

The keystone system

Which is your "keystone system"?
What might that mean for you?
How can you resource yourself differently?

Appendix Three – Learning points

LP1   It is much easier to have all dates set prior to the course commencement.

LP2   Participant application and exploration in group and cross learning gave the course greater impact than just my teaching and coaching.

LP3   It's experiential – the group needed less didactic input from me and more time to explore their own understandings and application of the systems and the model.

LP4   Maximise the ways in which we communicate if we want to communicate.

LP5   Do we really consider the nature of the spaces we use for training and learning?

LP6 Group dynamics (in workplaces as well as in therapeutic settings) are greatly benefited by clear and fair leadership of the group leader.

LP7 Everything is information, everything counts.

LP8 What would it be like to have caregivers assigned in a team, for a certain period of time, say?

LP9 Is it possible to use the wheel as a graphic plotter, diagnostic tool?

LP10 Could it be used as a check-in tool along the lines of where are you today? When having a staff reviews as a means to checking progress?

LP11 Is there a way to create an abridged version that might be deliverable in short bursts?

LP12 Can it be used as team activity – a tool kit?

LP13 When one person misses a session, get another who attended to do the catch-up – embedding the knowledge of the one who was there and fostering potential interest sharing and mutual learning between the two.

LP14 Consider catch-ups that could be run part way through the course.

LP15 Think about running it as a longer course.

LP16 Think carefully about the timing of the sessions not 12-2, 10-12 much better for wellbeing.

LP17 Think about how you clarify the pitch and articulate the payoff to organisations. Align the course much more closely to wellbeing.

LP18 Recognise the real value of group shared learning as opposed to tutor or didactic led learning.

LP19 It is okay to experience fear at work, and noticing this is a strength not a weakness.

LP20 Noticing odd careseeking behaviour, can be the signal for stopping and trying a different intervention.

LP21 Some learning just can't be delivered in a shorter period of time.

LP22 A programme of events using a model which will help you tune in to relational and situational aspects of coming to work. It helps explain the interactions which take place, the situations you can find yourself in, and why they might have developed that way.

LP23 A good learning alliance will stand the test of time.

References

Ackerman, N. W. (1959). Transference and counter-transference. *Psychoanalytic Review*, 46(3): pp. 17–28.

Agazarian, Y. M. (1997). Glossary of SCT terms. *SCT Journal: Systems Centred Theory and Practice*, 2(1): pp. 3–10.

Ainsworth, M. D. S. and Wittig, B. A. (1969). Attachment and exploratory behavior of one year-olds in a strange situation. In B. M. Foss (Ed.), *Determinants of Infant Behavior, Vol. 4*: pp. 111–136. London: Methuen.

Ainsworth, M.D.S. (1969). Object relations, dependency, and attachment: a theoretical review of the infant-mother relationship. *Child Development*, 40: pp. 969–1025.

Ainsworth, M. D., and Bell, S. M. (1970). Attachment, exploration, and separation: illustrated by the behavior of one-year-olds in a strange situation. *Child Development*, 41: pp. 49–67.

Aristotle. (1941). *The Basic Works of Aristotle*. Edited with an introduction by R. McKeon. New York: Random House.

Bar-On, R. (Ed.) and Parker, J.D.A. (2000). *The Handbook of Emotional Intelligence: Theory, Development, Assessment, and Application at Home, School, and in the Workplace*. San Francisco: Jossey-Bass.

British Association for Counselling and Psychotherapy (BACP). (2016). *The Ethical Framework for the Counselling Professions*. Lutterworth: BACP.

Baobab Centre, The. (2016). Description of company ethos. Retrieved on 14/5/2016 from http://www.baobabcentre.com/

Berne, E. (1961). *Transactional Analysis in Psychotherapy*. New York: Grove Press, Inc.

Berne, E. (1964). *Games People Play: The Basic Hand Book of Transactional Analysis*. New York: Ballantine Books.

Berne, E. (1975). *What Do You Say After You Say Hello*. Beverly Hills: Corgi.

Bion, W. R. (1961). *Experiences in Groups*. London: Tavistock Publications.

Biggs. J., and Tang, C. (2007). *Teaching for Quality Learning at University. What the Student Does* (3rd Edition). Maidenhead: Open University Press.

Black, Dame Carol. (2008). *Review of the health of Britain's working age population. Presented to the Secretary of State for Health and the Secretary of State for Work and Pensions*. Retrieved on 12/09/2016 from https://www.gov.uk/government/uploads/system/uploads/attachment_data/file/209782/hwwb-working-for-a-healthier-tomorrow.pdf

Blatz, W. (1940). *Hostages to Peace: Parents and the Children of Democracy*. New York: Morrow.

Bowlby, J. (1982). *Attachment and Loss: Attachment*. New York: Basic Books.

Bowlby, J. (1988). *A Secure Base: Clinical Applications of Attachment Theory*. London: Routledge.

Brandão, C., Miguez, J. and McCluskey, U. (2016). The dynamics of fear in the workplace: the contribution of attachment theory to leadership training and behaviour. *Revista E-Psi*, 6(2): pp. 4–25.

Cannon, W. B. (1929). Organisation for physiological homeostasis. *Physiological Reviews*, 9(3): pp. 399–430.

Cannon, W.B. (1932). *The Wisdom of the Body*. New York: W.W. Norton and Company.

Bretherton, I. (1992). The origins of attachment theory: John Bowlby and Mary Ainsworth. *Developmental Psychology*, 28: pp. 759–775.

Chapman-Clarke, M. (Ed.). (2016). *Mindfulness in the Workplace: An Evidence-Based Approach to Improving Welding and Maximising Performance*. London: Kogan Page.

Chartered Institute of Personnel and Development (CIPD). (2016). *Growing the Health and Well-being Agenda: From First Steps to Full Potential*. London: CIPD.

Damasio, A. (2006). *Descartes Error*. London: Vintage Books.

Darwin, C. (1859). *On the origin of species by means of natural selection, or, the preservation of favoured races in the struggle for life*. London: J. Murray.

Department of Health. (2011). *No Health Without Mental Health: A Cross-Government Mental Health Outcomes Strategy for People of All Ages*. London: COI.

Department of Health (2014). *Wellbeing – Why it Matters to Health Policy*. Retrieved on 12/19/2016 from https://www.gov.uk/government/uploads/system/uploads/attachment_data/file/277568/Wellbeing_-_why_it_matters_to_health_summary_of_key_points.pdf

Druskat, V. U., Sala, F., and Mount, G. (Eds). (2005). *Linking Emotional Intelligence and Performance at Work: Current Research Evidence with Individuals and Groups*. Mahwah, NJ: Lawrence Erlbaum Associates Inc.

Egan, G. (2001). *The Skilled Helper: A Problem-Management and Opportunity-Development Approach to Helping* (10th edition). Belmont, CA: Brooks/Cole.

Emde, R.N. (1983). The prerepresentational self and its affective core. *The Psychoanalytic Study of the Child*, 38(1): pp. 165–192.

Emery, F. and Trist, E. (1973). *Towards a Social Ecology: Contextual Appreciations of the Future in the Present*. London: Plenum Publishing Company Ltd.

Fairbairn, W.R.D. (1952). *Psychoanalytic Studies of the Personality*. London: Tavistock Publications Limited.

Fleming, N.D., and Mills. C. (1992). Not another inventory, rather a catalyst for reflection. *To Improve the Academy*, 11(1): pp. 137–155.

Freud, S. (1949). *An Outline of Psychoanalysis*. London: W.W. Norton and Company, Inc.

Freud, S. (1961). The ego and the Id. In J. Strachey (Ed. and Trans.), *The Standard Edition of the Complete Psychological Works of Sigmund Freud* (Vol. 19, pp. 3–66). London: Hogarth Press. (Original work published 1923)

Gallese, V., Eagle, M. N., and Migone, P. (2007). Intentional attunement: mirror neurons and the neural underpinnings of interpersonal relations. *Journal of American Psychoanalytic Association*, 55(1): pp. 131–175.

Gibson, E. J., and Walk, R. D. (1960). The "visual cliff". *Scientific American*, 202(4): pp. 67–71.

Goleman, D. (1995). *Emotional Intelligence*. New York: Bantam Books, Inc.

Griffiths, S. (2009). Teaching and learning in small groups. In H. Fry, S. Ketteridge, and S. Marshall (Eds.), *A Handbook for Teaching and Learning in Higher Education* (pp. 72–84). New York: Routledge.

Haldane, J. D., McCluskey, U., and Peacey, M. (1980). A residential facility for families in Scotland: developments in prospect and retrospect. *International Journal of Family Psychiatry*, 1: pp. 357–372.

Harms, P. D. (2011). *Adult Attachment Styles in the Workplace*. Lincoln: University of Nebraska – DigitalCommons@University of Nebraska.

Heard, D. (1982). Family systems and the attachment dynamic. *Journal of Family Therapy*, 4: pp. 99–116.

Heard, D. and Lake, B. (1986). The attachment dynamic in adult life. *British Journal of Psychiatry*, 149: pp. 430–439.

Heard, D., and Lake, B. (2009 [1997]). *The Challenge of Attachment for Caregiving*. London: Karnac.

Heard, D., Lake, B., and McCluskey, U. (2012). *Attachment Therapy with Adolescents and Adults: Theory and Practice Post-Bowlby*. London: Karnac.

Heidegger, M. (1929). *What Is Metaphysics? The Basic Text of Heidegger's Inaugural Lecture at the U. of Freiburg in 1929*. Translated by Miles Groth, PhD.

Honey, P., and Mumford, A. (1982). *Manual of Learning Styles*. London: Peter Honey Associates.

Health and Safety Executive (HSE). (2016). *Work related Stress, Anxiety and Depression Statistics in Great Britain 2016*. London: HSE.

Institute of Psychoanalysis. (2017). *Sigmund Freud*. Retrieved on 24/6/17 from http://psychoanalysis.org.uk/our-authors-and-theorists/sigmund-freud.

International Transactional Analysis Association (ITAA). 2017. *What Is Transactional Analysis?* Retrieved on 12/11/17 from http://www.itaaworld.org/what-transactional-analysis.

Karpman, S.B. (2014). *A Game Free Life: The Definitive Book on the Drama Triangle and Compassion Triangle by the Originator and Author – The New Transactional Analysis of Intimacy, Openness, and Happiness*. Self published.

Keller, H., Scholmerich, A., and Eibl-Eibesfeldt, I. (1988). Communication patterns in adult-infant interactions in Western and non-Western cultures. *Journal of Cross-Cultural Psychology, Western Washington University*, 19(4): pp. 427–445.

Klein, M. (1952). Some theoretical conclusions regarding the emotional life of the infant. In M. Klein, P. Heimann, S. Isaacs, and J. Riviere (Eds.), *Developments in Psychoanalysis* (pp. 198–236). London: Hogarth.

Kuhn, T. S. (1962). *The Structure of Scientific Revolutions*. Chicago: University of Chicago Press.

Konorski, J. (1948). *Conditioned Reflexes and Neuron Organisation*. Cambridge: Cambridge University Press.

LeDoux, J. (1998). *The Emotional Brain*. London: Weidenfeld and Nicolson.

Lewin, K. (1952). Group decision and social change. In: G. E. Swanson, T. M. Newcomb and E. L. Harley (Eds.), *Readings in Social Psychology* (pp. 459–73). New York: Holt.

Livingston, R.B. (1966). Brain mechanisms in conditioning and learning. *Neurosciences Research Program Bulletin*, 4(3): pp. 349–354.

Macmurray, J. (1995 [1961]). *Persons in Relation*. London: Faber and Faber.

McCluskey, U. (1983). Teddy Bears: facilitators of therapy. *Journal of Social Work Practice*, 1: pp. 14–35.

McCluskey, U. (1987). In praise of feeling, the ethics of intervention. In S.Walrond-Skinner and D. Watson (Eds.), *The Ethics of Family Therapy* (pp. 56–71). London and New York: Routledge and Kegan Paul.

McCluskey, U. (2001). *A Theory of Caregiving in Adult Life: Developing and Measuring the Concept of Goal-Corrected Empathic Attunement, Vol. I and II.* York: University of York Library.

McCluskey, U. (2005). *To Be Met as a Person: The Dynamics of Attachment in Professional Encounters.* London and New York: Karnac.

McCluskey, U. (2005a). Object relations and attachment dynamics in group psychotherapy: the communication, regulation and exploration of affective states. In J. Savage Scharff and D. E Scharff (Eds.), *The Legacy of Fairbairn and Sutherland.* London: Brunner-Routledge.

McCluskey, U. (2010). Understanding the self and understanding therapy: an attachment perspective. *Context,* February: pp. 29–32.

McCluskey, U. (2017). Keynote presentation, given at the 2017 Biennial Residential Conference for those who are new to or experienced in Exploratory Goal-Corrected Psychotherapy (EGCP)©.

McCluskey, U., and Bingley Miller, L. (1995). Theme-focused family therapy: the inner emotional world of the family. *Journal of Family Therapy,* 17: pp. 411–434.

McCluskey, U., Roger, D, and Nash, P. (1997). A preliminary study of the role of attunement in adult psychotherapy. *Human Relations,* 50: pp. 1261–1273.

Merleau-Ponty, M. (1964). *Signs.* Evanston, IL: Northwestern University Press.

McCluskey, U., Hooper, C.A., and Bingley Miller, L. (1999). Goal-corrected empathic attunement: developing and rating the concept within an attachment perspective. *Psychotherapy: Theory, Research, Training and Practice,* 36(1): pp. 80–90.

McCluskey, U. and Gunn, J. (2015). The dynamics of caregiving: why are professional caregivers vulnerable to anxiety and burnout, and how do we support their well-being? *ATTACHMENT: New Directions in Psychotherapy and Relational Psychoanalysis,* 9(2), July: pp. 188–200.

Merleau-Ponty, M. (1973). *Prose of the World.* Evanston, IL: Northwestern University Press.

Meyer, J., and Land, R. (2003). Threshold concepts and troublesome knowledge: linkages to ways of thinking and practising within the disciplines. *ETL Project Occasional Report 4, May 2003*: pp. 1–12.

Plato. (1987). *The Republic.* London: Penguin Classics.

Palmer, P. J. (1998). *The Courage to Teach.* San Francisco: Jossey-Bass Inc.

Quinby, L. (1994). *The Durable Triangle.* The Glowman Consulting Group. TA-Tutor. com. Retrieved on 27/11/17 from http://ta-tutor.com/tatutor/durable-triangle.

Porges, S.W. (2001). The polyvagal theory: phylogenetic substrates of a social nervous system. *International Journal of Psychophysiology,* 42(2): pp. 123–146.

Racker, H. (2012). *Transference and Countertransference.* London: Karnac.

Rice, A.K. (1965). *Learning for Leadership: Interpersonal and Intergroup Relations.* London: Karnac.

Rock, D. (2009). *Your Brain at Work.* New York: HarperCollins.

Rogers, C. (1951). *Client-Centred Therapy: Its Current Practice, Implications and Theory.* London: Constable and Company.

Rogers, C. (1957). The necessary and sufficient conditions of therapeutic personality change. *Journal of Consulting Psychology,* 21(2): pp. 95–103.

Rogers, C.R. (1959). A theory of therapy, personality and interpersonal relationships, as developed in the client-centred framework. In S. Koch (Ed.), *Psychology: A Study of a Science, Vol. 3: Formulations of the Person and the Social Context* (pp. 184–256). New York and Boston: McGraw-Hill.

Rogers, C. (1980). *A Way of Being*. New York: Houghton Miflin.

Rose, S. (2016). Appraising the implementation of mindfulness within a strategic approach to psychological health. In M. Chapman-Clarke (Ed.), *Mindfulness in the Workplace: An Evidence-based Approach to Improving Well-being and Maximizing Performance* (pp. 181–208). London: Kogan Page.

Schutte, N. S., and Loi, N. M. (2014). Connections between emotional intelligence and workplace flourishing. *Personality and Individual Differences*, 66: pp. 134–139.

Siddiqui, S. V., Chatterjee, U., Kumar, D., Siddiqui, A., and Goyal, N. (2008). Neuropsychology of prefrontal cortex. *Indian Journal of Psychiatry*, 50(3): pp. 202–208.

Siegel, D. J. W. W. (2007). *The Mindful Brain: Reflection and Attunement in the Cultivation of Well-Being*. New York: Norton and Company.

Sorce, J.F., Emde, R.E., Campos, J., and Klinnert, M.D. (1985). Maternal emotional signaling: its effect on the visual cliff behavior of 1-Year-Olds. *Developmental Psychology*, 21(1): pp. 195–200.

Spenceley, D. (2016). *TA 101 – Official Introduction to Transactional Analysis*. Introduction to TA . . . "101 Notes". Retrieved on 24/06/2017 from http://www.ta-psychotherapy.co.uk/pdf/101.pdf

Steiner, C. (1971). The stroke economy. *Transactional Analysis Journal*, 1(3): pp. 9–15.

Stern, D. (1985). *The Interpersonal World of the Infant: A View from Psychoanalysis and Developmental Psychology*. London: Karnac.

Stern, D. (2002). *The First Relationship: Infant and Mother*. London: Harvard University Press.

Stevens, J. (2015). *How I Grew a Tail: A Reflection on Exploratory Interest Sharing*. Conference proceedings. 7th Biennial Residential Conference. Exploratory Goal Corrected Psychotherapy.

Trades Union Congress. (2016). *Still Just a Bit of Banter? Sexual Harassment in the Workplace in 2016*. London: TUC.

Wheeler, R. E. (2016). Soft skills: the importance of cultivating emotional intelligence. *AALL Spectrum*, January/February: pp. 16–06.

Yalom, I. (2004). *The Gift of Therapy*. London: Piatkus.

Index